PROPOSITIONAL STRUCTURE
AND ILLOCUTIONARY FORCE

The Language & Thought Series

SERIES EDITORS
JERROLD J. KATZ, THE GRADUATE CENTER, CITY UNIVERSITY OF NEW YORK
D. TERENCE LANGENDOEN, THE GRADUATE CENTER, CITY UNIVERSITY OF NEW YORK
GEORGE A. MILLER, PRINCETON UNIVERSITY

Readings in Philosophy of Psychology
    Ned Block
    Editor

Semantics: Theories of Meaning in Generative Grammar
    Janet Dean Fodor

The Language of Thought
    Jerry A. Fodor

Propositional Structure and Illocutionary Force
    Jerrold J. Katz

An Integrated Theory of Linguistic Ability
    Thomas Bever, Jerrold J. Katz, and D. Terence Langendoen,
    Editors (Distributed by Harper & Row, Publishers)

PROPOSITIONAL STRUCTURE AND ILLOCUTIONARY FORCE:

A Study of the Contribution of Sentence Meaning to Speech Acts

JERROLD J. KATZ

Harvard University Press
Cambridge, Massachusetts
1980

First paperback printing, 1980

This Harvard University Press paperback is published by arrangement with Thomas Y. Crowell Company, Inc. It contains the complete text of the original hardcover edition.

Library of Congress Catalogue Card Number: 79–92561

ISBN 0–674–71615–9

What then finally is left of the distinction of the performative and constative utterance? Really we may say that what we had in mind here was this:
(a) With the constative utterance, we abstract from the illocutionary (let alone the perlocutionary) aspects of the speech act, and we concentrate on the locutionary: moreover, we use an over-simplified notion of correspondence with the facts—over-simplified because essentially it brings in the illocutionary aspect. We aim at the ideal of what would be right to say in all circumstances, for any purpose, to any audience, etc. Perhaps this is sometimes realized.
(b) With the performative utterance, we attend as much as possible to the illocutionary force of the utterance, and abstract from the dimension of correspondence with facts.
Perhaps neither of these abstractions is so very expedient: Perhaps we have here not really two poles, but rather an historical development. Now in certain cases, perhaps with mathematical formulas in physics books as examples of constatives, or with the issuing of simple executive orders or the giving of simple names, say, as examples of performatives, we approximate in real life to finding such things. It was examples of this kind, like "I apologize", and "The cat is on the mat", said for no conceivable reason, extreme marginal cases, that gave rise to the idea of two distinct utterances.

J. L. AUSTIN

The direct analysis of [natural languages], which has been prevalent hitherto, must inevitably fail, just as a physicist would be frustrated were he from the outset to attempt to relate his laws to natural things—trees, stones, and so on. In the first place, the physicist relates his laws to the simplest of constructed forms; to a thin straight lever, to a simple pendulum, to punctiform masses, etc. Then with the help of the laws relating to these constructed forms, he is later in a position to analyze into suitable elements the complicated behavior of real bodies. . . .

R. CARNAP

To Virginia, Seth, and Jesse

CONTENTS

PREFACE

The theory of speech acts and the theory of generative grammar went their separate ways. It could have been otherwise. Austin had planned to hold discussions on Chomsky's *Syntactic Structures* to acquaint himself and other Oxford philosophers with the technicalities of the new theory. But he became fatally ill before he could carry out his plan. There is, of course, no way of knowing what might have happened if Austin had had the chance to assess the significance of the transformational revolution in linguistics for his own work in linguistic philosophy.

As it was, Searle and Austin's other followers took over the development of speech act theory and refined it within the framework Austin had set down.[1] Similarly, Chomsky and his followers developed and refined the theory of generative grammar within a framework that paid as little attention to speech acts as the Austinians paid to transformations. The reasons for the separation of speech act theory and generative grammar are varied. On the one hand, there is the traditional suspicion on the part of ordinary language-style philosophers toward the use of formal systems in connection with natural language and the strong performance slant that Austin gave speech act theory by making it part of the theory of acts. On the other hand, early generative grammarians were preoccupied with the more highly formalized and more traditionally respectable areas of phonology and syntax and had their hands full trying to overcome Bloomfieldian and Quinian skepticism against according semantics a place in the theory of language. Moreover, semantics—although of increasingly greater importance as time went on—was initially preoccupied with the question of how semantic representations are mapped onto syntactic representations (in particular, whether semantic representations are assigned only to underlying phrase markers). Further, the design of semantic representations was almost exclusively

1. J. L. Austin, *How To Do Things with Words* (Oxford: Oxford University Press, 1962).

under the influence of constativist assumptions about propositional structure. Finally, the interest in speech act theory within linguistics was confined largely to linguists who, as a matter of doctrine, had forsworn the study of grammatical competence and formal methods in favor of describing the contextual factors influencing the use of sentences in speech.

Speech act theorists and generative grammarians, of course, occasionally commented on each other's work (though usually critically), and obviously, from time to time, ideas from one tradition found their way into the other. But even considering the stir in linguistics made by Ross's so-called higher performative analysis and Grice's theory of conversational logic, it is still correct to say that the main lines of theory construction in the traditions of speech act theory and generative grammar have in no real sense come together to form a generative grammar account of the illocutionary force of sentences in natural language.

The present book is an attempt to bring these traditions together. It proposes a theory in generative grammar showing how to formally represent the illocutionary force of sentences. To construct this theory, the performance slant that Austin gave speech act theory had to be eliminated, and the basic ideas of the theory had to be removed from the theory of acts and relocated in the theory of grammatical competence. It was even necessary to reject speech act theory itself, insofar as it is taken as an account of a *uniform* type of knowledge speakers exercise in performing and identifying speech acts. In place of the familar speech act theory, say, as presented in Searle's writings, I propose two distinct theories about two separate types of knowledge underlying the performance of speech acts. One theory is part of the theory of competence. It is a theory about what the ideal speaker-hearer knows about the illocutionary information embodied in the grammatical structure of sentences. The other is part of the theory of performance. It is a theory about the pragmatic principles that determine how the information about illocutionary force embodied in the structure of a sentence and the information about a speech context assign an utterance meaning to a use of the sentence.

To develop the theory of illocutionary competence, I had to extend significantly the formalism of semantic representation previously constructed to describe the meaning of constative sentences. The new apparatus for describing the meaning of performative sentences also constitutes an important increase in the explanatory power of semantic theory, particularly, in connection with the theory of semantic roles, the notion of assertive proposition, and the treatment of presupposition. To develop the theory of pragmatic performance, I had to resurrect and refine the notion, proposed several years ago in "The Structure of a Semantic Theory", that the meaning of a sentence in the language can be taken as the utterance meaning of a use of the sentence in a context devoid of anything that might contribute to contextual construal. Such a "null context" is, of course, an idealization, like the physicist's notion of a perfect vacuum or frictionless plane. Because it is constructed by abstracting away from those features of real situations that only complicate the formulation of purely grammatical principles, it permits us to characterize the theory of pragmatic performance as a theory about how speakers and hearers figure out the utterance meaning of sentences used in non-null contexts on the basis of their knowledge of grammatical principles and information about the contexts. Particular theories of pragmatic performance are thus explications of the principles speakers and hearers employ to work out the contribution that specific contextual information makes to utterance meanings, relative to the overall assumption that the closer a context is to the null context the larger the proportion of sentence meaning in utterance meaning and the less these principles are required to work out. Although various suggestions are made about the character of such principles, I make no attempt to develop a particular pragmatic theory. The conception of a theory of pragmatic performance is introduced only to provide a theoretically motivated distinction between the domains of semantics and pragmatics that will enable us to keep questions about the use of sentences out of semantics. By our keeping them in the domain of pragmatics where they belong, they do not interfere with the formalization of the speaker-hearer's knowledge of the illocutionary potential of sentences. My major claim in this book is that, without such interference, we can construct a rich and revealing theory of illocutionary force within the theory of generative grammar.

Apart from the inherent desirability of a formal theory of illocutionary force, there are a number of important consequences that can be anticipated. One is that semantics will be put on a far firmer foundation. Not only will we obtain a formal systematization that brings order to a wide range of linguistic facts but we will, in the process, have extended and much clarified every aspect of semantic theory. Another consequence is that the many controversies in linguistics that now exist because of a confused conception of the relation between grammar and pragmatics can be satisfactorily settled within the present framework. A particular example of this is the controversy about the nature of presupposition that D. T. Langendoen and I address ourselves to in "Pragmatics and Presupposition".[2] Still another consequence of the present study is the light it sheds on the assumptions underlying the important tradition in Oxford philosophy begun by Austin. It shows, I think, which of those assumptions must be abandoned to achieve that "true and comprehensive *science of language*" which Austin once prophesied.

The "linguistic turn" taken by philosophy in this century and the "semantic turn" taken by linguistics in the last decade have undeniably led to significant in-

2. *Language* 52, no. 1 (1976). Reprinted in Bever, Katz, and Langendoen, *An Integrated Theory of Linguistic Ability* (New York: Thomas Y. Crowell, 1976).

sights into the logical structure of natural language and to the philosophical issues about logic that turn on matters of language. Perhaps the most intriguing consequence is the prospect of a new conception of the nature of logic and its relation to natural language. The semantic theory that I have tried to develop over the last decade or so challenges the orthodox view of the nature of logic, roughly, that it is the study of truth-preserving inferences based on properties of the so-called logical particles. I tried to show that truth-preserving inferences also turn on properties of words in the "persuasively defined" category of non-logical vocabulary. One of the major objectives in the early stages of constructing semantic theory was to show how logical relations between nouns, verbs, and other allegedly nonlogical words can be formalized under the standard notion of validity. Austin's original idea of performativeness contained a related, and in some ways more radical, challenge to this orthodoxy, since it denied that truth and falsehood are appropriate notions to use in evaluating all inferences. The significant question that it raises is whether implication relations between performative propositions can be logical if such propositions are neither true nor false, and if they can, whether the sense in which they are logical implications undermines the orthodox view of logic.

But Austin's promising idea, undercut by Austin's own hand, never developed into such a challenge. In this book, I try to work out this challenge to the orthodox view of logic in a way that cannot be ignored. I try to confront the orthodox view with a formal theory of semantic representation that explicates logical relations between performative sentences on exactly the same semantic basis as logical relations between constative sentences. Also, in place of Austin's intuition that truth and falsity are inapplicable to performative sentences, I try to offer strong arguments to show that they are inapplicable, together with a theoretically defensible account of the performative/constative distinction. Having shown that performative sentences give rise to logical inferences that do not fit under the standard conception of validity, I propose a new interpretation of deductive connections, one abstract enough to encompass both implication relations between constatives and implication relations between performatives. This new notion of validity leads immediately to an unorthodox theory of the nature of logic, *viz.*, that it is the study inferences that preserve the property specified in this new interpretation of deductive connections, such connections being based on the semantic structure of all words.

A sabbatical grant from the Massachusetts Institute of Technology and a fellowship from the Guggenheim Foundation enabled me to begin this work in 1973-1974. A grant from The City University of New York, Faculty Research Award Program, received for the year 1975-1976, helped considerably in enabling me to finish the work. I hereby happily perform the orthographic act of thanking all three of these institutions.

A number of colleagues, students, and friends provided welcome intellectual stimulation in the process of carrying out this work. Initially, this book was to be one of three chapters in a volume with Robert M. Harnish and Bruce Fraser on meaning and use. That project was abandoned when our contributions all grew beyond chapters into full book-length manuscripts. The project, while it existed, and the seminar at M.I.T. that I taught with Fraser in 1972 were an early stimulus. Subsequent seminars at M.I.T. and at The Graduate Center of the City University of New York helped to further clarify my thinking. I am grateful to the students and colleagues at M.I.T., The Graduate Center, and elsewhere with whom I discussed this material. I want to thank D. T. Langendoen, Robert M. Harnish, Ned Block, Yuji Nishiyama, Fred Katz, Bill Stewart, Richard Mendelsohn, James F. Thomson, Robert Fiengo, Manfred Bierwisch, Edward K. Borchardt, Robert J. Matthews, Denis Newman, John Dore, Bruce Fraser, and Virgina Valian. I owe a special thanks to George Smith and Anita Janda, both of whom read the entire manuscript and made numerous valuable suggestions. My debt to Anita Janda is double because she prepared the index. I thank Joan Levinson for her editorial comments which much improved the book.

PROPOSITIONAL STRUCTURE
AND ILLOCUTIONARY FORCE

"Last week, the management of this station wished our listeners a happy New Year. Here now is Mr. Clyde Wilmer with an opposing view."

(Drawing by Dana Fradon; © 1979 The New Yorker Magazine, Inc.)

INTRODUCTION

The question this book addresses is what is the structure of propositions. The proposition has a unique interdisciplinary status. It represents the intersection of philosophy, logic, and linguistics. Each has its own special concern with an aspect of propositions. Philosophy conceives of them as the things that are asserted and denied in controversies about knowledge and thus as the proper things to analyze in order to better understand such controversies. Logic conceives of them as the objects to which laws of logic apply. Linguistics conceives of propositions as the result of the compositional combination of the senses of the words in sentences, that is, the senses of sentences. But, as central as propositions are to these disciplines separately and to the construction of interdisciplinary bridges between them, we have no general theory about the structure of propositions. I do not mean that we have nothing like the comprehensive, highly articulated theories found in the physical sciences, but that we lack an integrative conception of the various aspects of propositional structure, the first step toward such theories. I am not claiming that philosophy, logic, and linguistics do not say things of great theoretical importance about aspects of propositional structure. The point is simply that there is no general conception of how what we know about various aspects can be pulled together. The principal stumbling block to this, as I see it, is how to bring constatives and performatives under the same conception of proposition.

Grammars are accounts of how sounds and meanings are related in terms of their structure. Syntactic theory describes the forms into which sounds are organized, such as simple subject-predicate structures, coordination of sentential structures, subordination, and so on. Recent work in syntactic theory has contributed significantly to our knowledge of such patterns and their details. Semantic theory, whose job it is to describe the structure of the meaning side of the sound-meaning correlation, has recently developed as a serious part of the theory of grammar but it has not yet offered us a general theory of the structure

1

of senses of sentences. Thus, the question we take up here is the semantic parallel to the question syntacticians have been answering in their theory of the patterns by which words, phrases, clauses, and so on, form sentences. Our question is what is the internal structure of a sense of a sentence? What are its constituents, and what are the relations that make propositions out of them?

There are a number of special reasons for taking up this question beyond its purely intellectual interest. First, the project of constructing a general theory about the structure of senses of sentences in natural language constitutes the logical next step beyond my previous work in semantic theory.[1] So far, semantic theory has had two primary explanatory concerns. One is the understanding of the *componential structure* of the senses of linguistic forms, that is, the decomposition of senses into their component concepts, and these, ultimately, into the primitives of our conceptual system. The other is the understanding of *compositional construction*, that is, the composition of the senses of syntactically complex linguistic forms out of the meaning of their constituent lexical items and their syntactic relations. Neither of these explanatory goals could be achieved without a general theory of the structure of senses of sentences. We could not fully understand componential structure without taking componential analysis beyond the level of morphemes, words, and phrases to the level of clauses and sentences. And our theory of the compositional construction of meanings must remain radically incomplete until we obtain some reasonably satisfactory conception of the final stage of the compositional process, that is, the kind of semantic structures that the meanings of morphemes are mapped into at the sentential level.

The point can be put this way. An ideal speaker-hearer knows infinitely many distinct senses of infinitely many distinct sentences, and this could not be so unless these sentences obtained their senses compositionally. Thus a theory of this knowledge, a grammar, explains semantic competence on the basis of projection principles that assign semantic representations to sentences in a way that formally reconstructs compositionality. Our formal representations of meaning must enable us to predict the semantic properties and relations of the senses to which they are assigned. Hence, semantic representations cannot be single symbols, such as numerals, because we would then have no formal basis for predicting that an expression like "unmarried bachelor" is redundant but "unhappy bachelor" is not. Thus, we come to think of the objects represented by semantic representations of morphemes, words, and phrases as complex con-

1. See J. J. Katz, *Semantic Theory* (New York: Harper & Row, 1972); and J. J. Katz, 'Logic and Language: An Examination of Recent Criticisms of Intensionalism," in *Language, Mind, and Knowledge*, Minnesota Studies in the Philosophy of Science, vol. VII, ed. K. Gunderson (Minneapolis: University of Minnesota Press, 1975), pp. 36–130.

cepts. But the objects represented by semantic representations of clauses and sentences cannot be merely complex concepts. Simple declarative sentences like "Snow is white" express assertions, and therefore their sense must contain their truth conditions.[2] We have some ideas from formal logic about how to represent truth conditions for sentences, which could be adapted to serve as a partial theory about the meaning of simple declarative sentences, and we could adjust and supplement where these ideas fail to do full justice to sentences of natural language. But there are all sorts of sentences that do not express assertions: interrogatives, imperatives, hortatories, and the many kinds of complex declaratives with performative verbs, first-person subjects, and present tense that we use to make promises, warn, order, congratulate, and so on. Here, we do not have very much of an idea about the kind of object that should be represented by a semantic representation of these sentences. Efforts by some philosophers and logicians to tell us that such sentences are really assertive, too, have always come to grief simply because a sentence like "I apologize" cannot be responded to by saying "What you asserted is true (false)." Austin was quite correct in saying:

> In these examples it seems clear that to utter the sentence ... is not to *describe* my doing of what I should be said in so uttering to be doing or to state that I am doing it: it is to do it. None of the utterances cited is either true or false: I assert this as obvious and do not argue it.[3]

Until we obtain some reasonable idea of what the meanings of such performative sentences are, our attempt to construct a formal theory of the crucial property of compositionality is essentially incomplete. We might obtain sophisticated hypotheses about the formal representation of morphemes, words, and phrases and about the dictionary and projection rules, but without a conception of what kind of objects the senses of performative sentences are, our theory of the semantic structure of natural language is like a syntactic theory with no conception of the constituent structure of interrogatives and other nondeclarative sentences.

A second reason for taking up the problem of constructing a theory of the senses of sentences is related to a long-standing interest of mine in the philosophy

2. I, of course, do not mean that any notion of truth conditions will do. The Davidsonian notion and the modal notion are both too inclusive (see Katz, "Logic and Language: An Examination of Recent Criticisms of Intensionalism" and F. M. Katz and J. J. Katz, "Is Necessity the Mother of Intension?" *The Philosophical Review* 86, no. 1 (January 1977).
3. J. L. Austin, *How To Do Things with Words* (Cambridge, Mass.: Harvard University Press, 1962), p. 6. Lacking Austin's authority, we shall argue for this claim later.

of language and logic. To explain this reason, I have to say something about those interests.

For some time I have argued that the orthodox conception of the nature of logic is mistaken. This conception makes two incorrect assumptions about logical form (the grammatical aspects of sentences that determine their implication relations). One is that, according to Quine, the chief theoretician of this orthodoxy, logical form "rests wholly on how the truth functions, quantifiers, and variables stack up".[4] That is, the logical form of sentences is determined exclusively by the properties of the so-called logical particles ("and", "not", "or", "all", "if, then", and so on). The other assumption is that implication relations are those connections between sentences under which the property of truth is preserved. That is, the only sense of validity with which logic is concerned is that in which the truth of the premises makes it necessary that the conclusion also be true.

My disagreement with the first assumption is that it excludes from logic proper any implication that depends on the meaning of the nouns, verbs, adjectives, and so on, that is, on what advocates of the orthodox conception term the "extralogical" or "nonlogical" vocabulary.[5] In fact, inferences like (b) are no less necessary than inferences like (a):

(a) If Sally is a feminist, then she is either a feminist or a Marxist.

(b) If Sally had a nightmare, then she had a dream.

My disagreement with the second assumption is that it excludes implications holding between performative sentences because they cannot be considered bearers of truth values. Yet inferences like (c) and (d) involve the same deductive connection that appears between the constatives in the antecedent and consequent of (b).

(c) Did Sally have a nightmare? Did Sally have a dream?

(d) Do what you can to have a nightmare! Do what you can to have a dream!

My general criticism of the orthodox conception of logic is that its assumptions overly restrict the domain of logic, so that the theory of its subject matter and the systems of logic developed do justice to only a small fraction of the full range of logical implications.

4. W. V. O. Quine, *Philosophy of Logic*, (Englewood Cliffs, N.J.: Prentice-Hall, 1970), p. 48.

5. Also that it excludes traditional bread-and-butter logical apparatus. See J. J. Katz, "The Dilemma between Orthodoxy and Identity" in *Language in Focus*, ed. A. Kasher (Dordrect. D. Reidel Publishing Co., 1976), pp. 165-175.

Much of the plausibility of the orthodox view is due to the fact that it is in this narrow area of language where the most systematic and fruitful work of formalizing implication has been done. People reasonably tend to think the theoretical scheme that has achieved a uniform treatment of an area is the last word on the subject as a whole. Also the longer a scheme remains unchallenged, the more credibility it obtains. Euclidean geometry is a prime example. Moreover, its credibility is reinforced by the development of professionalism in the use of the formalization. As more and more practitioners become more specialized and more concerned with technical questions within the theoretical scheme, it becomes less and less likely that serious philosophical questions about the soundness of the entire theoretical scheme will be raised.[6]

The alternative view of logic I advocate eliminates both the restrictions in the orthodox view, but it maintains the traditional notion that logic is the study of valid implications between sentences. Thus logical forms of sentences are determined by the meaning of *all* the words appearing in them. The sentences between which valid implicational relations can hold are not restricted to those that can be either true or false, but include all the performative sentences in a language. The natural way to express this alternative view is to assert it as a *theoretical identity*—that is, as the claim that propositions, the objects to which laws of logic apply, *are* actually senses of sentences in natural language.[7] Thus the principles that represent valid implicational relations apply to all sentences and apply on the basis of their full linguistic meaning.

To identify linguistic meaning with logical form has essentially the same justification as other theoretical identifications in science, namely, to increase the simplicity of our overall account of the nature of things and to eliminate unanswerable questions about why there are correlations between objects of two different kinds. Without our identification, one would have to ask questions like "Why is it that whenever two sentences are synonymous they express the same proposition (and vice versa)?", "Why is it that whenever a sentence does not express a proposition (that is, has no logical consequences) it is meaningless (and vice versa)?", and so on. With our identification, such questions can no more be asked than can questions like "Why is it that whenever and wherever there is water there is H_2O?". Our identification also reduces the number of separate objects we have to countenance, because the sense of a sentence and the proposition that the sentence expresses are not two things but one.

Thus far the attempt to support this alternative against the orthodox view has concentrated almost exclusively on trying to refute the distinction between

6. This is discussed further in the preface to Katz, *Semantic Theory*.

7. See Katz, "Logic and Language: An Examination of Recent Criticisms of Intensionalism," pp. 36–40.

the logical and extralogical vocabularies. Very little has been done to support the assumption of the alternative view that logical implication holds between sentences that cannot bear truth values.[8] This gives the defender of the orthodox view the opportunity to argue that the objects to which laws of logic apply cannot be identified with senses of sentences because, insofar as validity involves the notion of truth, logical implication can hold only between objects about which it makes sense to predicate truth and falsity. Therefore, the second reason for constructing a theory of the structure of propositions is to deny the defender of the orthodox view this line of argument by providing a theoretical account of how logical relations can hold between performative sentences. Thus we seek a theory that provides an account of propositions on which the features of assertive propositions by virtue of which laws of logic apply to them are also features of nonassertive propositions generally (not only questions, but requests, promises, and other performative types). We want a theory that will explain the applicability of laws of logic to nonassertive propositions in terms of their common semantic structure and will provide a family of validity concepts that makes sense of the notion of a valid argument involving performatives.

A third reason for constructing a theory of propositional structure is to clarify the relation between meaning and use. It is reasonable to take one goal of the study of linguistic communication to be the explanation of how speakers of a language use its sentences to do the things they do with them. Two further facts are also clear. One is that the speakers' competence, what they know about the phonology, syntax, and semantics of the sentence types in the language (by virtue of being fluent speakers of the language), plays a crucial role in sentence use. The other is that knowledge of the grammatical structure of sentences does not exhaust what speakers must know to say or do things in real communication situations. Besides grammatical principles, there must be pragmatic principles. In even the simplest uses of language, the grammatical meaning of a sentence type is changed, on the basis of aspects of the context, to become the special utterance meaning of that token of the sentence. For example, consider cases of irony or instances in which we imply more than we say. These cases also show that our pragmatic principles involve subtle and highly intricate relations to our grammatical principles. Questions about where to draw the line between grammatical meaning and utterance meaning are inevitable. A theory of the structure of all propositions will provide us with a principled basis for drawing this line in constructing explanations of how speakers use sentences.

The particular form of the question about where one ought to draw the line between meaning and use with which we shall deal will be, "What does the semantic structure of a sentence contribute to the speech acts the sentence can

8. See Katz, *Semantic Theory*, pp. 203–232.

perform?" The attempt to answer this question is both an attempt to develop Austin's original insights systematically and a way of divesting ourselves from his methodological assumptions. Our answer will be a theory of propositional structure that makes an Austinian distinction between constatives and performatives, that classifies performative propositions into types on the basis of the information in their semantic structure, and that determines the illocutionary force of sentences independently of pragmatic considerations.

1
THE RELATION BETWEEN
SPEECH ACT THEORY
AND SEMANTIC THEORY

INTRODUCTION

An account of the contribution of sentence meaning to speech acts rests on some conception of the relation between speech act theory and semantic theory. Speech act theories from Austin[1] to the present are theories about acts, whereas semantic theories are theories about the grammatical structure of languages, and hence, in Chomsky's framework,[2] theories about the semantic competence exercised by an ideal speaker in performing speech acts. Thus, semantic theories can be expected to describe the common stock of grammatical information (in particular, semantic information) that speakers of a language bring to the situations in which they perform speech acts. The question about the contribution of sentence meaning to speech acts we are interested in is, then: What stock of semantic information about speech acts do speakers of a language bring to these situations? This stock of information is what we want to represent in the semantic component of a grammar of the language. To determine what we want to represent in the semantic component of a grammar, we need to know something about the kinds of information represented in an adequate speech act theory. This information will comprise the superset that includes the information represented in a grammar. Therefore, if we can determine the relation between speech act theory and semantic theory, we can determine which part of this superset is semantic information and which part is pragmatic, that is, information about how semantic competence is exercised in the performance of speech acts. Then we can use the principles on which this partition is based to determine what semantic representations have to represent and what they need not.

In this chapter we shall try to determine the relation between speech act

1. J. L. Austin, *How To Do Things with Words* (Cambridge, Mass.: Harvard University Press, 1962).
2. N. Chomsky, *Aspects of the Theory of Syntax*, (Cambridge, Mass.: M.I.T. Press, 1965).

theory and semantic theory so that we can exploit this relation later to construct a formal theory of the representation of illocutionary force information in the grammar. The leading idea of our approach, as already suggested, is that clarification in this area of linguistic phenomena requires a sharp competence/performance distinction, separating grammar from pragmatics. Indeed, our chief departures from Austin's ideas, which in very general terms we follow, arise where he fails to draw this distinction and is led to change essential features of his original theory. Austin began with a set of neat, clean distinctions, for example, between constatives and performatives, but in the course of his investigations he undermined, blurred, and erased almost all of them. We shall argue that these changes were unnecessary because the considerations that led Austin to eliminate the distinctions could be handled in a way that preserved them if competence and performance were sharply separated.

PROPOSITIONAL CONTENT
AND PROPOSITIONAL TYPE

A natural starting point for a study of the place of illocutionary force information in the meaning of sentences is Frege's remark:

> An interrogative sentence and an indicative one contain the same thought; but the indicative contains something else as well, namely, the assertion. The interrogative sentence contains something more too, namely a request. Therefore, two things must be distinguished in an indicative sentence: the content, which it has in common with the corresponding sentence-question, and the assertion.[3]

Extending Frege's observation, we may say that the propositions expressed by (1.1)–(1.6) have one substructure, which is the same from proposition to proposition, and one that varies from proposition to proposition.

    (1.1) Someone will eat the cookies.
    (1.2) Who will eat the cookies?
    (1.3) Eat the cookies!
    (1.4) I promise to eat the cookies.
    (1.5) I warn you to eat the cookies.
    (1.6) I allow you to eat the cookies.

3. G. Frege, "The Thought: A Logical Inquiry," in *Essays on Frege*, ed. E. D. Klemke, (Urbana, Ill.: Illini Books, 1968), p. 513.

Roughly speaking, the common component of the meaning of (1.1)-(1.6) is the information that someone eats certain cookies at some indefinite future time; the idiosyncratic component is the information which determines that (1.1) expresses an assertion, (1.2) and (1.3) requests, (1.4) a promise, (1.5) a warning, and (1.6) a permission. We shall impose a further distinction and say that there is a partly common and partly idiosyncratic component, which we shall call the "propositional content" to distinguish it from Frege's "content". The common part consists of Frege's content and the variable part consists of the relations of someone asking something in the case of (1.2), someone requesting something in the case of (1.3), someone promising someone in the case of (1.4), someone warning someone in the case of (1.5), and someone giving someone permission (1.6). The proposition content, as we are using this term, is thus the maximal predicate in the proposition together with terms occupying the places of this predicate. We use the term "propositional type" to refer to the wholly variable semantic substructure in such cases, that is, what makes (1.1) an assertion, (1.2) a request, and so on.[4]

The concepts of propositional content and propositional type go beyond Frege's notions in another important respect. These concepts defined here are purely semantic, as Frege's were not. Their formulation attaches no direct significance to the syntactic structure of sentences. Although differences of propositional type in cases (1.1) and (1.2) are correlated with differences in sentence type, the semantic characterization of (1.1) as an assertive and of (1.2) as a requestive does not reflect this correlation. Thus, (1.7), which is the same sentence type as (1.1), is a requestive like (1.2) and (1.3).[5]

(1.7) I request that you tell me who will eat the cookies.

The notion of propositional type can no more reflect such differences in sentence type (or the fact that the syntactic carrier of semantic information about propositional type in (1.1)-(1.3) is sentential type whereas the syntactic carrier in (1.4)-(1.6) is choice of main verb) than the shared sense of "bachelor" and

4. It should be said right at the outset that this work will depart radically from the approach sketched in J. J. Katz, *Semantic Theory* (New York: Harper & Row, 1972), pp. 150-157.

5. Frege, "The Thought: A Logical Inquiry," seems to tie his analysis of propositions to the syntactic form of the sentences expressing them. He says "One does not want to deny sense to an imperative sentence, but this sense is not such that the question of truth could arise for it. Therefore, I shall not call the sense of an imperative sentence a thought." (p. 512). On the other hand, "yes/no" questions are treated as having a thought as their sense (p. 513). Thus, Frege's commitment to syntactic structure will lead to problems with pairs like "Tell me whether you will go!" and "Will you go?".

"adult human male who has never married" can reflect the differences in the syntactic structure of these expressions.

Just as (1.1)–(1.7) have the same propositional content but different propositional type, so sentences might differ in having the same propositional type but different propositional content. Compare (1.4) with (1.8).

(1.8) I promise to pay all my debts.

Also, the notions of propositional content and propositional type ought to be thought of as expressing a decomposition of the structure of propositions similar to the decomposition of the structure of sentences expressed by the phrasal analysis in (1.9).

(1.9) S → NP Predicate Phrase

Finally, just as the notions "NP" and "Predicate Phrase" characterize the structure of simple *sentences*, so the notions "propositional content" and "propositional type" characterize the structure of simple *propositions*. In the case of simple propositions, propositional structure is simply a propositional type and a propositional content.

SIMPLE AND
COMPOUND PROPOSITIONS

Sentences classify into simple and compound depending on whether or not they have two or more *independent* clauses in them. Propositions might be classified into simple and compound on a similar basis, namely, whether or not they contain two or more *independent* propositions. Thus, in both cases further clarification depends on specifying this notion of simplicity. Roughly, we can take simplicity to mean this: A grammatical whole is simple just in case, for any components of the whole that are of the same category as the whole itself (sentences in the one case, and propositions in the other), there are relations between these components that determine aspects of their internal structure. For example, a sentence formed by conjoining (1.10) and (1.11) with "and", such as (1.12), is compound, whereas a sentence like (1.13), which results from (1.10) and (1.11) by relative clause formation, is simple.

(1.10) John eats cookies.
(1.11) John eats jam.
(1.12) John eats cookies and John eats jam.
(1.13) John who eats cookies eats jam.

Similarly, propositions formed with connectives that do not affect the logical form of the component propositions are compound. For example, propositions formed with logical conjunction or disjunction are compound because these connectives provide a context for propositions that leaves the logical form of propositions appearing in them unaltered.

Since our investigation here concerns itself with the structure of simple propositions, we may assume for the time being that propositional logic constitutes a complete theory of compound propositions. We recognize that this assumption is highly questionable, but we make it to get on with the analysis of simple propositions. One of the most questionable aspects of the assumption is that standard propositional logic says nothing about the compounding of nonassertive propositions, that is, propositions like those expressed by (1.2)-(1.6), to which truth and falsity do not apply. It is not clear whether standard propositional logic should be or could be extended to deal with the compounding of nonassertive propositions. But, clearly, to decide on the logical status of conjunctions, disjunctions, and other compound propositions with sentences expressing requests, questions, promises, warnings, and so forth, as their components, it would be necessary, in each case, to work out the properties corresponding to truth and falsity. In some cases, some of this work has already been done, and there are plausible hypotheses about such properties. For example, in the case of questions, the property corresponding to truth would seem to be *answer-hood*.[6] If this is right, then we can say that the conjunction of two questions is the joint asking of both, and the answer to a compound question is the answer to each of the component questions. In Chapter 6, we work out the properties corresponding to truth for other nonassertive propositions, formulate a general property encompassing truth, answerhood, and such further properties, and apply our results to the question of how close standard propositional logic is to a complete theory of compound propositions in natural language.

GRAMMAR AND PRAGMATICS

We now want to set up a framework for our formal investigation of the propositional structure of simple propositions that will tell us what kind of facts we should represent in our account of sentence meaning. As indicated above, our strategy will be to frame a model of the relation between grammar and pragmatics and then use it to enable us to decide what facts a theory of sentence meaning is responsible for and what facts it can leave to a separate account of how aspects of propositional type and content function in the use of language to perform speech acts.

The model in question goes back to the first attempts to characterize a

6. See Katz, *Semantic Theory*, chap. 5.

semantic component of a transformational grammar.[7] In order to decide what linguistic phenomena should be represented in a semantic component, we proposed the principle that semantic phenomena were any that fell beyond the phonological and syntactic competence of a fluent speaker (as determined by phonological and syntactic theory) but short of pragmatics. This attempt to set the domain of semantic representation by fixing an upper and lower limit would succeed, we recognized, only if something could be said to indicate what pragmatics is. We tried to do this by characterizing pragmatic phenomena, generally, as those in which knowledge of the setting or context of an utterance plays a role in how utterances are understood. Hence, semantic competence was pictured in terms of what an ideal speaker would know about the meaning of a sentence when no information is available about its context, that is, when it is used in a "null context" such as the "anonymous letter situation".[8]

The anonymous letter situation is the case where an ideal speaker of a language receives an anonymous letter containing just one sentence of that language, with no clue whatever about the motive, circumstances of transmission, or any other factor relevant to understanding the sentence on the basis of its context of utterance. We recognized, of course, that no such situation ever occurs, but we put it forth as an idealization, in the same spirit as Chomsky's ideal speaker-hearer or the physicist's perfect vacuum or frictionless plane. We intended to draw a theoretical line between semantic interpretation and pragmatic interpretation by taking the semantic component to properly represent only those aspects of the meaning of a sentence that an ideal speaker-hearer of the language would know in such an anonymous letter situation.

This immediately provides a distinction between "grammatical meaning" (or "sentence meaning") and "contextual meaning" (or "utterance meaning"), where the former is what a semantic interpretation represents and the latter is what a pragmatic interpretation represents. Sentence meaning is the meaning of a sentence type *in the language*, whereas utterance meaning is the meaning of a particular use, or token, of a sentence type *on that particular occasion*. Grammars represent sentence meaning because the meaning of a sentence in the language is the meaning it has by virtue of its having a particular grammatical structure. Pragmatic theories represent utterance meaning because the meaning of an utterance is the meaning it has by virtue of its being a specific spatio-temporal occurrence of a sentence in a particular contextual structure.

Thus, a grammar is responsible for representing the fact that (1.14) is *meaningful* in English and that (1.15) is not (is deviant to some extent).

---

7. J. J. Katz and J. A. Fodor, "The Structure of a Semantic Theory," *Language* 39, no. 2, part 1 (April–June 1963): 170–210.
8. Ibid., pp. 172–176.

(1.14) I pledge allegiance to the flag of the United States of America.

(1.15) Golf plays John.

But a pragmatic theory would be responsible for representing the fact that a token of (1.14) spoken uncomprehendingly by rote by nursery school children would not be meaningful in the context and that a token of (1.15) used by John's golfing partners to describe his generally poor golf performance might be fully meaningful in the context.

This distinction between sentence meaning and utterance meaning is the direct parallel of Chomsky's distinction between well-formedness (grammaticality) and acceptability.[9] Chomsky drew this distinction in the framework of his distinction between competence and performance by construing a performance theory as a theory about how real speakers of a language employ competence principles in their on-line processing mechanisms for producing and understanding speech. So far, the relation between competence and performance has been studied most extensively in connection with syntax and phonology. But it is clear that a complete treatment of this relation requires also an examination of semantic principles in performance, and that the notions of sentence meaning and utterance meaning play the roles of well-formedness and acceptability, respectively. Pragmatics is performance theory at the semantic level.

A pragmatic theory deals with the various mechanisms real speakers use to exploit the richness of the context in order to produce utterances whose meaning in the context diverges predictably from the meaning of the sentences of which they are tokens. There are three aspects of this exploitation that call for further discussion: how much an utterance meaning depends on its context, the function of such dependency, and the objectivity of contextually determined features of utterance meaning.

The fact that utterance meaning can be more or less dependent on speech context suggests the metaphor of dimension. At the origin of this dimension, we have the zero point, where the context of an utterance contributes nothing to its meaning. This is the anonymous letter situation, the idealization of a null context. The semantic component of the grammar is, by definition, a theory of the meaning of utterances at the zero point. Since the dimension represents the degree to which the utterance meaning of a sentence can be a function of features of its context, as we move toward the other extreme of this dimension, we encounter points representing increasing exploitation of features of the physical environment, the knowledge of the speaker about the beliefs, attitudes, and so on, of the audience, and other aspects of the context, to bring about a greater and greater dependency of utterance meaning on context, with cor-

9. Chomsky, *Aspects of the Theory of Syntax*, pp. 3-9.

respondingly less and less dependency on the sentence meaning of the sentence type to which the tokens belong. There will be a limit point at which utterance meaning is completely a product of context. At this point, where sentence meaning contributes nothing to utterance meaning, are utterances understood only on the basis of codes. When we consider different tokens of the same sentence type located at various points on this dimension from the zero point to the limit point, we are considering the larger and larger role of pragmatic principles in communication.

A pragmatic theory that systematically handlés the utterance meaning of sentence tokens beyond the zero point but short of the limit point does so on the basis of principles expressing how the grammatical meaning of sentence types interacts with features of context to determine utterance meaning. We may thus take a pragmatic theory to be a function of the form (1.16)—which we refer to as "PRAG".

$$(1.16) \quad \text{PRAG}\,(D(S_i), I(C(t))\,) = \{R_1, \ldots, R_n\}$$

Its arguments are $D(S_i)$, the full grammatical description of a sentence S_i, and $I(C(t))$, a specification of all the information about the context C in which the token t of S_i occurs that is relevant to t's utterance meaning. The output of PRAG is the set of sentence readings $R_1, \ldots, R_n$. If the context $C(t) = 0$, then, technically speaking, the set of readings $\{R_1, \ldots, R_n\}$ is the set of readings assigned to S_i in $D(S_i)$, that is, the set of readings that the grammar assigns to the type S_i as an account of its range of ambiguity. We shall make the simplifying assumption that, except for semantically anomalous sentences, $n = 1$ in the context $C(t) = 0$. This enables us to talk about the illocutionary potential of a sentence on one of its senses without involving ourselves in irrelevant discussion of the others. If the context $C(t) \neq 0$, then the output set $\{R_1, \ldots, R_n\}$ can be null or not. If the token t is meaningless in the context, then $n = 0$, as for instance an utterance of (1.14) by nursery school children.[10] If t has an utterance meaning, then $n \neq 0$. We shall assume, again for purposes of convenience, that $n = 1$.

This assumption has certain theoretical advantages. We can characterize the notion of equivocation as the case in which $n > 1$, that is, as the case in which the context allows the sentence token to bear two or more utterance meanings. This in turn enables us to characterize, contrastively, the notion of vagueness,

10. The grammatical description in a case like the use of (1.15) to express how poor a golfer someone is will come from a theory of semisentences, since such a theory relates semigrammatical strings to the grammatical strings they are understood in terms of. See J. A. Fodor and J. J. Katz, eds., *The Structure of Language: Readings in the Philosophy of Language* (Englewood Cliffs, N.J.: Prentice Hall, 1964) pp. 384–416.

roughly, as the case in which the context underdetermines features of a unique utterance meaning. Other pragmatic notions like evasiveness involve complex relations between the utterance meaning of a sentence token and certain contextually fixed expectations that the utterance meaning fails to satisfy.[11] These possibilities of definition depend on the assumption in question and make its acceptance desirable. I recognize, of course, that there is room for argument as to whether a given utterance can have more than one utterance meaning (make more than one statement, for example). Such cases exist, but I am tempted to think that the reason they do not count as equivocations is that it is clear that each statement is directed to a different audience.

We take the full grammatical description of S_i as an argument because, in principle, any aspect of S_i's grammatical structure, its sound pattern, morphology, syntax, or meaning, can play a role in determining the utterance meaning of S_i in a context. We choose sentences rather than smaller or larger linguistic forms because we take the proposition, the sense of a sentence, to be the basic unit of communication. We could take constituents of sentences of any kind in place of sentences, but the use of a word or phrase can always be seen as elliptical for the use of a sentence. The choice of the sentence as the unit of pragmatic analysis, then, represents the decision to view pragmatics as part of how people understand what they hear. There is nothing sacrosanct about this choice, particularly for those whose primary interest is in the study of language use. Our choice was motivated primarily by our interest in semantic structure.

On the other hand, taking single sentences rather than sequences of sentences is motivated by the fact that the contextual interpretation of discourses presupposes the interpretation of the individual utterances of which they consist. Nonetheless, here, too, we suppose that pragmatics in our narrow sense is only part of a full account of how people understand what they hear. Questions about how we are able to understand someone to have performed some speech act in producing a discourse even though that act is not performed by any of the utterances comprising it are to be answered in a theory of "discourse pragmatics", rather than in a theory of "sentence pragmatics". For example, a politician's two-hour speech may constitute his making the statement that economic conditions will improve, or his asking for a vote of confidence, or his calling for the overthrow of the government, even though none of the speech acts he performs in producing the utterances making up the speech perform the speech act. Such phenomena call for a broader theory than any represented by (1.16), but such a discourse pragmatics would need to be based on the utterance meanings of sentence tokens.

The output of PRAG is a reading rather than a full grammatical description

11. See Katz, *Semantic Theory*, pp. 213–216.

because all we wish to represent in the output is what the speaker states, asks, requests, and so on. Note also that we employ the notation of readings (that is, the same notation that represents the meaning of sentence types) to represent utterance meaning. This is the simplest way of obtaining a notation for utterance meaning, since we already need such a notation for sentence meaning and we describe what people assert, ask, request, and so on, using sentences such as (1.17), (1.18), or (1.19).

(1.17) He asserted that the book is silly.
(1.18) She asked whether George thought the book silly.
(1.19) They requested that the book be returned.

In an optimal grammar, such sentences will receive readings suitable as output for PRAG virtually as they stand. Moreover, if someone speaks ironically or sarcastically in saying (1.20), we would normally describe what was said by a token of the sentence type (1.21) or some similar sentence type.

(1.20) Ex-president Ford is a genius.
(1.21) Ex-president Ford is an idiot.

Since it is reasonable to think that the meaning of the sentence we use to describe what the speaker actually said [*viz.*, (1.21)] expresses[12] the utterance meaning of the sentence the speaker used [*viz.*, (1.20)], it seems natural to represent utterance meaning in the same notation that the grammar uses to represent sentence meaning.[13]

Adoption of the schema (1.16) as a normal form for pragmatic theories means that such theories are like grammars because they too are accounts of sound-meaning correlations. The difference is just that a grammar is an account of the sound-meaning correlation in a language, whereas a pragmatic theory is an account of the sound-meaning correlation in contexts of use. The correlation in the language is determined by the structural relations between the constitu-

12. A pragmatic theory, on this conception, thus assumes as a theoretical ideal that we can describe what the speaker actually says with perfect accuracy, that is, the whole proposition and nothing but that proposition. See Katz, *Semantic Theory*, pp. 120–127.

13. The proposal to use the same notation for both grammar and pragmatics is motivated by the economy of not using two separate notations for semantic representation. Although effability is not strictly a condition for achieving this economy, it is the most reasonable explanation of why it is that we would be generally justified in preferring the more economical grammar-pragmatic theory pairs in accounting for linguistic communication. See J. J. Katz, "Effability and Translation," in *The Theory of Translation: Linguistic and Philosophical Approaches*, ed. M. Guenthner-Reutter and F. Guenthner, (London: Duckworth, in press).

ents of sentences (that is, the syntactic and lexical relations that provide a basis for compositional meaning, on the one hand, and pronunciation, on the other). The correlation in context, that between tokens of sentences and their utterance meaning in the context, is determined by both the grammatical structure of the sentence type to which the token belongs and the special features of the context (such as the knowledge and beliefs of the speaker and the audience). The principal difference between grammars and pragmatic theories, then, is the following. The former are theories about the structure of sentence types, the sentences of a language. Their characterization of the structure of sentences, if optimal, determines all the grammatical properties and relations of each sentence in the language, whether it is well formed, whether it is declarative, imperative, ambiguous, what its metric structure is, whether it is analytic, and so on. This characterization is the basis on which these properties and relations are formally defined in the theory of grammars. Pragmatic theories, in contrast, do nothing to explicate the structure of linguistic constructions or grammatical properties and relations.[14] What they do is to assign sentence tokens to semantic types. They explicate the reasoning of speakers and hearers in working out the correlation in a context of a sentence token with a proposition. In this respect, a pragmatic theory is part of the theory of performance. It is like models of phonological and syntactic recognition, which assign sentence tokens to their proper phonological and syntactic types, thereby recognizing the sentence type to which the utterance belongs. Similarly, a theory of pragmatics, because an utterance meaning is represented as the sentence meaning of some (usually different) sentence, assigns sentence tokens to semantic types. It can thus be thought of as the recognition model at the semantic level. (It is equally natural to think of a pragmatic theory as a production model, insofar as it is reasonable to suppose that the speaker must reason by the same principles as the hearers in correlating sentence tokens with the propositions that exemplify the message communicated in the context. This duality is characteristic of models of phonological and syntactic processing, too.)

Given that the utterance meaning of a sentence S can be expressed as the grammatical meaning of another sentence S′, why isn't our performance mechanism designed to use S′ in the first place? What purpose is served by having it produce S and depend on information about the context to supply the hearers with part of the utterance meaning of S? One function performed by such a mechanism is to increase our repertoire of verbal behavior by permitting us to speak nonliterally. Its principal function, however, is that it allows speakers to make use of contextual features to speak far more concisely than otherwise.

14. J. J. Katz and D. T. Langendoen, "Pragmatics and Presupposition," *Language* 52, no. 1 (March 1976):1–17.

Imagine how lengthy utterances would be if everything we wanted to express had to be spelled out explicitly in the grammar of our sentences. Pragmatics saves us from this wasteful verbosity. Thus, instead of using sentences like (1.22), we can, on occasion, use sentences like (1.23).

> (1.22) The man who just asked the stupid question about the relation be-
> tween the mental and the physical has, thank God, left the room.
> (1.23) Thank God, he's gone.

Further, our pragmatic theory rests on the assumption that utterance mean-ing is as objective as sentence meaning. We assume that observers of the speech situation can be right or wrong about what was said, asked, requested, and so on. The main philosophical and linguistic issues concern the question of what, exactly, determines that such-and-such *is* the utterance meaning of a particular sentence token. (Is it the intention of the speaker to express such-and-such?) There are various theories,[15] but they are theories about the content of the function PRAG and as such do not concern us directly. The issue between them concerns only how it should be determined who is right in such disagreements about what was said, asked, requested, and so on, not whether there is some-thing to be right about. The basis for our assumption that utterance meaning is an objective notion is our conception of pragmatic theories of the form (1.16) as performance models. On such a conception, to suppose that particular in-stances of (1.16) are true or false theories about the semantic mechanism under-lying linguistic communication is as justified as supposing that particular schemes for phonological or syntactic processing are true or false theories about the phonological or syntactic mechanism. As performance models, these func-tions are theories of how the ideal speaker-hearer uses sentences of the language to communicate propositions that are not senses of these sentences in the language. These functions can be viewed as simulations of the principles that speaker-hearers use to exploit their knowledge of the grammar and their infor-mation about contexts to convey utterance meanings that are not equal in information to the grammatical meaning of the sentence that conveys them. Accordingly, questions about the truth or falsity of claims concerning what proposition is the utterance meaning of the sentence token in the context at hand are, in their most general and systematic form, questions about what particular instance of (1.16) is the simplest assignment of sentence tokens to semantic types that matches the speaker-hearer's clear intuitions about how tokens are understood in the speech contexts and about what such an optimal

15. The most promising, in my opinion, follow Grice and Searle in emphasizing the essential role of the speaker's intentions, e.g., see K. Bach and R. M. Harnish, *A Theory of Speech Acts* (New York: Thomas Y. Crowell, forthcoming).

instance of (1.16) predicts about the utterance meaning of the sentence token in the context at hand.

Finally, this conception of semantics and pragmatics offers a unification of the traditions of ordinary language philosophy and generative grammar. What has made these traditions seem irreconcilable are their apparently incompatible accounts of meaning: in the former tradition, a functionally oriented account in which meaning is identified with use, and in the latter, a formalistically oriented account in which meaning is identified with what the ideal speaker-hearer knows about the semantic structure of the sentences of a language. Our conception of semantics and pragmatics finds these two accounts of meaning to be reconcilable on the thesis that *meaning is the information that determines use in the null context*. This thesis preserves the fundamental insight in both traditions. We obtain a notion of meaning that is the same for the language and for speech contexts and is capable of formal analysis. We also obtain a notion that reflects the function of language in its semantic structure.

This thesis constitutes a significantly narrower claim about the relation of meaning and use than some philosophers in the ordinary language tradition would accept. They would object to the fact that our notion of use in the null context excludes things from the domain of semantics that influence the way speakers habitually employ words in speaking. For instance, the use of words like "bunny", "doggie", and so forth is governed by a convention of appropriateness that requires the speaker or the audience to be a child, whereas the use of words like "rabbit", "dog", and so forth is not. Insofar as utilizing this convention requires contextual information about the speaker and audience not available in the null context, our meaning and use equation excludes it from the domain of semantics. But the exclusion of this convention—as well as others such as those governing the employment of obscene words and offensive names of minority groups—is, in fact, an advantage. Synonymous words like "bunny" and "rabbit" that differ in their use in actual speech situations have frequently been cited as counter-examples to broader, more inclusive, identifications of meaning with use. We avoid such counter-examples.

On the other side, our equation meets a criticism that many ordinary language philosophers make of the tradition of semantic theory within generative grammar, namely, that it is not clear what abstract, formalized theories of semantic competence claim about how people actually use their language. Our conception of semantics and pragmatics clarifies this question by taking such theories to be descriptions of the contribution that speakers' knowledge of the language makes to their use of language. By treating theories of semantic competence in this way, it identifies the objects that a theory of use will assign to particular utterances as an interpretation of their meaning in context with propositions expressed by sentences in the language. This makes theories of semantic competence responsible for the logical structure of such interpretations; theories of pragmatics are responsible for explaining how such interpretations are assigned to utterances.

We make no further attempt to justify our conception of a pragmatic theory. To do so would require us to construct explanations of particular pragmatic phenomena and bring together the successful explanations to form an account of how the ideal speaker-hearer uses sentences to communicate. Then we would be in a position to determine whether our conception of a pragmatic theory accommodates these successful explanations. This should be done, but it is not part of our aim. Our aim here is confined to semantics. Thus, we shall adopt this conception of pragmatic theory and on the basis of it draw the line between semantics and pragmatics. This will provide us with a delimitation of what the semantic representation has to represent, that is, what it does and does not have to say about speech acts. Then we can set about the business of writing semantic representations that formalize the grammatically determined aspects of illocutionary force. This approach provides the possibility of an indirect justification of our conception of a pragmatic theory. For should the delimitation implied by our conception turn out to yield revealing semantic representations that can be obtained in no other way, it would be very strong support for our conception of a pragmatic theory.

COMPETENCE/PERFORMANCE
AND EXPLICIT FORMULAS

We are now ready to cash in on our conception of the relation between grammar and pragmatics to tell us what a semantic representation of the propositional type of a sentence should include.

For Austin and his followers in the speech act tradition, a theory of speech acts is a theory of acts, of utterances that constitute, in and of themselves, acts of one kind or another. This is why, instead of talking as we now do about the phonetic, phonological, morphological, syntactic, and semantic structure of sentences, Austin talked of "phonetic acts", "phatic acts", and "rhetic acts". In a theory like his, which lacks a competence/performance distinction, the various features that one wants to characterize have to be specified in terms of acts. Therefore, sorting out performative types is done in terms of types of utterances, and their relation to aspects of the grammar of sentences is expressed in terms of notions like "normal form", "explicit formulas", and "explicit performative". For instance, consider the following quote from Austin:

> . . . it is not in the least necessary that an utterance, if it is to be performative, should be expressed in one of these so-called normal forms. To say "Shut

the door", plainly enough, is every bit as performative . . . as to say "I order you to shut the door". Even the word "Dog" by itself can sometimes . . . stand in place of an explicit and formal performative; . . . To make our utterance performative, and quite unambiguously so, we can make use, in place of the explicit formula, of a whole lot of more primitive devices such as intonation, for instance, or gesture; further, and above all, the very context in which the words are uttered can make it entirely certain how they are to be taken.[16]

Hence, among (1.24)–(1.29), the only case that is an instance of the explicit formula for the act of requesting is (1.24).

    (1.24)   I request that you close the door.
    (1.25)   Close the door!
    (1.26)   The door!
    (1.27)   The damn cat is getting back in.
    (1.28)   The door is open.
    (1.29)   Were you brought up in a barn?

(1.25)–(1.29) are not in the appropriate normal form but, nonetheless, utterances of them can perform the same speech act of requesting that (1.24) normally does. Now, if we look at these cases within the framework set up in the previous section, the difference between (1.24) and (1.26)–(1.29)[17] is that the normal form of the former and the nonexplicitness of the latter are determined by the contrasting grammatical structure of these sentences in the language. Furthermore, the facts about usage that Austin insists on in the quotation above reflect the role that context plays in determining the requestive status of utterances (1.26)–(1.29). To understand (1.28) as a performative utterance issuing a request to close the door, we have to imagine a context in which it functions as, and was intended to function as, a reminder to the addressee. The reminder is that the door is in an undesirable position and is given by way of asking that the addressee put the door in the desired position. Without supplying such a context for a token of (1.28), it has the normal form of a constative rather than a performative. Within our framework, then, an explicit requestive formula like (1.24) can

16. J. L. Austin, "Performative-Constative," in *Philosophy and Ordinary Language*, ed. C. E. Caton (Urbana, Ill: University of Illinois Press, 1963), p. 26.
17. I omit (1.25) because it, too, might be considered an instance of the explicit formula for requesting. It might be argued that Austin's ideas about grammar were oriented to surface form. Considering what some transformational grammarians have said about the underlying form of imperatives [see J. J. Katz and P. Postal, *An Integrated Theory of Linguistic Descriptions* (Cambridge, Mass.: M.I.T. Press, 1964), pp. 74–79; and Katz, *Semantic Theory*, pp. 201–232], (1.25) might be regarded as explicit.

be described as a case where the null context suffices for its tokens to perform the speech act of requesting, whereas nonexplicit (requestive) formulas like (1.27)–(1.29) are cases where the null context does not suffice. Since (1.27) and (1.28) make statements in the null context and (1.29) asks a question, (1.27) and (1.28) are explicit assertive formulas and (1.29) is an explicit erotetic formula.

Just as the information about propositional content represented in the semantic representation of a sentence is the propositional content information it has in the null context, for example, the propositional content of (1.20) contains the concept of a genius, so the information about propositional type represented in the semantic representation of a sentence is the propositional-type information it has in the null context. Thus, the propositional type of (1.24) and (1.25) is requestive whereas the propositional type of (1.27) and (1.28) is assertive and the propositional type of (1.29) is erotetic. Accordingly, we may provide (1.30).

(1.30) The propositional type of a sentence (on a sense) is the information that determines the type of speech act that a token performs in the null context.

(1.31) The propositional content of a sentence (on a sense) is the information that determines the particular speech act (within the categories specified by its propositional type, and subtypes) a token performs in the null context.

(1.31) says that the part of a semantic representation that represents the propositional content of sentences like (1.4) and (1.8) has to specify that they are semantically equipped to make different promises in the null context, in the case of (1.4) to eat the cookies, and in the case of (1.8) to pay debts. We note that, although for convenience we speak about a token of a sentence type performing a speech act, this is to be understood to mean that the speaker performs the act in the use of the token.

Given (1.30) and (1.31), the grammar is responsible for representing all illocutionary force information contained in the structure of sentence types, just as it is responsible for representing all information about reference and predication contained in the structure of sentence types (on most everyone's theory).[18] Of course, we have not as yet argued that the semantic component is responsible for representing this information, as opposed to, say, the syntactic component. This is shown in Chapter 2, so we may overlook this point for the

18. Not everyone's, however; see L. Karttunen, "The Presuppositions of Compound Sentences," *Linguistic Inquiry* 4 (1973): 169–193. But see the rejoinder in Katz and Langendoen, "Pragmatics and Presupposition."

present. Thus, semantic representation becomes, in Austin's terminology, semantic representation of "explicit formulas". Since every sentence type is an explicit formula of some kind, semantic representation of propositional type will contain just the information that determines the illocutionary force of a sentence at the zero point. Correspondingly, semantic representation of propositional content will contain all the information that determines the differences between the particular speech acts performed at the zero point by sentences of the same propositional type. Thus, pragmatic theory is relieved of the burden of information about propositional type and content in its account of the utterance meaning of sentence tokens at any nonzero point. Just as on Chomsky's view[19] a performance theory dealing with the recognition of syntactic structure employs a theory of syntactic competence, so on our view a performance theory dealing with recognizing utterance meaning employs a theory of semantic competence. Thus, its account of utterance meaning can be given as an account of the divergence of utterance meaning from sentence meaning, using the semantic component's account of sentence meaning. The principles that explain how such divergence can occur without loss of comprehensibility to other speakers take the form (1.16) and constitute an explication of speakers' extragrammatical ability to use their beliefs about the context to speak more concisely, more subtly, more sarcastically, and so on.[20] The relation between the grammar of a language and a pragmatic theory is that the latter employs the sound-meaning correlations defined in the former to produce new sound-meaning correlations that are valid only for particular situations.

SEARLE'S CONCEPTION OF THE RELATION OF GRAMMAR TO SPEECH ACT THEORY

Speech act theory, since Austin, has undergone various modifications and attempts at systematization. At present, the most sophisticated and systematic version is found in the work of John .Searle. Searle was the first speech act theorist in the development of speech act theory to take into account the work of transformational grammarians. Searle's writings contain two conceptions of the relation of grammar to speech act theory. The first, which appears in his book,[21] is tentative and only suggestive, but seems to be essentially the same as ours. The second is definite and spelled out. It appears shortly after and

19. Chomsky, *Aspects of the Theory of Syntax*, p. 10.
20. Also, as in the case of a use of (1.27), we can express the reason for the urgency of the request in the making of it.
21. J. Searle, *Speech Acts* (Cambridge: Cambridge University Press, 1969), p. 64.

formulates an entirely different relation between grammar and speech act theory. In this section, we shall consider this alternative conception.

Searle's most explicit statement of his conception of how grammar and speech act theory are related is expressed in the following:

> The limitations of Chomsky's assumptions become clear only when we attempt to account for the meaning of sentences within his system, because there is no way to account for the meaning of a sentence without considering its role in communication, since the two are essentially connected. So long as we confine our research to syntax, where in fact most of Chomsky's work has been done, it is possible to conceal the limitations of the approach, because syntax can be studied as a formal system independently of its use. . . . But as soon as we attempt to account for meaning, for semantic competence, such a purely formalistic approach breaks down, because it cannot account for the fact that semantic competence is mostly a matter of knowing how to talk, i.e., how to perform speech acts.

> The Chomsky revolution is largely a revolution in the study of syntax. The obvious next step in the development of the study of language is to graft the study of syntax onto the study of speech acts.[22]

Searle's conception, put succinctly, comes to the claim that grammar (in the sense of generative grammar) is a formal system describing the syntactic (and we may assume, the phonological) structure of sentences to which speech act theory hooks up directly as a (nonformal) account of how speakers use sentences to perform speech acts. Thus, Austin's phonetic acts and phatic acts can be treated in grammar, but sense, reference, and rhetic acts all require a new theory.

The issue between this conception and ours is whether what hooks up with a theory of use is syntax, as Searle claims, or semantics, as we have claimed. The crux of the issue is whether there is a system of formal semantics in the grammar, which explicates the ideal speaker-hearer's knowledge of the meaning of sentence types. Searle offers two considerations to persuade the reader that there is no system of formal semantics in the grammar. First, he argues that "the semantic theory of Chomsky's grammar"[23] offers

> . . . a useful and interesting adjunct to the theory of semantic competence, since it gives us a model that duplicates the speaker's competence in recog-

---

22. J. Searle, "Chomsky's Revolution in Linguistics," originally published in *The New York Review of Books* (1972), reprinted in G. Harman, ed., *On Noam Chomsky* (New York: Anchor Books, 1974), p. 30.

23. This is one of various Searlelocutions referring to my work.

nizing ambiguity, synonymy, nonsense, etc. But as soon as we ask *what* exactly the speaker is recognizing when he recognizes one of these semantic properties. . . , it cannot cope with the dilemma. Either it gives us a sterile formalism, an uninterpreted list of elements, or it gives us paraphrases, which explain nothing.[24]

This argument, that a formal theory of semantics within grammar is either empty or vacuous, is easily seen to beg the question. Elsewhere,[25] I have examined Searle's argument in detail, but here it suffices to observe that there is no basis whatever for Searle to say that the formalism is sterile because he has no grounds for saying that its elements are uninterpreted. The theory he is criticizing is at great pains to provide a systematic interpretation of this formalism in terms of concepts and propositions. It takes the elementary components of the semantic representations of lexical items to stand for simple concepts and the grouping notation in such representations to express the relations between the simple concepts that comprise complex concepts and propositions.[26] And it provides rules to specify how the formation of such complex concepts and propositions takes place.[27] If Searle were to neglect the interpretation of the formalism for syntactic representation, as he neglects the interpretation of the formalism for semantic representation, he could accuse Chomsky's syntactic theories of the same sterility. Searle quite correctly points out that as far as the formalism is concerned, it does not matter whether we use the standard symbols or piles of stones. But Searle goes on to make this criticism:

Suppose we decide to interpret the readings as piles of stones. Then for a three-ways ambiguous sentence the theory will give us three piles of stones, for a nonsense sentence, no piles of stones, for an analytic sentence the arrangement of stones in the predicate pile will be duplicated in the subject pile, and so on. There is nothing in the formal properties of the semantic component to prevent us from interpreting it in this way. But clearly this will not do because now instead of explaining the relationships between sound and meaning the theory has produced an unexplained relationship between sounds and stones.[28]

24. Searle, "Chomsky's Revolution in Linguistics," p. 28.

25. J. J. Katz, "Logic and Language: An Examination of Recent Criticisms of Intensionalism," in *Language, Mind, and Knowledge*, Minnesota Studies in the Philosophy of Science, vol. VII, ed. K. Gunderson (Minneapolis: University of Minnesota Press, 1975), pp. 107–113.

26. See J. J. Katz, *The Philosophy of Language*, (New York: Harper & Row, 1966), pp. 155–157.

27. In particular, the projection rule, see Katz, *Semantic Theory*, pp. 98–116.

28. Searle, "Chomsky's Revolution in Linguistics," p. 27.

THE RELATION BETWEEN SPEECH ACT THEORY
AND SEMANTIC THEORY

Searle assumes that there has to be something in "the formal properties of a component" of the grammar to prevent bizarre contruals of its formalism. If this assumption were accepted, the formalism of syntax and phonology could provide no explanation of constituent structure and pronunciation. This reductio shows that Searle is simply confused about where to look. One looks not in the formal properties of the components but in the informal statements of the metatheory. These statements interpret such properties in the object language, that is, of the formalism. These statements interpret the formalism at the semantic level in terms of concepts just as they interpret the formalism at the phonological level in terms of speech sounds.

The second way Searle tries to make the reader think that there is no system of formal semantics in the grammar amounts to a definitional trick. The trick is to define "semantic competence", which is understood in the theory of grammar to be the ideal speaker-hearer's knowledge of the meaning of sentence types in the language, as follows:

> . . . a person's knowledge of the meaning of sentences consists in large part in his knowledge of how to use sentences to make statements, ask questions, give orders, make requests, make promises, warnings, etc., and to understand other people when they use sentences for such purposes. Semantic competence is in large part the ability to perform and understand what philosophers and linguists call *speech acts*.[29]

It is customary to expose such definitional tricks by distinguishing between the old and new meanings of the expression in terms of subscripts. Thus, we may distinguish between "semantic competence$_1$", which is the ideal speaker-hearer's knowledge of the meaning of sentence types in the language, and "semantic competence$_2$", which is a person's knowledge of how to use sentences to perform speech acts. Our conception is that semantic competence$_2$ contains semantic competence$_1$ plus a theory of pragmatics. Searle's is that it is a mistake to think that there is any semantic competence$_1$ and, contrary to our conception of the relation of grammar to speech act theory, that speech act theory is not simply part of the theory of performance. We have already dealt with Searle's claim that a theory of semantic competence$_1$ is either empty or vacuous. His claim that semantic competence$_2$ is not part of the theory of performance is based on the rather implausible view that Chomsky "has a mistaken conception of the distinction between performance and competence".[30] Searle says:

> He seems to think that a theory of speech acts must be a theory of performance rather than of competence, because he fails to see that competence is

29. Ibid., pp. 28-29.
30. Ibid., p. 31.

ultimately the competence to perform, and that for this reason a study of the linguistic aspects of the ability to perform speech acts is a study of linguistic competence.[31]

It is Searle, however, who has a mistaken conception of the competence/performance distinction. "Competence", as Chomsky uses it,[32] is a technical term. It refers to the idealized speaker-hearer's perfect (phonological, syntactic, and semantic) knowledge of the language. Hence, it is not clear what Searle means to say when he equates competence with "competence to perform". He cannot mean that Chomsky provides no connection between competence and a speaker's ability to use the language, since Searle must know that Chomsky has proposed that performance models incorporate a theory of competence.[33] One is forced to interpret Searle to be equating the theory of competence with the theory of the speaker's ability to use language, in spite of the fact that earlier Searle seems to grant Chomsky an independent notion of competence for syntax. This interpretation is necessary if Searle is to have a basis for the conclusion he goes on to draw. It is also confirmed by Searle's recent more radical position. He writes: ". . . so far as we can tell structure, function, and meaning in natural languages interact in all sorts of interesting and complex ways and it is extremely unlikely that all of the rules of structure can be stated completely independently of any of the rules for the use of the structures in question".[34]

On this construal, Searle has a mistaken conception of the competence/performance distinction. On Searle's account, "the linguistic aspects of the ability to perform speech acts", which for Searle means the ability to use sentences to perform speech acts, includes all sorts of things (for example, the exercise of what Searle calls "preparatory rules"[35]), which cannot be part of competence in Chomsky's sense. Therefore, Searle's conclusion that the study of linguistic competence *is* "the study of the linguistic aspects of the ability to perform speech acts" turns out to be the empty claim that the study of competence$_2$ is "the study of the linguistic aspects of the ability to perform speech acts", namely, competence$_2$.

What makes Searle's conception seem plausible is that a semantic theory that accounts for the idealized speaker-hearer's ability to recognize semantic properties and relations like analyticity, synonymy, ambiguity, anomaly, and so on, has not as yet offered an account of the illocutionary potential of sentence

31. Ibid., p. 31.

32. Chomsky, *Aspects of the Theory of Syntax*, pp. 3-4.

33. Ibid., p. 10.

34. J. Searle, "The Rules of The Language Game," *The Times Literary Supplement* (September 1976): 1119.

35. Searle, *Speech Acts*, pp. 66-67.

types. In the chapters to follow, we shall show how such a semantic theory can be extended to account for the illocutionary potential of sentences. In the remainder of this chapter, we present arguments to show that the development of semantic theory leads naturally to such an account.

Semantic theory explicates the semantic competence to determine semantic properties and relations on the basis of a hypothesis about the way that sentences obtain their meaning as a compositional function of the meanings of their constituents. This hypothesis expresses an isomorphism between the formal representations of compositional meaning and the defining conditions for semantic properties and relations. The question at issue, then, is whether, as a consequence of the principles already introduced to represent compositional meaning and define semantic properties and relations, such a theory comes to embrace the illocutionary potential of sentences within the same theoretical scheme. Will these principles permit us to represent the illocutionary potential of sentences in the account of their compositional meaning? This question leads immediately to two arguments against Searle's conception of the relation between speech act theory and grammar.

Semantic entailment is one semantic relation that a semantic theory is required to explicate, and the semantic entailment of a sentence is one of its properties that a semantic component of the grammar is required to predict.[36] A reading of a sense of a sentence that permits us to predict *all* its semantic entailments (and nothing that is not a semantic entailment of the sentence) adequately represents its logical form. If the sentence expresses an assertive proposition, such a reading will represent the truth conditions of the sentence (on the appropriate sense).[37] Thus, the semantic component of a grammar of English has to represent the truth condition of (1.32) as the condition that the referents of the noun phrases "I", "you", and "the movie" stand in the relation "x promised y to see z".

(1.32)   I promised you to see the movie.

Another way of saying this is to say that a semantic component has to represent (1.32), (1.33), and (1.34) in such a way that the entailment of (1.33) and (1.34) by (1.32) can be predicted.

(1.33)   The speaker referred to a future act of his own.[38]
(1.34)   The speaker undertook an obligation.

36. Katz, *Semantic Theory*, pp. 4–7, and pp. 188–191.

37. Ibid., p. 41.

38. The notion of future here is simply occurrence after the speech point associated with the performative verb.

Now, (1.32) differs from the performative sentence (1.35) only in having a past rather than a present tense.

(1.35)   I promise you to see the movie.

This difference concerns only when the action is supposed to occur. It does not concern aspects of the meaning of (1.32) and (1.35) related to their predicative structure. The argument runs as follows. For (1.32), we have to construct a semantic representation of the sentence that contains the notion of the futurity of the act described by the verb in the underlying complement sentence and the notion of undertaking of an obligation. These representations are necessary to predict the entailments of (1.33) and (1.34), and to state the truth conditions of (1.32). We would have to get such a semantic representation of (1.32), however, from the mechanism that reconstructs its compositional meaning. Hence, we would have to represent these notions as deriving, compositionally, from the meaning of the verb "promise". Since the notions of futurity and of undertaking an obligation are part of the lexical meaning of "promise", and since the meaning of performative sentences are just as compositional as the meaning of nonperformative sentences, it is reasonable to say that the meaning of (1.35) contains these notions, too, because (1.35) has the same lexical source as (1.32). The difference in tense is not the kind that can bring about a difference in the lexical aspect of the meaning of sentences like (1.32) and (1.35). If the lexical meaning of "promise" makes the same semantic contribution to performative sentences and nonperformatives and both kinds of sentence obtain their meaning compositionally, then a theory that describes the compositional meaning of one must also describe the compositional meaning of the other. It would be absurd to claim that the speaker's knowledge of the truth conditions of (1.32) is explained by hypothesizing that the speaker has an internal representation of the rules of the semantic component of English grammar but to deny that the speaker's knowledge of the illocutionary conditions of (1.35) (corresponding to these truth conditions) is explained by the same hypothesis.

The second argument against Searle's conception of the relation between semantic theory and speech act theory is based on an area of agreement. Searle acknowledges that a semantic theory provides a model of the knowledge used by speakers to recognize semantic properties and relations. Like other theories, semantic theory has every right to claim that anything it must assume, in order to account for the properties and relations acknowledged to fall in its domain, is part of what the theory is about. If performative sentences exhibit the same semantic properties and relations as nonperformative sentences, and if explaining these properties and relations requires that the dictionary representation of performative verbs contain significant aspects of the illocutionary potential of the sentences containing them, then semantic theory may claim to be as much about the illocutionary potential of sentences as it is about other aspects of sentence meaning.[39]

A few examples will establish that the constituents of performative sentences that embody their illocutionary potential do exhibit semantic properties and relations. First, (1.36) is synonymous with (1.37), and (1.38) is synonymous with (1.39).

(1.36) Who knows a secret that he will not tell?
(1.37) I request that you tell me who knows a secret he will not tell.
(1.38) Do not stick your fingers in the wall outlet.
(1.39) I request that you do not stick your fingers in the wall outlet.

Second, both (1.36) and (1.37) entail (1.40), and (1.41) entails (1.42).

(1.40) Someone knows a secret that he will not tell.
(1.41) I promise to support the old man.
(1.42) I undertake the obligation to support the old man.
(1.43) I confess I never heard about it.

Third, the sentence (1.43) is ambiguous (between a genuine confession and an ordinary statement of fact to the effect that the speaker never heard about it). Fourth, the sentence (1.44) is analytic and (1.45) is contradictory.

(1.44) Is breakfast a meal?
(1.45) . I warn you that no harm of any kind will come to you.

Fifth, the sentence (1.46) is semantically anomalous.

(1.46) I authorize the truth.

The semantic properties and relations of these sentences depend on the sense of their performative verbs and other syntactic devices indicating illocutionary force. It follows that the semantic component of a grammar will explain these properties and relations by providing readings for these verbs and the other appropriate syntactic devices, which will be combined in accord with the constituent structure of the sentences to form sentence readings whose formal structure satisfies the appropriate definitions. The aspects of meaning represented by

39. This argument is due to R. M. Harnish, "Semantic Theory and Speech Acts" (unpublished, University of Arizona). I have changed some examples to make the cases more natural to my idiolect.

readings in this kind of semantic explanation are part of what the semantic component is a theory about. Hence, semantic theory accounts for illocutionary force potential of sentences on the same basis as it accounts for other aspects of the grammatical meaning of sentences.

If these arguments are correct, there is no such thing as speech act theory in Searle's sense of the term. That is, there is no system of principles offering a uniform account of how sentences are used to perform speech acts that covers every aspect of such phenomena beyond the syntax and phonology of the sentences. The key word is "uniform". As Searle stresses, no part of our semantic ability to perform speech acts can be separated out and "studied as a formal system independently of its use".[40]

"Speech act theory" turns out to be a hybrid, part semantic component and part pragmatic theory, the former telling us what sentences, performative and nonperformative alike, mean in the language, and the latter telling us what they mean in various contexts. We should therefore be able to run through sets of speech act rules such as Searle has,[41] and exhaustively parcel out each rule to the category of semantic rules in the grammar or to the category of use rules in a pragmatic theory, depending on whether they express information about the meaning of a performative verb or other illocutionary force-indicating device, or information about how features of a context influence the illocutionary status of tokens of sentences occurring in them. It is plausible to think that such a parceling out is possible because the speech act rules Searle proposes for the illocutionary act of promising, namely, (1.47), are of two very different kinds.

(1.47)   Rule 1. *Pr* is to be uttered only in the context of a sentence (or larger stretch of discourse) T, the utterance of which predicates some future act A of the speaker S.

Rule 2. *Pr* is to be uttered only if the hearer H would prefer S's doing A to his not doing A, and S believes H would prefer S's doing A to his not doing A.

Rule 3. *Pr* is to be uttered only if it is not obvious to both S and H that S will do A in the normal course of events.

Rule 4. *Pr* is to be uttered only if S intends to do A.

Rule 5. The utterance of *Pr* counts as the undertaking of an obligation to do A.[42]

40. Searle, "Chomsky's Revolution in Linguistics," p. 30.

41. Searle, *Speech Acts*, p. 63.

42. Ibid., p. 63.

Rules 1, 2, and 5 are about the kind of information a dictionary would give about the lexical meaning of "promise". Rules 3 and 4 provide the kind of information given in principles about how highly structured behavioral interactions are coordinated by their participants.

For example, rule 1 provides the lexical information needed in a compositional semantic analysis to account for the fact that one of the truth conditions of (1.32) is that the act of seeing the movie predicated of the speaker postdates the speaker's uttering the promise to see the movie. Moreover, the contrast between this rule and the corresponding rule for the verb "thank" is part of the basis on which a semantic component marks the semantic difference between these verbs (the illocutionary force-indicating device for "thanking" is to be uttered only in the context of a sentence predicating some past act of the hearer). On the other hand, rule 4 seems to be only a special case of the general social convention underlying the coordination of behavioral interactions we expect people to follow. We expect speakers to act sincerely in their interactions with the audience, just as we expect automobile drivers' hand signals to express their true intention to turn as the signal indicates. Rules 2 and 5, or something like them, seem also to be semantic: The former helps to distinguish the verb "promise" from the verb "threaten", and the latter helps to account for entailments like that between (1.41) and (1.42). Rule 3, which seems to be a special case of some general convention against wasting one's breath, does not even reflect a condition on promising, since there are cases of promising that violate it.[43] It seems reasonable to think that Searle's rules for illocutionary acts parcel out into the two categories of semantic rules and rules of use, reducing speech act theory, in Searle's sense, to the theory of grammar and the theory of pragmatics.

Interestingly, when Searle held his earlier conception of the relation of grammar to speech act theory, he wrote several things that seem to endorse such a reduction. At one point in *Speech Acts*, he writes:

> Notice also that the rather tiresome analogy with games is holding up remarkably well. If we ask ourselves under what conditions a player could be said to move a knight correctly, we would find preparatory conditions such as that it must be his turn to move, as well as the essential condition stating the actual positions the knight can move to. There are even sincerity conditions for competitive games, such as that one does not cheat or attempt to "throw" the game. *Of course, the corresponding sincerity "rules" are not peculiar to this or that game but apply to competitive games generally.*[44]

43. This volume, pp. 150–152.
44. Searle, *Speech Acts*, p. 63. Italics mine.

Searle also says:

> . . . In particular, the non-obviousness preparatory condition runs through so many kinds of illocutionary acts that I think that it is not a matter of separate rules for the utterance of particular illocutionary force indicating devices at all, but rather is a general condition on illocutionary acts (and analoguously for other kinds of behavior) to the effect that the act is defective if the point to be achieved by the satisfaction of the essential rule is already achieved. There is, e.g., no point in telling somebody to do something if it is completely obvious that is is going to do it anyhow. But that is no more a *special* rule for requests than it is a matter of a special rule for moving the knight that the player can only move the knight when it is his turn to move.[45]

If what he says here is right, and it surely seems to be, then his later conception mistakenly states "general conditions" on illocutionary acts as idiosyncratic features of individual types. The nature, and to some extent the seriousness, of this mistake is the same as the mistake of stating rules in a generative grammar in a form that fails to reflect their true generality. Generative grammarians have set up a notion of simplicity for grammatical rules that measures the loss of generality by how many times a rule has to be unnecessarily stated because it was not formulated originally with sufficient generality. Thus, the failure to state as a single general condition on acts the principle that acts are defective if there is no point to performing them makes it necessary for Searle to state it over and over again in the case of each particular (relevant) illocutionary act type.[46] From the generative grammarian's point of view, this extravagance ought to cost Searle dearly when his theory is compared with others that use a more general formulation of the condition. If we follow this line of thought to its logical conclusion, our preference for theories with minimal cost makes us bifurcate speech act theory into a theory about the general conditions or "ground rules" on the coordination of complex behavior in structured interaction situations and a theory about the idiosyncratic features of particular illocutionary force-indicating devices in the syntax of sentences. That is, we are led directly to a reduction of speech act theory to the grammar and a pragmatic theory.

The orientation of the chapters to follow is this. We assume (fully appreciating of the enormity of the assumption) that there is nothing to prevent the construction of a pragmatic theory that, among other things, will be capable of stating with sufficient generality the information in rules like Searle's rules 3 and

45. Ibid., pp. 69-70.
46. As, for instance, for the types listed by Searle in his chart in Ibid., pp. 66-67.

4.[47] We then set as our goal the task of accomplishing the grammatical side of the reduction. That is, we shall try to set up a formal theory of the structure of propositions that states information like that in Searle's rules 1, 2, and 5 as part of the speaker's competence, that is, knowledge of the grammatical meaning of sentence types in the language. Our discussion of grammar and pragmatics has served, for our purposes, to set an appropriate goal for explicating of the notion of propositional type.[48]

47. It might, for example, be an expanded version of Grice's theory of conversational logic. See P. Grice, "Logic and Conversation," in *Syntax and Semantics: Speech Acts*, ed. P. Cole and J. L. Morgan (New York: Academic Press, 1975), pp. 41-58. But such an expansion would have to overcome serious difficulties, for example, see J. J. Katz, and D. T. Langendoen, "Pragmatics and Presupposition," Section 5, pp. 13-14.

48. A full critique of Searle's position would also consider the difficulties with his positive account of meaning (see H. P. Grice, "Meaning," *The Philosophical Review* 66, no. 3 (1957): 377-388 and Searle, *Speech Acts*, pp. 42-50). For example, the acute criticism of this account found in P. Ziff, "On Grice's Account of Meaning," *Analysis* 28, no. 1 (1967): 1-8, has, to the best of my knowledge, never been answered. Ziff makes the point that an account of this kind fails as an account of meaning because it neglects the "set of projection devices," the recursive character of the semantic structure of a natural language, that is, just what Searle now denies as a matter of doctrine.

2
SENTENCE TYPE AND PROPOSITIONAL TYPE

INTRODUCTION

We have argued that the explication of propositional type is a job for grammar. Ultimately we shall claim that it is to be carried out in the semantic component. The logic of our argument requires us to provide support for thinking that neither of the other two components of the grammar, the phonological and the syntactic, is the proper place to formally represent propositional type. The phonological component is concerned primarily with pronunciation, so we may dismiss it, which leaves the syntactic component. The question then becomes how much of propositional type can be explicated within the framework that explicates sentence type.

To answer it, we shall consider the most promising proposals of linguists about the syntactic structure underlying the propositional type of sentences. We shall try to show that these proposals fail to make a case for a syntactic explication of propositional type, and furthermore that they fail in ways that make it reasonable to think that the explication of propositional type belongs in the semantic component. We shall also determine which aspects of sentence structure are interpreted in the semantic component as illocutionary force-indicating devices. This question is important in a compositional theory of sentence meaning (in which sentence meaning contains information about illocutionary potential), since this information must derive from the meaning of constituents of sentences and such a theory must identify these constituents.

THE INTEGRATED-THEORY THEORY
AND ROSS'S ALTERNATIVE THEORY

English sentence types include *declaratives*, *interrogatives*, *imperatives*, and *hortatories*. Propositional types include *assertives*, *requestives*, *promisories*, and *permissives*. In accord with (1.30), different propositional types are to be

37

thought of as what it is about propositions that is responsible for their performing different illocutionary acts in the null context. *An Integrated Theory of
Linguistic Descriptions* made the first attempt to relate sentence type and
propositional type in the theory of transformational grammar.[1] This book relates them in two ways. First, propositional-type information was held to come
from the meaning of certain different abstract syntactic elements underlying
the surface form of declaratives, interrogatives, imperatives, and hortatories,
for example, the Q morpheme, the I morphemes, intonational contour structures.
Second, such information was held to come from the meaning of performative
verbs.[2] Thus, both (2.1) and (2.2) express requestive propositions, but in (2.1)
the type is derived from the meaning of the Q morpheme in the underlying
phrase marker, whereas in (2.2) it is derived from the meaning of the performative verb "request".

(2.1) Who did the deed?
(2.2) I request that you tell me who did the deed.

The obvious advantage of this account, which we shall refer to as "the integrated-
theory theory", is that by postulating different underlying structures it preserves
the simplest relation between the deep syntactic structure of sentences and their
surface structure. The deep syntactic structure of neither type of sentence needs
to be made more complex just to obtain the correct propositional type for each
sentence.

Recently, Ross proposed an alternative theory that sacrifices this simple
relation in order to gain uniformity in the underlying syntactic source.[3] In the
integrated-theory theory, the underlying syntactic sources of (2.1) and (2.2)
are different, as are the underlying syntactic sources of (2.3) and (2.4).

(2.3) The dog barked.
(2.4) I say that the dog barked.

In Ross's theory, this difference disappears, but at the price of more complex
deep syntactic structures and more complex transformational relations to
surface structure. In the integrated-theory theory, the underlying phrase marker
for a sentence like (2.3) would be something like (2.5).

1. J. J. Katz and P. Postal, *An Integrated Theory of Linguistic Descriptions* (Cambridge,
Mass.: M.I.T. Press, 1964).
2. Ibid., p. 89.
3. J. R. Ross, "On Declarative Sentences," in *Readings in Transformational Grammar*,
ed. R. A. Jacobs and P. S. Rosenbaum (Boston: Ginn-Blaisdell, 1970), pp. 222–272.

(2.5)

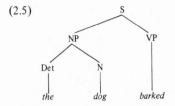

In Ross's theory, the underlying phrase marker for (2.3) would be something like (2.6).[4]

(2.6)

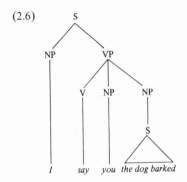

Embedding phrase markers like (2.5) in higher sentence structures like (2.6), whose main verb is an appropriate performative verb, increases the homogeneity of the underlying source. But there is a corresponding loss in simplicity, because the transformational relation to surface structure must involve the application of an erasure transformation that strips away the higher sentence structure to leave something close to the structure represented in (2.5).

To justify these more complex deep syntactic structures and tranformational relations, Ross must justify each of the main features of his higher sentence structures. He has to show that there is independent motivation for positing the following: (1) a higher subject which takes the form of the first-person pronoun, (2) a higher verb which is performative and which in the case of simple declaratives like (2.3) is something more or less like "say", and (3) a second-person pronoun indirect object of this higher verb. Ross tries to do this, presenting a number of arguments for (1), (2), and (3). These arguments together with the criticisms that have been made of them may be briefly reviewed here to provide

4. I use the item "say", but Ross has in mind some abstract verb or bundle of features, including [+Performative], [+Communicative], [+Linguistic], and [+ Declarative]. Here it makes no difference, so that convenience decides in favor of the simpler form.

the reader with some idea of the controversy in syntactic theory. We shall make no attempt to provide more than a sketch, both because a more comprehensive treatment would leave things in much the same inconclusive state as our sketch and because there is a semantic argument against Ross's theory that definitively refutes it.[5] We shall present it after our brief review.

Ross claims that underlying a declarative sentence there is a higher sentence structure with a first-person singular subject. His first argument is based on the rule that turns a noun phrase into an anaphoric reflexive pronoun of a preceding coreferential noun phrase; this rule applies only if both noun phrases are in the same simplex sentence.[6] Thus the difference in grammaticality between (2.7) and (2.8):

(2.7) I think that I will win.
(2.8) *I think that myself will win.

Ross notes that this rule is not general enough to account for the difference in grammaticality between sentences like (2.9) and (2.10).

(2.9) Tom believed that the paper had been written by Ann and (him) himself.
(2.10) *Tom believed that the paper had been written by Ann and themselves.

He suggests that these examples, together with examples like (2.11) and (2.12), show that a sufficiently general rule would determine the occurrence of reflexive pronouns on the basis of an anaphoric relation to an appropriate constituent of a higher sentence.

(2.11) This paper was written by Ann and myself.
(2.12) *This paper was written by Ann and himself.

Though Ross offers no formulation of the rule, he claims that the principle in question must be embodied in any adequate formulation. He observes that if structures like (2.6) underlie surface forms like (2.5), then the grammaticality of (2.9) and (2.11) and the ungrammaticality of (2.10) and (2.12) could be predicted. The surface structure of (2.3) and (2.11) would be obtained by a rule of "performative deletion", which erases the higher sentence structure with the first-person singular subject (which determines the reflexive pronoun in (2.11)).

---

5. At best, the criticism could only show that there is no evidence for Ross's theory, whereas the semantic argument shows it to be false.

6. All the arguments of Ross's cited here are from "On Declarative Sentences."

Hence, (2.3), which is a simple sentence in the integrated-theory theory, is a complex sentence in Ross's theory.

Ross's chief critics, Anderson and Fraser,[7] point out counter-examples to Ross's principle of command by a higher constituent. Anderson cites the sentence (2.13) as a direct counter-example to Ross's account of the distribution of reflexive pronouns.

(2.13) The government approves the formation of a commission to be headed by Milton Eisenhower and yourself to look into the causes of violence in America.

The occurrence of the pronoun "yourself" in (2.13) is unpredictable on Ross's principle of command by a higher constituent, because the fact that "approves" takes only one object rules out command by a higher noun phrase as a basis for predicting the reflexive form. There can be no argument that the sentence is embedded in a deleted performative sentence structure insofar as the sentence in question is already performative.

Anderson offers further counter-examples that show that some account other than Ross's is required. Among them are (2.14) and (2.15).

(2.14) Was the paper which John mentioned finally written by just Mary and himself?

(2.15) Since the people who he expected yesterday haven't arrived yet, the work can't be completed by only Sue and myself.

Fraser adds (2.16) and (2.17).

(2.16) I agree (with you) that the letter should have been written by Harry and ourselves.

(2.17) The chair acknowledges that the question was directed at the secretary and myself.

Ross also argues that pronoun reflexivization in "like" phrases is determined by the commanding noun phrase, as illustrated in (2.18).

(2.18) I told Albert that physicists like himself were a godsend.

Accordingly, Ross takes the difference between the grammaticality of the sen-

7. S. Anderson, "On the Linguistic Status of the Performative/Constative Distinction," mimeo (Cambridge, Mass.: Harvard University, 1968); B. Fraser, "A Reply to 'On Declarative Sentences,' " (Cambridge, Mass.: Language Research Foundation, 1969). Subsequent examples from Anderson and Fraser will also come from these papers.

tences in (2.19) and the ungrammaticality of (2.20) to be evidence for his position.

(2.19) Physicists like $\begin{Bmatrix} \text{Albert} \\ \text{him} \\ \text{myself} \end{Bmatrix}$ don't often make mistakes.

(2.20) *Physicists like $\begin{Bmatrix} \text{herself} \\ \text{themselves} \end{Bmatrix}$ don't often make mistakes.

Fraser offers the counter-examples (2.21) and (2.22).

(2.21) I want to talk to you, Harry. John claimed to me that a man like yourself ought to be elected easily.

(2.22) I ask the advice of men like yourself.

In (2.21), an appropriate sentential context makes us realize that what at first blush seems to be ungrammaticality is only the unacceptability of a sentence lacking an appropriate context.[8] In (2.22) either the performative is embedded in an ellipsed higher sentence structure, contrary to Ross's account,[9] or else Ross's account cannot be extended to performative sentences generally. Anderson cites the example (2.23).[10]

(2.23) A good plumber like yourself can make thirty dollars an hour by soaking the rich.

Ross argues that the main verb of the higher performative structure underlying declarative sentences is something like "say", on the grounds that the verb "believe" can have an object that is a noun phrase marked as human provided this noun phrase is anaphoric to the subject of an appropriate verb of declaration in a higher sentence. Sentences like (2.24) and (2.25) illustrate this principle. (2.26) is now taken as evidence for the existence of a higher sentence with a verb of declaration.

8. See discussion in N. Chomsky, *Aspects of the Theory of Syntax* (Cambridge, Mass.: M.I.T. Press, 1965), pp. 10–15.

9. Since Ross must take "I ask" to be the undeleted higher structure.

10. Ross considers a number of other constructions in his attempt to marshall evidence for his claim about the existence of a higher commanding noun phrase, for example, "as for" phrases, picture nouns, passive sentences with first-person agentive nominals, "lurk" sentences, and "according to" forms, but in each instance Anderson and Fraser offer counter-examples. Note, too, R. M. Harnish, "The Argument from 'Lurk,'" *Linguistic Inquiry* 6, no. 1 (1975): 145–154.

(2.24) Tom$_i$ told him that Ann could swim but nobody believed him$_i$.

(2.25) Tom$_i$ smiled his$_i$ encouragment, but nobody believed him$_i$.

(2.26) Ann can swim, but if you don't believe me, just watch.

But not only is there a wide variety of sentences in which a nondeclarative verb allows "believe" to take a human object, for example, (2.27), as Fraser points out, there is a much better way of accounting for the facts in question here.

(2.27) The president is such a pathological liar that nobody ever believes him.

Sentences like (2.24) can be derived from underlying phrase markers whose terminal string is something like (2.28) by reducing the nominalized sentence that is the object of "believe" to the form "him" (under standard conditions of recoverability).

(2.28) Tom$_i$ told him$_j$ that Ann could swim but nobody believed what he$_i$ told him$_j$.

Ross also argues that no sentence containing the verb phrase "be damned if" followed by a sentence is grammatical unless the subject of this verb phrase is identical to the subject of the first verb phrase higher up whose verb is a verb of declaration. Given that the underlying phrase marker of (2.29) has the appropriate higher performative structure, its grammaticality is alleged to be a consequence of this principle.

(2.29) I'll be damned if I'll go.

But Anderson offers the counter-examples (2.30) and (2.31).

(2.30) Jones will be damned if he'll pay up.

(2.31) The president will be damned if he'll let a Kennedy succeed him.

Anderson points out further that, were Ross to try to derive these sentences from structures having higher sentences of the form "Jones says. . ." and "The president. . .", such derivations would assign the wrong semantic interpretations to (2.30) and (2.31). Such derivations would claim that Jones and the president actually took the "be damned if" stance on some occasion, whereas the sentences themselves simply attribute such a stance to them. The sentences express a prediction about Jones and the president.

Ross's last set of arguments are intended to show that "you" is the indirect object of the verb of the higher structure. One of these arguments is the deep structure subject of idioms like "hold one's breath", "lose one's cool", and so on, must be identical with the indirect object of the verb in the next higher sentence. We can thus explain why a sentence like (2.32) is ungrammatical and a sentence like (2.33) is grammatical:

(2.32) *I want Tom's breath held for two minutes.
(2.33) I want your breath held for two minutes.

(2.33) but not (2.32) is derivable from a structure having a higher performative sentence in which the indirect object of the verb is a second person pronoun. Anderson observes, however, that sentences like (2.34) are perfectly grammatical.

$(2.34) \begin{Bmatrix} \text{Your} \\ \text{Tom's} \end{Bmatrix}$ breath was held (longer than I thought possible).

Fraser claims that Ross's linguistic intuitions in these cases are highly idiosyncratic and so unacceptable.[11]

Another argument of Ross's is that the subject of verb phrases like "be tired" and "be bored" cannot be identical to the indirect object of the verb in the next higher sentence structure. This restriction, which has to be posited to handle cases like (2.35), together with the higher performative structure of sentences like (2.36), handles the contrast in grammaticality between the second-person subject and the first-person subject sentences of (2.36).

$(2.35) \quad \text{I told Jones that} \begin{Bmatrix} \text{I} \\ \text{you} \\ \text{*he} \end{Bmatrix} \text{felt bored (tired, and so on).}$

$(2.36) \quad \begin{Bmatrix} \text{*You} \\ \text{I} \end{Bmatrix} \text{feel bored (tired, and so on).}$

Again, Anderson and Fraser are ready with counter-examples (2.37)–(2.40).[12]

(2.37) I asked him why he felt bored.

11. There are more twists and turns to this argument; they are discussed by Anderson. Fraser's claim, however, seems right.

12. Ross's intuitions seem faulty here. Imagine a hypnotist saying, "You feel tired". Both Ross's further arguments in this connection and the replies of his critics are more of the same. We might mention another recent criticism of Ross's position, M. B. Kac, "Clauses of Saying and the Interpretation of *because*," *Language* 48, no. 3 (1972): 626–632.

(2.38) You can't tell someone that he feels bored.
(2.39) You are tired, aren't you?
(2.40) I told Jones that he probably feels tired.

Anderson's and Fraser's counter-examples are generally convincing, but it is too much to expect that this will settle the issue. Even if Ross were to concede that every one of his arguments fails to go through, this would only show that he had not succeeded as yet in justifying his theory. He could begin to patch it up and to construct new arguments. Hence, what is wanted is conclusive arguments that show that Ross's theory is wrong. We can supply such arguments if we turn from the syntactic implications of Ross's theory to its semantic implications.

Ross's theory, as we observed above, obtains homogeneity in the sources of performative sentences at the expense of complicating the derivation of simple declarative sentences. The burden of his syntactic arguments was to justify the complications by showing that his underlying phrase markers for declarative sentences with their higher performative structure are motivated on independent grounds. Semantically, all appears well. The first-person subject and the second-person object correspond nicely to the speaker/addressee form of illocutionary acts, and the properties of the performative verb accord well with the performative character of the sentences. But it has gone unnoticed that this account implies that *all* sentences are performative, semantically speaking. Constatives, in Ross's theory, are merely the particular form that declaratives take when their higher performative sentence structure is deleted by Ross's rule of performative deletion,[13] that is, when structures like (2.6) are transformed into ones like (2.5). That Ross's transformational analysis of sentences like (2.3) implies that they are performatives follows from the fact that, on this analysis, sentences like (2.3) and (2.4) are related in the same way as sentences like (2.41) and (2.42).

(2.41) Melvin bakes cakes as well as Ann.
(2.42) Melvin bakes cakes as well as Ann bakes cakes.

Thus, (2.3) must be counted as an ellipsed form and synonymous with the fully realized sentence structure (2.4). Hence, the notion of constativeness, in Ross's theory, is that of a special syntactic subtype under the syntactic type "declarative sentence", characterized, basically, in terms of the difference between the ellipsed and unreduced forms.

Any theory that claims that all declarative sentences are performatives, just like that, courts immediate disaster from the very distinction it pretends to re-

13. See Ross, "On Declarative Sentences," p. 249.

construct.[14] Austin's constative/performative distinction had in part to do with the difference between sentences whose meaning equipped them to express true or false statements and sentences whose meaning equipped them only to serve as instruments for performing an act. A theory like Ross's is incoherent because it asserts that sentences that express truths and falsehoods do not express truths and falsehoods. Ross explicitly sets out to reconstruct Austin's notion of performativeness, and consequently, his attempt to construe declaratives as genuine performatives has to be abandoned. Ross must either give up the attempt to so construe declaratives or give up Austin's notion of performativeness. Since the latter is the alternative that concerns us, let us look at it in some detail.

There are two possibilities. One is to say that there are no constatives at all, that is, no sentences that express truths or falsehoods, and the other is to say that, somehow, performatives can also express truths and falsehoods. Since the former is little better than a contradiction itself, and since there are serious views based on the latter (which we shall consider in Chapter 5), we can assume that Ross would opt for the latter. But even with this "improvement", there are overwhelming arguments against Ross's higher performative analysis.

On Ross's analysis, (2.3) is the same in meaning as (2.4); their common meaning is paraphrasable, roughly, as (2.43).

> (2.43) The speaker of the present sentence says that the dog in question barked at some time antecedent to the time at which the speaker is saying this.

Therefore, both (2.3) and (2.4) are about the speaker of the sentence, and both claim that the speaker is expressing a statement about a dog's behavior. But although this is reasonable as a paraphrase of (2.4), it is totally unacceptable as a paraphrase of (2.3). (2.3) is *not* about any speaker of (2.3), and it does *not* assert anything about the expression of a statement. (2.3) is about a dog, and it asserts something about what the dog did. Since (2.3) and (2.4) are about different things and make different assertions, they cannot be synonymous, and thus (2.3) cannot be derived from (2.6), as it is in Ross's theory.

The same point, that the truth conditions for (2.3) and (2.4) are different, can be made in a somewhat different form. Let us compare (2.3) and (2.4) for differences in their truth conditions by asking in what possible worlds they are true and false. Consider a possible world W_1 in which there are only dogs and

14. Ross seems to have confused the constative/performative distinction with the explicit/ implicit distinction, thus supposing (with the aid of a competence/performance confusion) that constatives could be reduced performatives in the way that implicit performatives are reduced explicit performatives. See "On Declarative Sentences," pp. 222–223.

these dogs bark occasionally, and another possible world W_2 in which there are only people, no dogs. (2.3) could be true in W_1 but not in W_2, whereas (2.4) could be true in W_2 but not in W_1. Hence, these sentences cannot be synonymous.

Since the entailments of a sentence correspond to its truth conditions, the point may be put in still another way. (2.3) entails (2.44) but (2.4) does not entail (2.44).

 (2.44) A barking sound occurred.

On the other hand, (2.4) does entail (2.45) but (2.3) does not entail (2.45).

 (2.45) Someone claimed something about something.

These entailment differences also emerge when we check the consistency of the original sentences with the denials of their alleged entailments. If (2.3) and (2.4) were synonymous, as Ross's theory holds, then not only would (2.46) and (2.47) be contradictory, so would both (2.48) and (2.49). Since neither is, (2.3) and (2.4) cannot be synonymous.

 (2.46) The dog barked but no barking sound occurred.
 (2.47) I say that the dog barked, but no claim about dogs ever occurred.
 (2.48) The dog barked but no claims about dogs ever occurred.
 (2.49) I say that the dog barked, but no barking sound occurred.

A further argument considers the implications of the differences in logical form exhibited by the previous arguments for the use of sentences like (2.3) and (2.4).[15] On Ross's account, other things being equal, I make the same statement using (2.3) that I make using (2.4). Thus, on the occasion of using (2.3) I make the statement expressed in (2.50).

 (2.50) Jerrold J. Katz says that the dog in question barked at sometime antecedent to the time he is saying this.

Now, suppose that Ross were to use (2.3). He would make the statement expressed in (2.51).

 (2.51) John R. Ross says that the dog in question barked at sometime antecedent to the time he is saying this.

15. I am indebted to James F. Thomson for this argument (personal communication).

Both these statements are made using (2.3) but they are different statements because the subject of (2.4) is an indexical, referring, variably, to whoever is the speaker of the sentence on the occasion of its use. From this, it follows that Ross's theory implies the falsehood that we cannot same-say with (2.3). For example, Ross does not say the same thing as I do when he uses (2.3), because my statement is (2.50) and his is (2.51). But clearly, if someone uses a sentence like (2.3), someone else can use the same sentence to agree. If A says (2.3), B can surely express agreement by saying (2.3), that is, "The dog barked, all right". This can never happen in Ross's theory because A's statement will always be about A and B's will be about B.[16] The only way out of this counter-intuitive consequence open to Ross is to deny that the first-person subject, the present tense, and the so-called performative verb of the higher sentence structure carry any semantic information. But in this case our criticism that Ross's approach offers no account of performativeness is conceded.

TRANSITION

This conclusion about Ross's approach can be reached in another way, namely, from the vacuity of Ross's feature analysis of Austin's notion of performativeness. Ross suggests that we characterize the illocutionary force information of constative sentences by associating the features [+Performative], [+Communicative], [+Linguistic], and [+Declarative] with the main verb of the highest clause in the deep syntactic structure.[17] Accordingly, the grammatical distinction between constatives and performatives is expressed by the contrast between this feature bundle and, for example, [+Performative], [+Communicative], [+Linguistic], and [+Promissory] associated with the main verb of the highest clause in the deep syntactic structure of sentences with the illocutionary force of promises. But it is hard to see how this suggestion amounts to anything more than an *ad hoc* record of what intuition tells us about the cases in question. Without offering some explication in terms of underlying principles, these feature bundles simply mark cases where intuition is clear. To characterize thus the distinction between propositional types is as vacuous as distinguishing sentence types by introducing features such as [+Declarative], [+Interrogative], [+Imperative], and [+Hortatory] without further phrase structure or transfor-

16. Indeed, not only does Ross's proposal deny that we can same-say, it even denies that we can ever assert anything about something other than our own sayings. This "linguistic solipsism" follows from the fact that there is no semantic category of constativeness. Thus, no use of (2.3) can assert simply that the dog barked.

17. Ross, "On Declarative Sentences," p. 224.

mational explication.[18] Ross's characterization requires us immediately to fall back on the intuitions that a formal theory of the constative/performative distinction should reconstruct. We are given no explication of our intuitions about the structure underlying illocutionary force.

Ross's approach fails at two levels. First, it makes every sentence performative, and second, it offers an empty characterization of performative types. But even these failures do not justify a purely semantic approach to propositional type because Ross's approach does not attempt enough. Ross's theory turns out not to attempt a syntactic distinction between constatives and performatives, and at the level of performative types, it turns out not to attempt a structural analysis of the notions of assertion, promise, request, and so on. What is required to justify a purely semantic approach is the failure of a serious syntactically oriented theory, which fails because the task it has taken on is too much for purely syntactic apparatus. In the next section, we shall consider such a theory. It will explicitly attempt to write syntactic representations for performative sentences that formally mark each piece of information that enables them to perform the particular illocutionary act they standardly perform. We shall show that the limitations of syntactic description preclude such syntactic representations, and on this basis, we shall assume that the illocutionary structure formalized in the semantic component is only loosely related to the syntactic structure underlying sentence type relations.[19]

18. Ross makes a vague reference to the goal of a "uniform deep structural configuration on which to base the semantic notion of *speech act*" (p. 248), but nothing is said about how such a feature bundle analysis could provide an adequate basis.

19. In effect, this approach contrasts with that of Ross and other generative semanticists, whose working assumption has been that one should always push syntactic analyses deeper toward more abstract structures. Their principle of explicating as much nonphonological grammatical structure with syntactic apparatus as possible has led to "grammars" that are a mish-mash of every sort of linguistic rule, because the principle has been applied in the absence of any notion of what properly belongs in syntactic description. Their conception of what is possible in extending the abstractness of syntactic representation to incorporate more linguistic phenomena never included a serious examination of the boundary between syntax and semantics or between grammar and pragmatics. Indeed, recently it has become a matter of doctrine among generative semanticists that there are no such boundaries. [See, for example, J. D. McCawley, "Interpretative Semantics Meets Frankenstein," *Foundations of Language* 7:285; G. Lakoff, "Presupposition and Relative Grammaticality," *Studies in Philosophical Linguistics* 1: 103-116, reprinted under the title "Presupposition and Relative Well-formedness," in *Semantics*, ed. D. D. Steinberg and L. A. Jakobovits, (London: Cambridge University Press, 1971), pp. 297-307.] The result has been that their grammars have become a dumping ground for every sort of language-related phenomena in psychology and sociology, with the consequence that instead of the structures in the grammar becoming more abstract they just become less formal. See J. J. Katz and T. G. Bever, "The Fall and Rise of Empiricism," in *An Integrated Theory of Linguistic Ability*, ed. T. G. Bever, J. J. Katz, D. T. Langendoen (New York: Thomas Y. Crowell, 1976), pp. 11-64.

VENDLER'S THEORY

Recently, Vendler has proposed a syntactically oriented theory that sticks to Austin's performative/constative distinction by reconstructing many of Austin's insights about speech acts within a more sophisticated theory of the nature and limits of syntactic description than Austin had available.[20] Yet Vendler's theory, cannot, in principle, handle questions about propositional type, not because of any mistakes of Vendler's in the elaboration of his theory, but because of the inherent limitations of syntactic apparatus. In examining Vendler's theory, we shall provide grounds for our claim that semantic apparatus is required for the representation of propositional type.

Vendler's theory was developed strictly within Zellig Harris's conception of transformational grammar.[21] Although in certain respects Harris's conception is close to that developed by Chomsky,[22] it is significantly different from it in some critical ways. The principal difference is that Harris's interpretation of his transformational formalism is strictly within the tradition of Bloomfieldian structuralism. Grammars are seen as taxonomic analyses of the corpus, and alternative grammars can be as valid as alternative ways of cataloguing books.[23] For Harris there is no notion "generative grammar" and hence no universal constraints on the form of grammars that make different grammars formalizations of conflicting theories about a natural language. The inadequacy in Vendler's account of performatives that will emerge from our examination is a direct result of the absence of universal constraints on what can count as a derivation of a sentence in grammars.

Vendler begins with Austin's intuition that performative verbs are akin to propositional attitude verbs and are thus "saying verbs".[24] The direct objects of such verbs, called *container verbs* in Harris's early nomenclature, ". . . are not simple nouns but sentences".[25] The object of "know", "believe", "doubt", and other verbs of propositional attitude is a nominalized sentence—a noun that has been transformationally derived from a sentence. More specifically, a nominalized sentence of the particular type that Vendler calls "imperfect nominals", which express propositions, are opposed to "perfect nominals", which express events, processes, or actions, for example, (2.52).[26]

20. Z. Vendler *Res Cogitans* (Ithaca, N.Y.: Cornell University Press, 1972).

21. Z. Harris, "Co-occurrence and Transformation in Linguistic Structure," *Language* 33, no. 3 (1957):283–340.

22. Katz and Bever, "The Fall and Rise of Empiricism," pp. 14–22.

23. Z. Harris, "Transformational Theory," *Language* 41, no. 3 (1965):363–401.

24. Vendler, *Res Cogitans*, pp. 8–10.

25. Ibid., p. 12.

26. Z. Vendler, *Linguistics in Philosophy* (Ithaca, N.Y.: Cornell University Press, 1967), chap. 5, pp. 122–146.

(2.52)   I am listening to his singing.

These container verbs have achievement time schemata and unmodified first-person singular present tense occurence.[27]

The claim that all performative verbs are container verbs is absolutely crucial because of the role it plays in distinguishing performative from nonperformative verbs. The details about the kind of illocutionary act that a particular performative verb is grammatically equipped to perform, and therefore the place of this verb in Vendler's taxonomy of performative types, must be obtained from the syntactic structure of the sentence whose nominalization fills the object slot of the verb.[28] The claim is, however, false: such syntactic notions cannot be stretched far enough to cover the full range of performative verbs.

There are an enormous number of sentences in which the surface structure of a verb phrase offers no reason to think that the verb is a container verb. Vendler's claim therefore requires that their underlying syntactic structure supply the missing surface indication. Derivations such as Vendler's (2.53) are essential.[29]

(2.53)   (i)   I appoint you so that you (shall) be(come) the president.

         (ii)   I appoint you to be(come) the president.

         (iii) I appoint you to the presidency.

The derivation of (2.53) (iii) enables us to classify "appoint" as a performative verb because it relates this sentence to the underlying form (2.53) (i), where there is a basis for saying that the verb has a sentential object. It also enables us to categorize "appoint" as an *operative*, a performative verb grammatically equipped to perform the act of changing the status of a person, by providing some basis for connecting the notion of change to constituents of the sentence, that is, to "(shall) be(come)".[30] Hence, if in principle such derivations are wrong, the claim that performative verbs are container verbs is refuted by the many cases where performative verbs take simple nouns as their objects or take other nonsentential objects.

27. Vendler, *Res Cogitans*, p. 16.

28. That performative verbs are container verbs is also crucial for Vendler's argument against behaviorism in *Res Cogitans*. I agree with his Cartesian viewpoint and I acknowledge that his argument against behaviorism requires that performative verbs, by their grammatical nature, express propositions. But I disagree that their propositional character derives from their syntactic status as container verbs. If my theory about the semantic basis for performativeness (to be set out in the next chapters) is correct, Vendler will have all he needs for his argument without having to claim that every performative verb is a container verb.

29. Vendler, *Res Cogitans*, pp. 21–22.

30. Ibid., pp. 21–22.

What is wrong with these derivations is glimpsed by Vendler when he observes that with negative operative verbs like "demote", "dismiss", and "fire", "the pattern has to be stretched. Some construction like [(2.54)] must be at the source."[31]

(2.54) I demote you so that you shall cease to be. . . .

Vendler tries to justify such a derivational source, and make the appearance of "stretching things" disappear, by observing that because "demote" is an operative we have to have "cease to be" rather than "is" in the underlying form.[32] This only makes matters worse, however, because it makes the whole business circular. The appeal here is to the illocutionary function of operatives in creating new situations, but it is just this function that the underlying structure (2.54) will be invoked to explain when we turn from grammatical structure to sentence use. The mystery deepens when we realize that even apart from this circularity, Vendler's observation about the operative use of the verb "demote" is irrelevant to the issue of what is the underlying syntactic form of sentences like (2.55) (without considerable supplementary argument).

(2.55) I demote you.

After all, both (2.56) and (2.57) function in speech to request information, but this is no reason to conclude that they have the same underlying syntactic form.

(2.56) I request that you tell me whether you are going or not.
(2.57) Are you going?

Vendler comes closer to seeing the problem in connection with the verbs "arrest" and "baptize". He observes that "the general pattern will work only in a seemingly trivial sense".[33] Nonetheless, he is forced to propose that the underlying form of sentences like (2.58) and (2.59) is something like (2.60) and (2.61), respectively,[34] because the standard transformational treatment of such sentences interprets them as simple transitive verb sentences with ordinary pronouns as the direct object.

(2.58) I arrest you.
(2.59) I baptize you.

31. Ibid., p. 22.
32. Ibid., p. 22.
33. Ibid., p. 22.
34. Ibid., p. 23.

(2.60) I arrest you so that you shall be(come) arrested.
(2.61) I baptize you so that you shall be(come) baptized.

Vendler almost puts his finger on the problem when he goes on to comment:

> This seems to be a travesty of a derivation. For, after all, what prevents one from claiming that, say, behind "I kick you", there must be something like [(2.62)]?

(2.62) I kick you so that you shall be kicked.

> This is a serious matter, for if this objection holds up, then our claim that all performatives are propositional verbs goes by the board.[35]

To counter this objection, Vendler argues[36] that verbs like "arrest" and "baptize" are similar in underlying syntactic structure to causatives like "grow", "bake", and "paint", in that simple sentences with any of these as the main verb have an underlying syntactic structure of the form (2.63), whereas simple sentences like (2.62) do not have this underlying structure because "kick" is not a causative verb.

(2.63) N_i C [=causes] (N_j becomes Ved)

This rejoinder fails because it misdiagnoses the problem. What makes derivations of sentences like (2.58) and (2.59) from underlying forms like (2.60) and (2.61) a travesty of a grammatical derivation is not that these derivations encourage us to think that certain noncausatives like (2.62) could be handled the way causatives are. What makes them a parody is rather that these derivations are *ad hoc*; they introduce extraordinary complexity into the *syntactic* description that serves no function in explaining any syntactic facts but exists only to make up for what would otherwise be a deficiency in the semantic description. The problem is not to show why simple "kick" sentences should not be analyzed in the manner of causatives, but to show why causatives (that is, according to Vendler, simple sentences with main verbs like "arrest", "grow," "baptize", "bake", "paint") should be syntactically represented as having an underlying form like (2.63).

Let us bring the problem into sharper focus by considering an example that makes the Vendlerian pattern of syntactic analysis exhibit its implausibility even more clearly. Since "apologize" is a performative verb, Vendler will have to analyze the underlying syntactic form of (2.64) as something like (2.65).

35. Ibid., p. 23.
36. For this argument, he refers us to his Appendix II, pp. 210–216.

(2.64) I apologize (to you).
(2.65) I apologize (to you) so that you shall be(come) aware that I regret the bad effect that an act of mine had on you.

What makes this so implausible is that an underlying form like (2.65) takes to its extreme the licence tolerated by the framework of Vendler's analyses. Even without the benefit of an alternative framework, we feel that there have to be constraints on what can be said about the syntactic structure of a sentence—not any syntactic analysis that we might want for semantic reasons can be allowed. There are such constraints, and derivations like the derivation of (2.64) from a structure like (2.65) flagrantly violate them, but they are not to be found in Harris's conception of transformational grammar, within which Vendler works. At this point, then, we must turn to Chomsky's conception of the constraints on derivations in generative grammars to see why the freedom enjoyed by one of Vendler's derivations is too licentious for proper theories of language.

To derive the surface form of (2.64) from the underlying form (2.65), we must employ an erasure transformation that deletes the complement construction entirely. There are, however, restrictions on the use of such transformations. According to Chomsky,

> . . . a deletion operation can eliminate only a dummy element, or a formative explicitly mentioned in the structure index (for example, *you* in imperatives), or the designated representative of a category (for example, the *wh*-question transformations that delete noun phrases are in fact limited to indefinite pronouns. . .), or an element that is otherwise represented in the sentence in a fixed position.[37]

Vendler's derivations are unacceptable because they violate these constraints on deletion operations in a grammar. These constraints are not arbitrary conventions, and derivations that violate them cannot be considered well formed in a transformational generative grammar.

To see why Vendler's derivations are unacceptable, we must look at the rationale for introducing constraints designed to guarantee recoverable deletion. The last clause of Chomsky's constraints covers the standard case of deleting formative material under identity conditions in the transformational explanation of ellipsis. Consider a genuine case of ellipsis like (2.66) or (2.67).

(2.66) Mary makes better bargains than Sally makes.
(2.67) Bachelors prefer blondes but marry brunettes.

37. Chomsky, *Aspects of the Theory of Syntax*, pp. 144-145; see also pp. 177-184.

We know that the ellipsed subject of the second clause of (2.67) is the noun "bachelors" and that the ellipsed object in the second clause of (2.66) is the noun "bargains". It is *this* fact that has to be explained in transformational derivations of these sentences that would account for the ellipsis in them. Note in particular that this is a syntactic, not a semantic, fact. The constituent missing in the surface structure of (2.66) is not any expression synonymous with "bargains", such as, say, (2.68), but the specific noun "bargains";

(2.68) Agreements between parties that settle what each gives or receives in a transaction between them or what course of action or policy each pursues in respect to the other

and the constituent missing in the surface structure of (2.67) is not some expression synonymous with "bachelors" like, say, (2.69), but the specific noun "bachelors".

(2.69) adult unmarried human males

Therefore, the basic rationale for requiring recoverable deletion in grammars is that we want syntactic derivations to offer a formal explanation of the intuition that in ellipsis a specific constituent of a sentence fails to appear in its surface structure. Grammars that do not satisfy this requirement, whose syntactic derivations do not permit us to formally recover such absent constituents, fail the fundamental empirical demand on theories of the syntactic structure of sentences, *viz.*, that these theories determine the constituents of sentences.

Vendler's derivations presuppose grammars in which transformations erase language-specific formative material that is neither mentioned in the structure index of the transformation nor identical to an antecedent in the sentence. They therefore violate the requirement of recoverable deletion. Hence, these derivations are illegitimate on three grounds. First, as Chomsky observes,[38] grammars allowing nonrecoverable deletion allow any sentence to be represented as meaning almost anything and as infinitely ambiguous. Vendler's conception of syntactic derivations offers us the very same basis for taking the embedded sentence structures in the underlying forms for (2.58), (2.59), and (2.64) to be any of an indefinitely wide range of arbitrarily chosen (synonymous and nonsynonymous) sentences, or to be all of them at once, as it offers for taking them to be those in (2.60), (2.61), and (2.65), respectively. Second, Vendler's grammars fail the fundamental empirical demand on syntactic representation to tell us

38. N. Chomsky, "Current Issues in Linguistic Theory," in *The Structure of Language: Readings in the Philosophy of Language*, p. 71.

what the constituents of a sentence are. Third, these grammars fail to explain ellipsis.

A possible, but by no means attractive, reply to this objection is for Vendler to say that he need not violate recoverability because he can obtain the erasure operations he requires under Chomsky's convention for recoverable deletion by introducing special transformations. Since Chomsky allows the erasure of formatives explicitly mentioned in the structure index of a transformation, technically, Vendler could introduce a transformation for each performative verb in which the structure index mentioned all the formatives that need to be erased to obtain the proper surface structure. The transformation for "apologize" would look something like (2.70).

(2.70)

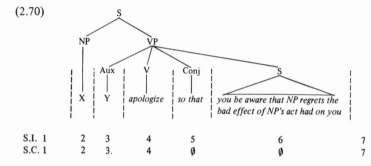

There would have to be such a transformation for each performative verb. Since there are only finitely many such verbs, this could be done in principle. (Even this wouldn't be enough, since a different transformation would be necessary for every synonymous sentence that can occur as an embedded sentence in the case of each performative verb.) But the *ad hocness* of the grammar resulting from the inclusion of such highly unproductive transformational rules would be staggering. Hence, we may conclude that, since the formative material that must be erased is furthermore neither a dummy element nor a designated representative of a major category, Vendler's derivations will be unacceptable. Thus, Vendler's theory has to be rejected.[39]

Our criticism shows why a syntactic account of propositional type is not possible. Syntactic representation is designed to explain such things as the constituents of a sentence, its degree of syntactic ambiguity, sentence type, and ellipsis. To do this, constraints like recoverability must be imposed on the rules

39. Although the example of "apologize" is an extreme one, chosen because it better illustrates the problem, the same problem arises with Vendler's own examples and the same radical form of the problem arises in connection with very many other (clearly) performative verbs, for example, "congratulate", "object", "protest", "volunteer", "consent".

of the syntactic component. Our criticism of Vendler shows that syntactic rules cannot be made to express the rich semantic information involved in propositional type without running afoul of these necessary constraints. The semantic structure needed to reflect the wealth of distinctions underlying the illocutionary potential of sentences is too elaborate to be expressed in syntactic derivations that satisfy the conditions of adequacy in linguistic theory for relating underlying and surface structures.

We may now conclude that the grounds for seeking a semantic explication of propositional type are not only that the semantic properties and relations of sentences depend on information about illocutionary force, but also that such an explication puts the structure needed to represent the illocutionary potential of sentences in the semantic component where it will not cause unnecessary problems for the syntactic component.

3
ASPECTS OF PROPOSITIONAL CONTENT

INTRODUCTION

This chapter is a transition from the previous chapters, which were concerned with motivating a semantic explication of propositional type, to the chapters that follow, which will be concerned with the explication itself. To explicate the illocutionary force of sentences within semantic theory, it will be necessary to extend the apparatus of semantic theory. The present chapter "tools up" for the job ahead. It could have been subtitled "what one has to know about propositional content to understand propositional type".[1]

PREDICATE STRUCTURE

Propositional content breaks down into two parts, a "term sequence" and a "condition". Roughly, a term sequence corresponds to sequence of individual constants and a condition corresponds to a predicate constant. In the present section, we shall consider the condition.

A condition is a representation, in the notation of readings, of predication. The notation of readings is also used to formulate terms, but the readings that constitute conditions represent meanings that play the role of predications in the sense of a sentence. These readings thus represent the properties and relations attributed to something in the assertive use of a sentence in the null context.

Although there is a parallel between conditions and predicate constants in standard applied predicate calculi, there is also an essential difference in how properties and relations are represented in these two notations. The notation

1. The background for this chapter may be found in J. J. Katz, *Semantic Theory* (New York: Harper & Row, 1972), chap. 1–4, although this chapter has been written to make it self-contained for most readers.

for a predicate constant in predicate calculus is a symbolization of an intension, but this symbolization is not a description of the logical structure of the intension. The notation of semantic markers and readings is both. That is, the formal structure of semantic markers and readings reflect the internal conceptual structure of the properties and relations they represent, whereas the formal structure of predicate constants (and individual constants, as well) serves only to assign symbol tokens to symbol types. The absence of a representation of internal conceptual structure follows from the character of the primitive basis for a predicate calculus. Predicate (and individual) constants are specified by a fixed number of infinite lists (singulary predicate constants, binary predicate constants, and so on) of primitive symbols.[2] For example, the two-place relations might be symbolized with the list $R_1, R_2, \ldots$, where each letter has parts only orthographically. The infinity of the lists is necessary to guarantee that there will always be enough symbols for any domain of relations. It makes up for the fact that predicate calculi contain no recursive rules that generate the representations of properties and relations in the way that well-formed formulas are generated. The logical structure of relations has to be stated in terms of special postulates of the predicate calculus.[3] These features of predicate calculi can be shown to make such systems less adequate as representations of the logical form of words and sentences in natural languages than systems of readings.[4]

In contrast, the primitive basis for a semantic component of a grammar contains a fixed number of finite lists of primitive symbols and a set of recursive rules for combining these symbols, thus providing an infinite stock of elementary and complex symbols for representing properties and relations. *Elementary symbols* represent intensions as predicate constants do. *Complex symbols* represent the logical structure of intensions in their formal structure. *Primitive symbols* may be either simple or complex, but symbols that result from the rules of combination are *ipso facto* complex. The customary methodological requirement to minimize the number of primitive symbols can be understood as the requirement to maximize the explanation of the logical structure of the properties and relations expressed in the language.

We have referred to the primitive and derived symbols as "semantic markers" because the way they represent conceptual structure in their formal structure is analogous to the way phrase markers represent constituent structure in their formal structure. A reading is simply a set of semantic markers. Each separate

2. A. Church, *Introduction to Mathematical Logic* vol. I (Princeton, N.J.: Princeton University Press, 1956), pp. 168–176.

3. R. Carnap, "Meaning Postulates," supplement B, in *Meaning and Necessity*, enlarged ed. (Chicago: University of Chicago Press, 1956), pp. 222–229.

4. J. J. Katz, "The Advantage of Semantic Theory over Predicate Calculus in the Representation of Logical Form in Natural Language," *New Directions in Semantics, The Monist* 60, no. 3 (July 1977). The demonstration is beyond the scope of the present study.

semantic marker in a reading stands for a distinct concept in the sense represented by the reading. Thus, the reading of the predicate nominal in (3.1) might be stated as the set {(Physical object), (Human), (Adult), (Male), (Single)}.

(3.1) Pat is a bachelor.

Intuitively, the reading of the predicate phrase of (3.1) represents the truth condition that what is designated by the subject of the sentence falls under the concepts represented by each of the semantic markers belonging to the reading. In the next chapter, we shall explicate the idea that the condition of the propositional content of an assertive proposition, like that expressed by (3.1), tells us what the sentence asserts when it is used in the null context. The point now is simply that the reading {(Physical object), (Human), (Adult), (Male), (Single)} involves five independent predications. In contrast, the semantic markers that appear within complex semantic markers stand for interdependent concepts in the sense represented by the complex semantic marker. For example, we might employ semantic markers like $((Sex)^{(Organs\ for\ begetting\ offspring)})$ instead of (Male) and $((Age)^{(Maturity)})$ instead of (Adult). The conventions for interpreting the formalism specify that superscript semantic markers represent the incompatible concepts in the domain represented by the semantic marker to which they are attached. In this finer-grained representation of the sense of "bachelor", we have two complex semantic markers, the first with the component semantic markers (Sex) and (Organs for begetting offspring) and the second with (Age) and (Maturity). The formal relation of superscripting under this interpretation represents the concepts of maleness and adulthood as having a structure that reflects their antonymy relations. Semantic theory distinguishes between concepts in a sense that function as independent predications and those that function as components of the internal structure by representing the former as semantic markers that are members of the reading of the sense, and the latter as semantic markers that are proper parts of the semantic marker for the sense.

Elementary semantic markers are written as single symbols enclosed in ordinary parentheses. These symbols are English words or phrases, but this is only a convention, adopted so that the symbol suggests the concept it represents. Other signs would serve just as well for representational purposes, but of course would be nowhere near as useful mnemonically. Complex semantic markers are tree structures whose nodes are labeled with elementary semantic markers.[5]

5. Although in previous publications we have used a parenthesis notation to represent semantic markers, we shall here employ an equivalent tree notation. There are two reasons for this notational change. First, it is easier to read tree notation. Second, certain generative semanticists can no longer make the mistake of thinking that semantic markers are not tree structures in the mathematical sense because they are not trees orthographically, for example, see G. Lakoff, "On Generative Semantics," in *Semantics*, pp. 268-269.

Bracketing relations in these tree structures and the labels on their nodes represent the logical relations within the internal conceptual structure of concepts. Such relations, which are what make the component concepts within such a conceptual structure dependent, can be referred to as "ordonnance relations".[6]

Let us illustrate how the notation of a semantic marker formally represents the logical structure of a concept in terms of elementary semantic markers and bracketing structure. We may use the familiar example of the English verb "chase".[7] Its lexical reading contains one semantic marker, namely (3.2).

(3.2)

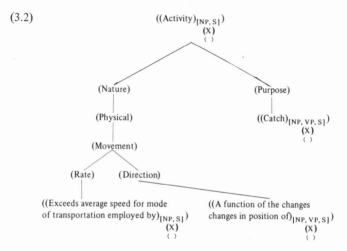

We interpret this tree structure in accord with the conventions that follow. Complex symbols like (3.2) represent a concept whose internal logical structure is displayed by the branching structure and the labeling of the tree. The labels may be either *primitive semantic markers* or *defined semantic markers*. Both kinds of semantic marker may have no categorized variables in them, or they may have one or more categorized variables in them. Both types are illustrated in (3.2). The categorized variables are written slightly below the component marker to indicate that they represent argument places of the predicate for which the marker stands.[8] Such variables determine the positions into which the projection

6. J. J. Katz and R. I. Nagel, "Meaning Postulates and Semantic Theory," *Foundations of Language* 11 (1974): 311–340.

7. J. J. Katz, "Recent Issues in Semantic Theory," *Foundations of Language* 3 (1967): 169–170; also idem, *Semantic Theory*, pp. 165–166. Actually, we should say that the example is of one lexical sense of the word "chase". A dictionary entry will consist of *n* lexical readings for an *n*-ways ambiguous lexical item.

8. These predicates are syncategoramatic in a sense to be explained.

rule substitutes readings to produce derived readings for constituents of a sentence. Above the categorized variables are syntactic symbols in brackets which tell the projection rule where to find the readings it can consider as substitutions. Thus, the grammatical function [NP, S] tells the projection rule to consider the reading of the subject of the sentence, whereas [NP, VP, S] tells it to consider the reading of the direct object.[9] Below the categorized variable are semantic symbols in angles; they express a *selection restriction* that tells the projection rule the condition under which a reading is substituted for the variable.[10] Categorized variables may either be enclosed by *heavy parentheses*, as indicated in (3.3), or not, as indicated in (3.4) [where (M) stands for a semantic marker].

$$(3.3) \quad ((M)_{[\ ]})$$
$$(x)$$
$$\langle\ \rangle$$
$$(3.4) \quad ((M)_{[\ ]})$$
$$X$$
$$\langle\ \rangle$$

Heavy parentheses mark the position as referential, so that the readings that appear in these positions, as a result of the projection rule, are represented as referential terms. The semantic marker representing a relation may have every one of its categorized variables enclosed in heavy parentheses, none so enclosed, or some enclosed and some not. For example, we might have the semantic marker $((Wants)_{[NP, S]} {}_{[NP, VP, S]})$ as our lexical reading of "wants" in order to
$$(X)\ , \quad X$$
$$\langle\ \rangle \quad \langle\ \rangle$$
state that the reading of the subject of this verb is a referential term and the reading of its object is nonreferential.

If a definition introduces a symbol as an abbreviation for a complex semantic marker, the symbol is a *defined semantic marker*. For example, $((Chase)_{[NP, S]} {}_{[NP, VP, S]})$ is a defined symbol in case a definition introducing
$$(X) \quad (X)$$
$$\langle\ \rangle \quad \langle\ \rangle$$
it as an abbreviation for (3.2) appears in semantic theory. Since the question of which semantic markers are defined and which are primitive can be answered only in a more advanced state of the discipline, we shall use semantic markers as node labels with no implication about their status in this respect.

The conventions of interpretation take the form of *correspondence definitions*, which state that some elementary semantic marker is the formal symbol

9. Katz, *Semantic Theory*, pp. 104–226.

10. Ibid., pp. 89–98.

that stands for some concept in the theory, and *interpretive principles*, which state, in general terms, how the particular formal structures built up out of a set of elementary symbols by the recursive rules for combining them represent the internal structure of a complex concept or proposition. For example, there might be a correspondence definition stating that the semantic marker (Movement) stands for the intuitive concept of a change in spatial position of an object over a temporal interval. The adequacy of the correspondence definitions of semantic theory consists in their matching up elementary concepts of the language with elementary symbols of the notation.

The interpretive principles explain the branching in formal structures like (3.2) as a notation for representing complex concepts and propositions. To try to state these principles systematically would be premature. Rather, we informally interpret various bracketing structures. For example, if, in an instance of (3.3), (M) had the form (3.5), it would represent the application of n independent predicate concepts to the argument place marked by the categorized variable.

(3.5) $((A_1), \ldots, (A_n))$

Another branching structure that occurs in complex semantic markers is an instance of (3.3) in which (M) has the form (3.6).[11]

(3.6)(i) $(((B_1), \ldots, (B_n))(A))$ (3.6)(ii)

$$(A)$$
$$(B_1) \quad \ldots \quad (B_n)$$

The domination relations express what I will refer to as the application of a *predicate function*, that is, an operation of converting a less specified predicate concept into a more specified one. A domination relation such as that which connects (Purpose) to $((Activity)_{[NP, S]})$ in (3.2) does not change the number
$$(X)$$
$$\langle \ \rangle$$
of argument places of the relation, but the domination relation that connects $((Catch)_{[NP, VP, S]})$ increases the number of argument places, converting the
$$(X)$$
$$\langle \ \rangle$$
representation of a property into that of a two-place relation.[12] The original

---

11. We introduce the device of putting dashes between semantic markers to represent branches. Thus, "$(A)-(B_n)$" represents one branch of (3.6), and "$(A)-(B)- \cdots -(Y)-(Z)$" represents one of indeterminate length rooted in "(A)" and terminating in "(Z)".

12. The definition of placedness is given in (3.9).

semantic marker with the predicate function applied to it together represent a more highly specified concept than the one represented by the original marker alone. The interpretive principle, then, treats the domination of (Physical) by $((\text{Activity})_{[\text{NP, S}]})$ in (3.2) as representing the conversion of the less specified

$$(\text{X})$$
$$\langle\ \rangle$$

concept of activity into the more specified concept of physical activity: the information in the concept of physicalness is used to qualify the concept of activity and thereby produce a new concept that is distinct from mental activity.[13]

Another possible bracketing structure internal to a semantic marker is illustrated in (3.7).

(3.7) (i) $((((C_1), \ldots, (C_n))(B))(A))$ (3.7) (ii)

13. This was what was intended in remarks like "The semantic marker '(Physical)', together with the bracketing, indicates that the activity is qualified as to its nature, that is, that chasing is a physical activity." (Katz, *Semantic Theory*, p. 102) However, an unfortunate loose usage of the term "higher predication" in connection with such qualification of markers has caused confusion about the intended interpretation of such bracketing notation (see, for example, M. Bierwisch, "On Certain Problems of Semantic Representation," *Foundations of Language* 5 (1969):153–184, where the notation is interpreted in terms of actual higher-order predication). One instance of such loose talk is my remark that "...the parenthesization that relates [semantic markers to those immediately dominating them, as, say, described in (3.6)] represents higher-order predications whereby certain concepts qualify others by specifying them further" (Katz, *Semantic Theory*, p. 166). I did not intend higher-order predication in the sense that the semantic markers $(B_1), \ldots,$ (B_n) in a case like (3.6) are understood such that the domination of (A) over (B_i), $1 \leqslant i \leqslant n$, formally represents a predication of some property B_i of order $k + 1$ of some property A of order k. Understanding the bracketing of semantic markers in this way would make nonsense of them. It makes no more sense to take the concept represented by (Physical) in (3.2) to be a higher predicate applied to the concept represented by (Activity) than it does to take the concept "is wise" to be a higher predicate of "is a virtue": the concept of an activity can no more have the property of being physical than the concept of virtue the property of wisdom. This contrasts with a genuine case of higher-order predication, in which we apply a predicate like "is self-applicable", "is truth functional", and so on, to a predicate to make an assertion about that predicate. I wish to thank Robert M. Harnish and Michael Houghtaling for calling this confusing usage to my attention; cf. R. M. Harnish and M. Houghtaling, "An Investigation of Algorithmic Translation Procedures from Semantic Feature Representation to Predicate Logic" (Tucson: University of Arizona, 1974).

Here n predicate functions are applied to the result of applying a predicate function to the base predicate concept represented by the semantic marker (A). Although such trees are finite, there is no upper limit on the degree of branching, just as there is no limit on the complexity of a concept.[14]

In terms of these conventions, (3.2) offers the following analysis of the logical structure of the verb "chase". The semantic marker labeling the highest node represents the concept serving as the base predicate, namely, the activity engaged in by whatever the reading of the subject refers to. (This is, of course, subject to the idealization of the previous chapter, that is, whatever the reading of the subject would refer to in the null context.) The reading of a sentence like (3.8) thus represents the police as those engaged in the activity.

(3.8) The police chased the demonstrators.

The semantic marker labeling the second node in the first branch qualifies the activity concept as having a definite nature and distinguishes the meaning of "chase" from the meaning of an expression like "doing something". The semantic marker labeling the third node in the first branch is a second-order predicate function applied to the result of the application of (Nature) to (Activity). It qualifies the nature of the activity as involving the behavior of a material body in space and time. This distinguishes "chase" from verbs expressing mental activities like "think", "remember", "plan", and so on. The semantic marker labeling the fourth node in the first branch is a third-order predicate function that qualifies the qualifying concept 'Physical' by indicating that the behavior oı the body involves its changing its spatial location through time. This distinguishes "chase" from verbs like "jump up and down", "run in place", "chin", and so on, which, respectively, involve changes in vertical location in space, the moving of parts of the body without the body changing location, and so on.[15] The semantic markers represented by the bracketing as qualifications of the concept of movement further specify this concept with the information that (a) the rate at which the changes in spatial location occur exceeds the average speed for the mode of conveyance employed by the referent of the subject and (b) these changes in spatial location are directed in their course by the movement of that

14. The various branches rooted in the semantic marker representing the base predicate (A) and their various subbranches rooted in (A), namely, $(A) - (B) - (C_1)$, $(A) - (B)$, $(A) - (B) - (C_1) - \cdots - (C_n)$, and so on, determine the $\alpha \sqsubset \beta$ condition used in the formulation of the definitions of analyticity and entailment (Katz, *Semantic Theory*, p. 174f).

15. For some discussion of the kind of semantic markers that will be needed to represent these spatial relations, see M. Bierwisch, "Some Semantic Universals of German Adjectivals," *Foundations of Language* 3 (1967):1-36; also, P. Teller, "Some Discussion and Extension of Bierwisch's Work on German Adjectivals," *Foundations of Language* 5 (1969):185-217.

to which the reading of the object noun phrase refers. (We regard the semantic marker (Fast) as a defined construct, to be replaced, eventually, by a semantic marker whose formal structure fully represents (a).) Thus, the verb "chase" is distinguished from verbs like "walk", "mope along", "crawl", and so on, on the one hand, and from verbs like "run", "swim", "walk", "submerge", and so on, on the other.

The second semantic marker in the second major branch in (3.2) is also a second-order predicate function applying to (Activity). It qualifies the activity as purposeful and so distinguishes it from the concept in the meaning of verbs like "wander". The semantic marker that expresses the predicate function applying to (Purpose) qualifies the purpose as that of catching that to which the direct object refers. This additional information distinguishes "chase" from "hunt", "search for", "destroy", and so on. In both these cases, what we are calling a predicate function applies in a way that specifies further information about the concept serving as the base predicate, and therefore the formalism represents a qualification of the activity attribution rather than a further attribution. Later on, we shall use this feature to distinguish formally between purposes of activities and the intentions of their agents.

We shall now consider how the argument places of a predicate concept can be determined from the reading of the linguistic construction that expresses it.[16] The entire treatment of the placedness of relations in semantics depends on the use of categorized variables in readings to mark the positions where the projection rule embeds readings. The earliest version of the theory does not utilize categorized variables but instead employs a number of projection rules, each formulated to handle a different grammatical relation and often a different operation of reading amalgamation.[17] Thus, the statement of semantic facts about how the compositional process makes use of information about the grammatical relations between constituents of a sentence is made in the projection rules. A change in the earlier version of semantic theory reduced these projection rules to a single substitution principle, relocating the instructions for using the information about grammatical relations to the symbols that mark the substitution positions in readings. As we shall see, this is absolutely crucial for developing an account in semantic theory of the placedness of relations.

The change, however, is motivated on independent grounds. One reason is that it simplifies the semantic component.[18] Another, perhaps even more com-

16. We can take it that our intuitions about semantic properties and relations include ones about the placedness of predicate concepts expressed by words and phrases of the language, and so we shall require a definition in semantic theory.

17. J. J. Katz and J. A. Fodor, "The Structure of a Semantic Theory," *Language* 39 (1964): 177-210.

18. Katz, *Semantic Theory*, pp. 113-116.

pelling reason, is that the explanatory and predictive power of the semantic component is increased in a way that could not otherwise be achieved. For example, the definition in semantic theory that explicates the converse relation and explains the logical equivalence between converse sentences as an instance of synonymy[19] must be stated in terms of a formal relation between the categorized variables in the readings for converse constituents like "buy" and "sell". We shall deal later with other analyses that exploit the appearance of categorized variables in readings.[20]

Looking at (3.2), we note that there are three *occurrences* of a categorized variable, but that only two distinct categorized variables appear, *viz.*, the variable categorized for subject readings and the variable categorized for direct object readings. Since the predicate concept that is expressed by "chase" has two argument places, one for terms referring to the chaser and one for terms referring to the chasee, it would seem reasonable to determine the placedness of a predicate concept in terms of the number of distinct categorized variables represented in the reading for the concept. This leads us to formulate the principle (3.9).[21]

(3.9)   The argument places of the concept represented by a semantic marker are given by the *n* distinct categorized variables that have occurrences in the semantic marker (that is, each instance of the same categorized variable in the semantic marker is merely another occurrence of the variable and so counts as the same argument place).

A semantic marker notation like (3.2) is designed to do two things at the same time. First, it is designed to exhibit the onion-like structure of predication in the system of concepts that comprise the internal constituents of a predicate concept. Thus, (3.2) reveals that the base predicate and the predicate functions stack up in a way that represents the concept of an activity that is a certain kind of purposeful, physical movement. Hence, (3.2) represents the meaning of "chase", and peeling the onion-like structure, layer by layer, we get parts that represent the meaning of analytically included predicate concepts, for example, "follow". The notation therefore provides a domain for the entailment definition. Second, it exhibits the association of the internal predicate concepts of a

19. Namely, (7.174) in ibid., p. 344.

20. For example, their use in stating the semantics of the reflexive element and in formulating a definition of presupposition.

21. Without entering into a survey of the empirical evidence for (3.9), we may note that it offers an intuitively natural account of the placedness of the predicate concepts expressed by common verbs like "hit", "kill", and so on, and that it even handles cases with syntactically hidden places like "buy" and "sell". In these two verbs, we have a four-place relation between a buyer, seller, article(s), and sum of money. See Katz, *Semantic Theory*, chap. 7.

predicate constant with its argument places, so that each argument place is associated with the proper internal predicate concepts. Thus, in (3.2) the bracketing, the choice of semantic markers as node labels, and the positioning of the categorized variables jointly determine how the predications distribute with respect to the two argument places of the relation. In a sentence like (3.8), the predication "engages in an activity that is physical movement of a certain kind with a certain purpose" applies to one argument place of the relation whereas the predications "its direction determines that of the movement of the activity" and "is what the activity seeks to catch" apply to the other. This distribution is determined, first, by the relation of semantic markers to occurrences of categorized variables in (3.2), and second, by (3.9), which collects the component semantic markers expressing predications applying to the same argument place as a consequence of pairing occurrences of categorized variables with argument places.

Since we shall depend heavily on (3.9) in this study, it will be worthwhile examining in detail a case where it might at first appear that (3.9) breaks down. We shall show why our first assumptions about the case are mistaken and why a better treatment is forthcoming if we make new assumptions consistent with (3.9). Perhaps the best example for this purpose is reflexive constructions, where at first glance (3.9) seems to assign too many argument places.[22] The sentence (3.10) has the same main verb as the sentence (3.11), which clearly has a logical form consisting of a two-place predicate concept.

(3.10) John intentionally killed himself.
(3.11) John intentionally killed Horace.

Thus, we might expect that (3.9) commits us to saying that (3.10) has a logical form consisting of a two-place predicate concept. The lexical reading of "kill" must contain occurrences of two distinct categorized variables, one categorized for readings of the subject and one categorized for readings of the direct object. Otherwise, how could the lexical reading for "kill" provide a basis for a compositional analysis of (3.11) on which its sense contains a two-place predicate concept? But it might be objected that (3.10) should not be represented as having a predicate concept with two argument places since it is synonymous with (3.12) which, clearly, has a logical form consisting of a one-place predicate concept.

(3.12) John committed suicide.

22. We do not have to worry about the assignment of too few argument places because semantic representation can always use categorized variables that do not correspond to any constituent of a sentence, as, for example, in the case of our treatment of "buy" and "sell" as four-place predicates.

The first step toward overcoming this objection is to recognize that the problem is not specifically about (3.9). The problem here, which we refer to as the "suicide paradox", constitutes a general problem that has to be faced by any theory of predicate structure in natural language. It may be expressed as follows. Since (3.12) is synonymous with (3.10), they have the same logical form, and in particular, their predicates have the same number of places. Since the predicate in (3.12) is a one-place predicate, the predicate in (3.10) is also. But since the verbs in (3.10) and (3.11) are the same, and since the verb "kill" expresses a two-place predicate in (3.11), the verb "kill" expresses a two-place predicate in (3.10) also. But then the predicate expressed by the verb in (3.10) is both two-place and one-place, which is absurd.[23]

The suicide paradox arises from a false assumption about the origin of the logical structure of predicate concepts in propositions, roughly, that their logical structure comes entirely from the sense of the lexical item from which they derive in the compositional determination of the proposition. Thus, it is taken for granted that the degree of placedness of a predicate concept in a proposition is the same as the degree of placedness of the sense of the verb from which the predicate concept comes. But in a semantic theory that treats the meaning of a sentence as a function of the senses of its constituents, some of the logical structure of a predicate concept in the sense of a sentence can come from the senses of constituents with which the verb is in construction. By denying the assumption in question, we obtain the following solution of the suicide paradox. Let NP_i be a noun phrase in a sentence S that is syntactically marked both [+Pro] and [+Reflexive]. Let NP_j be an anaphoric identity of NP_i in S. Let R_i and R_j be readings of NP_i and NP_j, respectively. Let C be a constituent in S such that NP_i bears the grammatical relation $[[\alpha] [\beta]]$ to C, and NP_j bears the grammatical relation $[[\gamma] [\beta]]$ to C (C has the grammatical function $[\beta]$ in S).[24] Let R_C be a reading of C containing the categorized variables $\overset{[\alpha]}{\underset{\langle\ \rangle}{X}}$ and $\overset{[\gamma]}{\underset{\langle\ \rangle}{X}}$. We introduce the rule (3.13) as the dictionary entry for the syntactic feature [+Reflexive].[25]

$$(3.13) \quad (\ldots \overset{[\gamma]}{\underset{\langle\ \rangle}{X}} \ldots) \longrightarrow (\ldots \overset{[\alpha]}{\underset{\langle\ \rangle}{X}} \ldots)$$

23. We assume that the logical form of (3.12) is not to be analyzed as a relation between John and a suicide, *viz.*, something like "Commits$_{x, y}$".

24. See Katz, *Semantic Theory*, pp. 104-113, for a discussion of this notation.

25. Other such rules are found in ibid., pp. 157-173, and J. J. Katz, "A Proper Theory of Names," *Philosophical Studies* (in press).

(3.13) says that the semantic contribution of this syntactic feature is to change the categorization of the variable in R_C that is categorized for the readings of constituents that bear $[[\gamma]\,[\beta]]$ to C, so that its categorization is the same as that of the variable in R_C that is categorized for the readings of constituents that bear $[[\alpha]\,[\beta]]$ to C. The application of (3.13) in the semantic interpretation of (3.10) illustrates how the suicide paradox is resolved. Let (3.14) be the phrase marker that is interpreted in the semantic interpretation of (3.10).

(3.14)

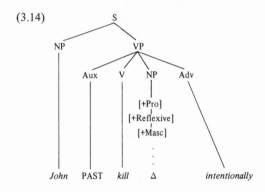

In the first stage of the interpretive cycle, lexical readings from dictionary entries are assigned to occurrences of lexical items in (3.10). The occurrence of "kill" in (3.14) will receive a lexical reading of the form (3.15).

$$(3.15) \quad (((\,\ldots\,\overset{[NP,\,VP,\,S]}{\underset{\langle\ \rangle}{(X)}}\,\ldots\,))\,(Act)_{[NP,\,S]}\,\underset{\langle\ \rangle}{(X)})$$

In the next stage of the cycle, those syntactic features assigned to lexical items in (3.14) that have dictionary entries are assigned the rule from their entry, and the rule applies where its conditions of application are met. Thus, (3.13) is assigned to the occurrence of [+Reflexive] in (3.14), and (3.13) applies under the conditions $\alpha = $ [NP, S] and $\gamma = $ [NP, VP, S]. The result of its application is, therefore, the assignment of the derived reading (3.16) to the verb constituent of (3.14).

$$(3.16) \quad (((\,\ldots\,\overset{[NP,\,S]}{\underset{\langle\ \rangle}{(X)}}\,\ldots\,))\,(Act)_{[NP,\,S]}\,\underset{\langle\ \rangle}{(X)})$$

This completes the characterization of the meaning of the lexical items in (3.14). Applying (3.9) at this point, we obtain the prediction that the predicate concept in the meaning of (3.10) is a one-place predicate, as it has to be to account for the synonymy of (3.10) and (3.12). We account for the verb being the same in (3.10) and (3.11) by assigning the occurrence of "kill" in the phrase marker underlying (3.11) the same lexical reading that its occurrence receives in (3.14). Since the object noun phrase in the phrase marker underlying (3.11) will not be marked [+Reflexive], there is no change from (3.15) to (3.16), and by (3.9), we have the prediction that the predicate concept in the meaning of (3.11) is a two-place predicate. Therefore, the suicide paradox dissolves, and with its dissolution, the objection to (3.9) disappears.

In the remainder of this section, I shall argue for using (3.13) as the dictionary entry for [Reflexive] on the independent grounds of its usefulness in handling two problems. One is how to represent the synonymy of sentences like (3.10) and (3.12). Regardless of whether we treat "commit suicide" as a single lexical item or as a compositional construction of two lexical items, we shall represent its meaning in something like the manner of (3.17).

(3.17)

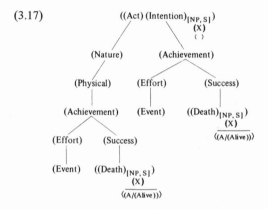

The meaning of "kill" is represented by a lexical reading identical to (3.17) except for two things: (a) the absence of a branch with the semantic marker (Intention) and the semantic marker below it, since committing suicide, unlike killing, must be intentional, and (b) the categorization of the variable in the semantic marker under (Success) being [NP, VP, S] instead of [NP, S], since the reading of the direct object is wanted here.[26] The meaning of the

26. Two points: First, we have not tried to represent the qualification of the event that states the condition under which it is "close enough" to the death for the agent to be the

constituent "kill intentionally" in sentences like (3.10) and (3.11) will be obtained in the projection process by a lexical reading for the adverbial "intentionally" like (3.18), which replaces a branch of the kind specified on the left-hand side of the arrow with one of the kind specified on the right-hand side.

(3.18)

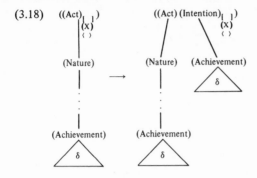

The problem of representing the synonymy of (3.10) and (3.12) boils down to how to change the syntactic categorization of the variables where the reading for the victim will go in the lexical reading of "kill" from [NP, VP, S] to [NP, S] , as in (3.17). But as we have already seen, the direct object categorizations in the reading of "kill" will be automatically changed to subject categorizations by the operation of (3.13) in the semantic intepretation of (3.10), and therefore, the reading of (3.10) will come out to be identical to that of (3.12), which is derived directly from (3.17).

The second grammatical problem that shows the usefulness of (3.13) concerns the distinction between what may be called *semantically determined coreference* and *semantically undetermined coreference*. Informally, the distinction is between a case like "John wants to leave" in which it is semantically determined that the person whom John wants to leave is himself and cases like "John wants someone to leave", "John wants the person with smelly shoes to leave", and so on where it is undetermined. We may pose the problem sharply by asking how we are to explain the ambiguity in a sentence like (3.19).[27]

killer rather than a cause of the death of the recipient. Second, in Chapter 5, we shall provide an interpretive convention under which lexical readings like these formally represent the fact that the event that constitutes the successful killing of the victim is the same event that the agent intends to bring about. We note also that the bar over the selection restriction in (3.17) represents the requirement that the value of this categorized variable cannot contain the semantic marker (A/(Alive)) .

27. I am indebted to Jerry A. Fodor for this form of the problem.

(3.19) Only Churchill can remember giving the famous blood-sweat-and-tears speech.

One of the senses of (3.19) is an *a priori* truth of some sort, whereas the other is an (obvious) empirical falsehood. The former is *a priori* true because no one other than the person who made the speech can recall making the speech. The latter is empirically false because a great number of people are old enough to recall Churchill's speech. We can distinguish these senses by the nonellipsed forms (3.20) and (3.21).

(3.20) Only Churchill can remember himself giving the famous blood-sweat-and-tears speech.

(3.21) Only Churchill can remember his giving the famous blood-sweat-and tears speech.

Standard approaches to pronominalization offer no satisfactory explanation of the difference in meaning (or truth conditions) for such cases. Such approaches posit an underlying phrase marker in which the subject noun phrase of the (embedded) complement sentence is identical or anaphoric to the subject of the matrix sentence structure. A sentence like (3.21) is derived by a pronominalization of the subject of the complement sentence (either by realizing an underlying subject noun "Churchill" as the surface pronoun "his" or by spelling an appropriate bundle of syntactic features as the surface pronoun "his"). A sentence like (3.20) is derived in essentially the same way, except that the subject of the complement sentence is marked with the syntactic feature [+Reflexive], which determines the reflexive form of the surface pronoun. A sentence like (3.19) is derived from both these underlying structures, but with an ellipsis of the subject of the complement sentence instead of a surface pronominal realization. It is clear that this difference in syntactic structure (that is, the appearance of a subject of a complement sentence marked for reflexivization in one underlying phrase marker and the appearance of a subject of a complement sentence not so marked in the other) does not offer an explanation of why a sentence like (3.20) and a sense of (3.19) should be *a priori* truths whereas a sense of a sentence like (3.21) and (3.19) should not be. The only interpretation of [+Reflexive] is in terms of the form of surface pronouns derived from nouns marked with this feature.

Although the syntactic difference does not solve the problem, it enables us to restate it as a question about the semantic contribution of [+Reflexive] to the meaning of sentences and thereby bring the semantic principles developed immediately above to bear. First, we shall propose a hypothesis about the nature of semantically determined coreference and then use it in conjunction with (3.13) to solve our problem.

This hypothesis follows from (3.9) together with the account of presupposition in *Semantic Theory*[28] and extended later in this chapter. Determination of the places of a predicate concept in accord with (3.9) is accomplished by taking all occurrences of a categorized variable in a semantic marker as a single place of the predicate concept represented by the semantic marker. Accordingly, the readings that the projection rule substitutes for these occurrences of the categorized variable are interpreted as the term occupying that place of the predicate concept. Given that the place is a referential position,[29] the term in question will occur referentially and the various predications associated with the individual occurrences of the categorized variable are thereby collected to constitute what is asserted of the referent of this term. Hence, the constituents (or better, the senses represented by the readings that the projection rule substitutes for the occurrences of the same categorized variable) will be semantically determined as coreferential; otherwise, semantically undetermined as coreferential.

The dictionary entry (3.13) now provides us with an explanation of the differences between (3.19)–(3.21). The underlying phrase marker for the sense of (3.19), which is also the sense of (3.20), is, roughly, (3.22).

(3.22)

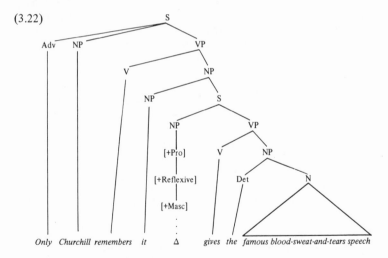

28. Katz, *Semantic Theory*, pp. 127–150.
29. See Katz, *Semantic Theory*, p. 167f., and this volume, pp. 97–112, where we discuss the use of heavy parentheses to represent a position's being referential.

In the semantic interpretation of (3.22), (3.13) applies to the reading of the verb in the complement sentence, which is something like (3.23).

(3.23)   ((Delivers publicly)$_{[NP, S, NP, VP, S]}$)
$$(X)$$
$$(\ \ )$$

(3.13) changes the categorization of the variable from [NP, S, NP, VP, S] to [NP, S]. This makes the reading of the sentence (3.20) and of the sense of (3.19) shared by (3.20) represent the attribution of a (complex) property to the referent of the term. Since there is no occurrence of [+Reflexive] in the phrase markers underlying the empirically false sense of (3.19) and (3.21), (3.13) does not apply in their semantic interpretation, and the reading of the verb in the complement sentence is left in the form (3.23). The reading in these cases is thus the representation of a relation R between the referent of one term and the referent of another. Hence, the truth conditions of the sentences in this latter case is something like that no one other than Churchill can bear R to the event in question, whereas the truth conditions of the sentences in the former case is something like that no one other than Churchill can have the property. The explanation of why the sentences in the latter case are empirically false whereas those in the former are *a priori* true is now straightforward. Many of us besides Churchill bear the relation "remembers" to the event of Churchill giving the speech in question, but no one other than Churchill can be both the person who gave the speech and someone who remembers Churchill giving it. The semantically determined coreferentiality of the occurrence of Churchill to which the predicate "giver of the famous blood-sweat-and-tears speech" is applied and the occurrence to which the predicate "rememberer of Churchill giving the famous blood-sweat-and-tears speech" is applied precludes anyone other than Churchill from satisfying both components of the truth conditions.

Before concluding this section, we take up a technical point that arises in connection with the use (3.13) in the semantic interpretation of an underlying phrase marker like (3.22).[30] As we have seen, the use of (3.13) changes the categorization from [NP, S, NP, VP, S] to [NP, S] for the variable in (3.23). On the other hand, the categorization for this variable in the reading of the verb "give" in a sentence like (3.21) does not change from [NP, S, NP, VP, S]. But the question arises of how this variable got the categorization [NP, S, NP, VP, S] in the first place. We have to suppose that in the dictionary "give" has a lexical reading in which this variable is categorized [NP, S], so that when "give" occurs as the main verb of simple sentences the values of the variable will be readings of the subject of such sentences. How, then, does [NP, S] become [NP, S, NP, VP, S] in a case like (3.21)? This problem is further compli-

30. I wish to thank Manfred Bierwisch for bringing this problem to my attention.

cated by the fact that any particular such variable can appear in the reading of a constituent that is *any* finite number of embeddings deep in its host sentence.

The solution requires adding a clause to the projection rule[31] that "completes" the categorization of variables in readings of embedded sentence structures on the basis of information in the formal structure of the phrase marker in which they occur. This clause would take the form of a rule that expands the lexically specified categorization of these variables by adding the sequence of nonterminal node labels that appear on the nodes of the branch from the constituent itself up to "#-S-#". Let "ψ" be the substring of the terminal string in the phrase marker that represents the constituent in question. Let the grammatical function "$\chi_1, \ldots, \chi_n$" represent the lexically specified categorization of the variable undergoing expansion. Let the sequence of nonterminal symbols "$\lambda_1, \ldots, \lambda_m$" represent the node labels appearing on the nodes of the branch from the node immediately dominating "ψ" to "#-S-#", that is, the phrase marker has the form in (3.24).

(3.24)

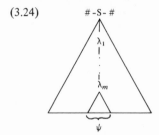

The rule for completing the categorization of variables is thus (3.25), where $\lambda_1, \ldots, \lambda_m$ is not null.

$$(3.25) \quad \begin{matrix} [\chi_1, \ldots, \chi_n] \\ X \\ \langle \; \rangle \end{matrix} \quad \longrightarrow \quad \begin{matrix} [\chi_1, \ldots, \chi_n, \lambda_m, \ldots, \lambda_1, S] \\ X \\ \langle \; \rangle \end{matrix}$$

In the example, (3.22), ψ is "gives the blood-sweat-and-tears speech", $n = 2$ and χ_1, χ_2 is "NP, S", and $\lambda_m, \ldots, \lambda_1$ is the sequence "NP, VP".

SEMANTIC ROLES

The previous section dealt with the structure of predicates. This section concerns semantic roles such as "Agent", "Recipient", and so on, that characterize the terms that can occur in argument places of a predicate.[32] We take up this

31. See Katz, *Semantic Theory*, pp. 313–316.
32. Ibid., pp. 104–113.

topic because a number of the theoretical constructions that will be needed in the explication of propositional type require that we know how to formally represent semantic roles. We shall first say a few words about why we reject the "case approach" to semantic roles and then describe the relational approach employed here.

Fillmore[33] was instrumental in bringing the topic of semantic roles to the attention of linguists. But his attempt to define them systematically in terms of case grammar is based on a misunderstanding of the function of grammatical relations in syntactic theory. This misunderstanding vitiates his argument for case grammars and leads to his setting up a framework for treating semantic roles that is, in principle, unsatisfactory. The misunderstanding, on which he bases his case for case grammars, is the notion that the function of definitions of grammatical relations in a standard, *Aspects*-type grammar is to predict semantic roles. On the basis of this notion, he argues that an *Aspects*-type account of grammatical relations is inadequate because its definitions do not distinguish the different semantic roles that may correspond to the grammatical relation "subject of" or "direct object of", nor do they show that different grammatical relations may correspond to the same semantic roles. Fillmore remarks:

> . . . the semantic role of deep structure subjects appears not to be univocal. . . . The involvement of the entity named by the subject NP . . . appears to be quite different in each case . . . there appears to be no common notional property of "subjectness" which semantic descriptions of these sentences can exploit.[34]

Thus, to identify "the boy" as the subject of the sentence in examples like (3.26)–(3.31) fails to predict such semantic facts about roles as that "the boy" is agentive in (3.26) but not in (3.27)–(3.30).[35]

    (3.26) The boy slapped the girl.
    (3.27) The boy fell down.
    (3.28) The boy received a blow.
    (3.29) The boy has a toothache.

33. C. Fillmore, "The Case for Case," in *Universals in Linguistic Theory*, ed. E. Bach and R. Harms (New York: Holt, Rinehard, & Winston, 1968).

34. C. Fillmore, "Subjects, Speakers, and Roles," *Synthese* 21, no. 3/4 (October 1970): 252–255.

35. Fillmore says that "the boy" is the "Experiencer" in (3.29) and the object acted on in (3.27) and (3.28).

(3.30) The boy has blue eyes.

(3.31) The boy [= his appearance] shocked me.

Fillmore sets out to revise the form of the rules in *Aspects* grammars so that their base components no longer represent subjects, direct objects, and other grammatical relations in the sense of Chomsky's relational notions, but represent semantic roles instead, such as "Agent", "Experiencer", "Instrument", "Object", "Goal", and so on.

As I argued elsewhere,[36] Fillmore mistakenly assumes that the account of grammatical relations in *Aspects* is intended to specify semantic roles of constituents directly. Otherwise, it is not at all clear why Chomsky's treatment of grammatical relations should be criticized for failing to perform the function of specifying semantic roles. My argument against Fillmore was simply that grammatical relations were never intended to represent semantic roles. Their function, which Fillmore totally ignores, is to provide the most abstract generalization about the syntactic relations among the constituents in a sentence that together with the lexical readings of its morphemes determine its semantic interpretation.[37] Hence, it is no surprise to find that the claim that grammatical relations are supposed to express semantic roles is easily falsified, in that the inherent meaning of lexical items is a critical factor in determining semantic roles and syntactically defined grammatical relations can make no reference to the meaning of lexical items in *Aspects* grammars.[38]

Ironically, this fact about the importance of the meaning of lexical items in determining semantic roles also prevents Fillmore's own attempt to handle semantic roles from succeeding. His approach is based on the idea that a deep syntactic structure in which the marking of case relations directly determines semantic roles overcomes the alleged failures of an *Aspects*-type deep syntactic structure. In (3.32) and (3.33) the case markers "Object" and "Instrument" would be

(3.32) The car broke the window with its fender.

(3.33) The car's fender broke the window.

assigned to "the window" and "the car's fender", respectively, in a common deep case structure underlying both sentences. Chomsky has observed, however,

---

36. Katz, *Semantic Theory*, pp. 111–113.

37. Chomsky also suggests from time to time that his relational definitions of grammatical relations are explications of notions from traditional syntax.

38. See P. Mellema, "A Brief Case against Case," *Foundations of Language* 11, (1974): 39–76 for further criticism.

that this approach seems to be nothing more than a thinly disguised version of the *Aspects* conception of grammars.[39] Fillmore's case grammar treatment is essentially the same as that in an *Aspects* base component of a somewhat eccentric sort, namely, one in which the nonterminal vocabulary includes case symbols so that the relational definitions of the semantic roles that replace grammatical relations take a particularly simple form. For example, the definitions of *Object role* and *Instrument role*, on which the constituents "the window" and "the fender of the car" in (3.32) and (3.33) would be picked out as playing object and instrument roles, respectively, would be stated in terms of the domination of a substring by the case markers "Object" and "Instrument". Now, Fillmore's case treatment is essentially the same as an *Aspects* treatment and thus makes no use of semantic information from the lexical meaning of morphemes in determining semantic roles. The semantic information that explicates the nature of a role, for example, that the agent is the animate instigator of the action, is not part of the deep case structure but is given independently by definitions connecting case markers to role explications. Thus, his treatment ought to fail for precisely the same reasons that Fillmore's strawman version of the *Aspects* theory does. Fillmore's criticism that there is no direct correspondence between grammatical relations (read: case markers) and semantic roles applies to his own theory.

Indeed, counter-examples showing this were found almost immediately. Chomsky mentions (3.34) and (3.35) and Anderson discusses them in detail.[40]

(3.34)   Bees are swarming in the garden.
(3.35)   The garden is swarming with bees.

Here (3.34) and (3.35) must be derived from the same underlying case structure and hence these sentences receive the same semantic representation and are marked as synonymous. But as Chomsky and Anderson point out, they are not synonymous: (3.34) locates the swarming activity within the garden, whereas (3.35) describes the garden as having bees distributed all over it. Hence, the reason expressed in the subordinate clause of (3.36) does not make (3.36) contradictory in the way that the reason in the subordinate clause of (3.37) makes (3.37) contradictory.

(3.36)   Some children in the garden did not get stung because, although bees were swarming in the garden, the garden was not swarming with bees.

39. N. Chomsky, "Some Empirical Issues in the Theory of Transtormational Grammer," pp. 173–180.
40. S. Anderson, "On the Role of Deep Structure in Semantic Interpretation," *Foundations of Language* 6 (1971): 197–219.

(3.37) Some children did not finish the race because, although they did not eat too much, they overate.

These counter-examples work for the same reason that Fillmore's own examples do, because the theory against which they are directed fails to take account of the contribution of lexical meaning to the determination of semantic roles. Here the trouble arises from the lexical ambiguity in the meaning of the verb "swarm". On the one hand, it means "some aggregation of free-moving creatures thronging together in some area", and on the other, it means "an area covered with or teeming with some multitude of things". These senses differ in several ways. For one thing, in the latter sense, the things doing the swarming need not be creatures at all; for example, (3.38) is nonanomalous.

(3.38) Every page of the book is swarming with mistakes.

Second, in the latter sense, the things doing the swarming need not be free-moving, whereas they must in the former sense; thus, (3.39) is ambiguous.

(3.39) The club house is swarming with bats.

Third, the former sense requires that the swarming things be thronging together, whereas the latter sense does not. This is shown by the fact that the nominalization of "swarm" carries only the former sense and consequently sentences like (3.40) are unambiguous.

(3.40) The swarm of bats is in the clubhouse.

The reason for this is that the objectification of the things performing the action requires the concept of close assemblage in the former meaning but not in the latter: the concept of an object in the sense of "the swarm of bats" requires that each of the parts of the object, that is, each bat, be spatio-temporally proximate to the others.

The lesson is obvious. Semantic roles have to be represented at the semantic level in the grammar where the explication of them can avail itself of what is said at that level about the meaning of lexical items. The proposal in *Semantic Theory* of relational definitions of semantic roles, stated in terms of readings, was intended as the simplest means of making use of what is said about the meaning of lexical items.[41] These definitions of semantic roles were modeled on Chomsky's definitions of grammatical relations. Since our definitions specify

41. Katz, *Semantic Theory*, pp. 104–113.

semantic roles in terms of configurations of symbols in semantic markers, just as grammatical relations are specified in terms of configurations of symbols in phrase markers, our definitions offer explications of semantic roles that are, from the viewpoint of simplicity, free. They cost us nothing because they do not introduce additional theoretical apparatus in order to gain this substantial increase in explanatory power. Relational definitions employ the already existing representational apparatus for constructing semantic markers by being stated exclusively in terms of the structure of these markers. On general methodological grounds, then, any solution that can be given in the form of a set of relational definitions is preferable, other things equal, to any solution based on a special notation for semantic roles because the introduction of such a notation enlarges our stock of theoretical apparatus.[42]

The full elaboration of our proposal to define semantic roles relationally requires an appropriate configuration of semantic constructs to define each of the semantic roles recognized by speakers of the language. We may suppose that speakers of the language have semantic intuitions about these roles in the same sense as they do about such properties and relations as synonymy, ambiguity, analyticity, meaningfulness, and so on. We may thus suppose that the definitions of semantic roles fall together with the definitions of other semantic properties and relations. Fillmore's definitions serve to interpret otherwise uninterpreted case markers; ours, like other definitions of semantic properties and relations, constitute generalizations over semantic representations. Our definitions express hypotheses about what formal features a reading has to have in order that the constituent it represents be associated with some particular semantic role.

Before considering the definitions of the semantic roles that will be utilized in the remainder of the book, we must say a few words about terminology. The terms "agent", "recipient", "instrument", and so on, refer to the persons and things involved in the action. In (3.41), John is the agent in the act of killing the fly

(3.41)   John killed a fly.

42. It should be pointed out that my own thinking on the question of what such dictionary entries look like is different from that in Mellema's "A Brief Case against Case". For the "some aggregation of free-moving creatures thronging together in some area" sense, I would use a variable categorized for readings of the subject with appropriate selection restriction to ensure only values that represent living creatures and another variable categorized for readings of the object of the prepositional phrase in the verb phrase with a selection restriction to ensure only values that represent a location. For the "an area covered with or teeming with a multitude of things" sense, I would use a variable categorized for readings of the subject with a selection restriction to ensure only values that represent a location and another variable categorized for readings of the object (or object of the prepositional phrase) with a selection restriction to ensure only values that represent concrete objects.

and the fly is the recipient, the object acted upon. Nothing in such a report or in the sentence type used to make the report is an agent or a recipient. Therefore, we properly speak about linguistic expressions *referring* to agents, recipients, instruments, and so on. But we shall speak about their senses in the same way. Calling a constituent or its sense an "agent", "recipient", or "instrument" will simply be a loose way of speaking, indulged in for convenience and to be understood in terms of these conventions. We shall use the notions "agent reading" or "recipient reading" to mean the reading that represents the sense of the constituent that refers to the agent or recipient in a standard use of the sentence. Our definitions will be definitions of these notions.

The concept of agent that Fillmore and others employ is that of the animate instigator of the action. Assuming that this is correct, we have to explicate this concept in terms of formal features of readings, and to do this so that the explication will permit us to predict which of its constituents, if any, is the agent. In sentences like (3.41)-(3.43) it will have to identify the agent reading with the reading of the subject, whereas in sentences like (3.44) and (3.45) it will have to differentiate the agent and subject readings.

(3.42)   John chased Mary.
(3.43)   Mary slapped John.
(3.44)   John received a slap.
(3.45)   Mary suffered an insult.

To arrive at such an explication, let us look at the readings for the action verbs "chase" and "kill" presented in (3.2) and (3.17) and ask where we find something like the informal notions "animate", "instigator", and "action" that comprise the intuitive concept of agentiveness. Clearly, the latter notion, that of an action, is represented primarily in the semantic markers (Activity) and (Act). The various component predications in this notion merely qualify the action, saying what kind of act or activity it is. The notion of instigator or performer of the action is, of course, specified in the bracketing that represents the association of the semantic marker (Act) or (Activity) with the topmost categorized variable, since this association expresses the application of the concept of act or activity in question to the referent of the reading that becomes the value of this variable. Finally, the notion of animate (or sentient[43]) would be specified in the reading that substitutes for the topmost categorized variable.

43. The proper notion here is probably 'sentient' rather than 'animate', since plants are animate but are not agents in sentences like "The plant killed the people who were warned not to eat it". This case is like (3.49) where the subject refers to the cause rather than the agent. Such cases contrast with "The venus flytrap killed two flies today".

For sentence (3.46) is semantically anomalous and sentence (3.47) can mean only that the table is the instrument that administered the blow to the child.

(3.46) The stone (chair, and so on) chased the boy.
(3.47) The table slapped the child.

To mark them as such, the selection restriction on the relevant categorized variable would have to contain the semantic marker (Living).[44] This would require that the reading that is the value of this variable have this semantic marker. Note also that this explains why the subject of (3.48) but not (3.49) is an agent.

(3.48) The soldier killed the people.
(3.49) The falling rocks killed the people.

We are thus led to the definition (3.50).

(3.50) R is the *agent reading* in the sentence reading R_S = df.
  (a) the part of R_S that represents the propositional content of the sentence S contains a semantic marker with a branch of the form[45]

$$(\left\{ \begin{array}{c} (\text{Act}) \\ (\text{Activity}) \end{array} \right\} ((M_{i_1}), \ldots, (M_{i_s})) - (M_{j_1}) - (M_{j_2}) - \ldots - (M_{j_n}))$$

  (b) R is the reading $(M_{i_1}), \ldots, (M_{i_s})$
  (c) $(\text{Sentient}) = (M_{i_k})$, where $1 \leqslant k \leqslant s$.

This formulation can be tightened to exclude the readings of the subjects of psychological verbs like "think" and "recall" from counting as agent readings simply by adding the clause that $(M_{j_1}) = (\text{Nature})$ and $(M_{j_2}) = (\text{Physical})$. The issue, on which I wish to remain neutral, is whether being an agent requires causing something to happen in a stronger sense of causation than is or could be involved in thinking or remembering.

(3.51) is the obvious corollary to (3.50).

(3.51) R is the *recipient reading* in the sentence reading R_S = df.

---

44. Stones cannot engage in activities or acts that have purposes. When we say of someone who is running to avoid being run over by a rolling bolder that he or she is being chased, we speak metaphorically, as is clear from the mild humor of the description.

45. The dash notation for branches is introduced in footnote 11. The braces in (3.50) indicate a choice of one of the enclosed elements. The dots indicate the possibility of other markers in the same category.

(a) the part of R_S that represents the propositional content of the sentence S contains a semantic marker with a branch of the form (3.50a),

(b) $(M_{j_1}) = $ (Nature) and $(M_{j_2}) = $ (Physical)

(c) there is a marker (M_{j_q}), $2 < q \leqslant n$, of the form $((M_r)$ $((M_{h_1}), \ldots, (M_{h_k})))$

(d) R is the reading $(M_{h_1}), \ldots, (M_{h_k})$.

No clause in (3.51) is comparable to (3.50c). The reason is, of course, that unlike the agent, the recipient of an action need not be sentient, as the sentences (3.52) and (3.53) show.

(3.52) Bill slapped his shoe.

(3.53) Mary killed the weed.

Looking at the readings (3.2) and (3.17) for "chase" and "commit suicide" or "kill", it is easy to see that (3.50) and (3.51) will predict correctly the agent and recipient in sentences like (3.41) and (3.42). Moreover, it will be no trick to devise a reading for "slap" such that applying (3.50) and (3.51) to it will just as correctly predict the agent and recipient in sentences like (3.43). It also turns out that handling cases like (3.44) and (3.45) is a simple matter. To convince oneself of this, it suffices to note that both "receive" and "suffer" (that is, "suffer" with a nominalized verb as its object) belong to converse pairs. For example, there are the pairs (3.54) and (3.55) and (3.56) and (3.57).

(3.54) John received a slap from Mary.

(3.55) Mary gave John a slap.

(3.56) Mary suffered an insult from John.

(3.57) John insulted Mary.

As has already been established,[46] converses are represented by identical readings except for the inverse positioning of some categorized variables. Thus, the lexical readings for the members of such converse pairs will have the form shown in (3.58a) and (3.58b), where the structure C but neither A or B may be null.

The lexical reading of "give" will have the form (3.58a) and the lexical reading of "receive" will have the form (3.58b).[47] The semantic interpretation of the sentence (3.55) will contain a projection rule operation that substitutes the read-

46. Katz, *Semantic Theory*, pp. 332–346.

(3.58) (a)

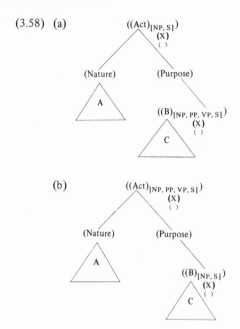

(b)

ing of the subject "Mary" for the occurrence of the categorized variable in the highest semantic marker in the reading of the verb and the reading of the indirect object "John" for the occurrence of the categorized variable in the semantic marker under the semantic marker (Purpose). The semantic interpretation of (3.54) will contain a projection operation that substitutes the reading of the indirect object "Mary" for the occurrence of the categorized variable in the highest semantic marker in the reading of the verb and the reading of the subject "John" for the occurrence of the categorized variable under the semantic marker (Purpose). Given these differences, applying (3.50) and (3.51) to the semantic interpretations of (3.54) and (3.55) correctly predicts their semantic roles. It predicts that "John" refers to the recipient of the act (the slap) and "Mary" refers to the agent in both sentences, even though "John" and "Mary" are, respectively, subject and indirect object of the verb in (3.54) and, respectively, indirect object and subject of the verb in (3.55).

Sentences (3.44) and (3.45) pose no significant problem, even though they do not contain an indirect object of the verb. The fact that, nonetheless, the

47. Given the present sorry state of the theory of grammatical relations, the use of the grammatical function '[NP, PP, VP, S]' to specify the indirect object of a string is not to be taken too seriously. Nothing in our argument hangs on this choice. As long as the syntactic component provides different grammatical functions for indirect object, subject, and so on, our argument will go through.

sense of (3.44) and the sense of (3.45) contain both an agent and a recipient is easily explained by the clause of the projection rule that supplies a reading as the value of a categorized variable from its own selection restriction when there is no constituent in the sentence that satisfies the grammatical function for the variable.[48] Consider (3.44). If we suppose that the selection restriction under the occurrence of the categorized variable in the highest semantic marker in the reading of "receive" is ⟨(Physical object), (Sentient)⟩, then the projection rule would provide the two semantic markers in this selection restriction as the value of this variable. Since, furthermore, the reading of the subject of (3.44) would be the value of the categorized variable in the semantic marker directly under (Purpose), (3.50) and (3.51) predict that the recipient of the slap is the referent of "John" and the agent is some unspecified, sentient creature.

We make no attempt to provide a complete or systematic treatment of semantic roles at this time. An approach such as ours, which seeks relational definitions of semantic roles, assumes a wide range of descriptively adequate readings for verbs. In the present state of semantic theory nothing approaching such a range is available. Nonetheless, as we develop the formalism of semantic representation in connection with our explication of propositional type, we shall provide definitions of those further semantic roles that are needed in this explication.

THE TERM SEQUENCE

Terms are represented by individual constants in the notation of standard predicate logic but by readings in the notation of semantic theory. Hence, the same things we said about the differences between these notations in connection with the representation of predicates can also be said in connection with the representation of terms.

The argument places of a predicate concept are determined by its reading by (3.9). This principle, as it were, collapses each occurrence of the same categorized variable into the same argument place and separates occurrences of different categorized variables by assigning them to different argument places. The terms to which a predicate concept is applied are the readings appearing in its argument places. The readings substituted for occurrences of categorized variables map into terms of the predicate concept in the mapping of these categorized variables into argument places. Thus, the terms in the propositional content of a sentence are represented by the n-tuple of distinct readings that the projection rule substitutes for the n distinct categorized variables in the reading for its condition. The term sequence is just an ordering of the n terms with respect to some ordering of the argument places, in which each term occupies the same position in the sequence that its argument place occupies in the ordering of argument places.

48. Katz, *Semantic Theory*, p. 107.

PRESUPPOSITION

The theory of presupposition, which comes down to us from Frege,[49] is an attempt to explain the notion of the application of a predicate to a term sequence. Roughly speaking, this theory, which is developed only for the case of assertive propositions, says that the terms pick out the objects or sets of objects that the proposition is about, the predicate expresses a concept, and the application of the predicate concept embodies the assertion that the objects picked out have the property or bear the relation in question. When the terms successfully refer and the objects to which they refer have the property or bear the relation, the proposition is a true statement. When the terms successfully refer but the objects do not have the property or do not bear the relation, the proposition is a false statement. When there is failure of reference, the proposition is neither true nor false. It is not a statement. The central feature of the theory of presupposition is that at least some instances of the application of a predicate can be understood in this way: some propositions have presuppositions; presuppositions are conditions whose satisfaction consists in an appropriate referential relation holding between the sense of a constituent or constituents and some object or objects; and satisfaction of a presupposition of an assertive proposition is necessary and sufficient for statementhood.

This theory of presupposition was adopted in *Semantic Theory*.[50] But in adopting it we revised and extended the theory in various ways. Since the discussion of presupposition in this section picks up where it is left in *Semantic Theory* and makes further revisions and extensions, it will be worthwhile mentioning some features of the earlier discussion.

First, we stipulated that the nature of the presupposition for a particular sentence, S, is a function of the semantic structure of S, that is, S's meaning in the language. This was done by adding presupposition to the list of semantic properties and relations. This has three major consequences. It made the specification of presuppositions for sentences a problem for the projection apparatus that explicates compositionality in the language. It made the notion of presupposition nonpragmatic.[51] It explicitly and generally formulated the Fregean notion of presupposition as a logical property of propositions.[52]

49. G. Frege, "On Sense and Reference," in *Translations from the Philosophical Writings of Gottleob Frege* (Oxford: Basil Blackwell, 1952), p. 69.

50. Katz, *Semantic Theory*, pp. 127–150.

51. I recognize that the claim that presupposition is a nonpragmatic notion is a controversial one in linguistics these days, but I think conclusive arguments can be given to show that critics of the purely grammatical notion of presupposition are simply confused about the relation between grammar and pragmatics. See J. J. Katz and D. T. Langendoen, "Pragmatics and Presupposition," *Language* 52, no. 1 (1976).

52. Hence, some things linguists call "presupposition" do not qualify as presupposition in the logical sense. For instance, Chomsky's notion of presupposition defined in terms of the

Second, we introduced a specific proposal concerning a notation for representing presuppositional information in propositions. We proposed that readings represent such information just in case they occur within heavy parentheses like those appearing in (3.3). The use of this notation will be discussed at length in this section.

Third, we presented a number of arguments for a presuppositional analysis of propositional structure as opposed to a Russellian analysis.[53] The principal argument was that Epimenedian sentences like "This sentence is not true" are counter-examples to Russell's assumption that meaningfulness is both a necessary and sufficient condition for statementhood, that is, for a sentence to be either true or false. The assumption is crucial because it allows Russell to treat the existential condition in the logical structure of definite descriptions as a component of the truth conditions of the sentences in which such descriptions appear. Our argument against this assumption was that it led to a contradiction when applied to Epimenedian sentences. We reasoned as follows. On Russell's assumption, an Epimenedian sentence makes a statement. It exhibits no semantic deviance. Further, if an Epimenedian sentence is true, then it is not true and if it is not true, then it is true. If we couple these conditionals with the previous consequence that an Epimenedian sentence fulfills the condition for statementhood, it follows that the sentence is both true and not true.[54] This is a *reductio* of Russell's assumption. The alternative to Russell's assumption is Frege's assumption that the existential condition in the logical structure of definite descriptions is a condition on the statementhood of appropriate sentences containing such descriptions. Since this is the only alternative theory about the logical status of such existential conditions, the *reductio* of Russell's assumption is an argument for a presuppositional condition of statementhood.

Another argument that we offered for a presuppositional analysis was that such an analysis of propositional structure enables us to define the words "true" and "false" in a way (as indicated above) that distinguishes "false" from "not true". We also argued for a presuppositional analysis on the grounds that the Russellian analysis forces us to adopt an unnatural account of what simple copula sentences, among others, are about. Intuitively, one would say that a

---

intonation center of a sentence is nonlogical. See N. Chomsky, "Deep Structure, Surface Structure, and Semantic Interpretation," in *Studies on Semantics in Generative Grammar* (The Hague: Mouton, 1972), pp. 89-103. In *Semantic Theory*, pp. 417-434, I argue that Chomsky's is a stylistic notion.

53. See Katz, *Semantic Theory*, pp. 127-150; idem, "On Defining the Notion 'Presupposition,'" *Linguistic Inquiry* 4, no. 2 (1973):256-260; and idem, "Interpretive Semantics Meets the Zombies," *Foundations of Language* 9 (1973):268-274.

54. A slightly different form of this argument now appears in Kripke's discussion of "truth value gaps" in his theory of truth. See S. Kripke, "Outline of a Theory of Truth," *Journal of Philosophy* 72, no. 19 (1975):690-716.

use of a sentence like "The president of the U.S. is bald" is about the president of the U.S. and that a use of a sentence like "The king of France is bald" is not about anything. But, on a Russellian analysis of the definite descriptions in these sentences, we have to say that they are both about everything, and hence about the same thing (or else resort to *ad hoc* machinery to avoid saying this). On a presuppositional analysis, we can frame a general definition of aboutness for such sentences to the effect that such sentences are about the referent of their subject term if it has one and about nothing if not. This definition conforms to our intuition by predicting that "The president of the U.S. is bald" and "The king of France is bald" are about different things, the president of the U.S. in the former case and nothing in the latter.

We may mention one new argument for presuppositional analysis: On such analysis, we get a swift and clean solution to one of the most troublesome paradoxes in the philosophy of science, namely, the confirmation paradox called the "paradox of the ravens". The paradox runs as follows. A statement like "All ravens are black" is confirmed by a statement to the effect that something is both a raven and black. By the same token, then, the statement "All nonblack things are nonravens" is confirmed by a statement to the effect that something is both nonblack and not a raven. But these two general statements are logically equivalent, and hence, they are confirmed by the same particular statements. Accordingly, the particular statement that something, this piece of paper, for example, is nonblack and not a raven must, paradoxically, confirm the generalization that all ravens are black. As Goodman once observed, accepting this argument is tantamount to endorsing indoor ornithology.

As might be expected, confirmation theorists have carefully examined the premises of this argument. Different theorists have challenged different premises, and there is now a large literature on the topic. Whatever the merits of these challenges, the paradox of the ravens is resolved immediately the moment we adopt a presuppositional analysis of the propositional structure of the two general statements. On a presuppositional analysis, "All ravens are black" presupposes the existence of ravens and asserts that each is black, whereas "All nonblack things are nonravens" presupposes the existence of nonblack things and asserts that each is a nonraven. Since these two sentences do not have the same presupposition and the same assertion, they do not express the same proposition. Since they express different propositions, we are not forced to say that they are confirmed by the same particular statements, even though they are logically equivalent. The implicit premise of the argument to indoor ornithology that we are challenging is that the logical form of the sentences in question is properly represented in accord with the Russellian analysis, so that the condition for sameness of logical form is logical equivalence. Once we adopt a richer conception of propositional structure, the logical forms of the two general sentences emerge as different and there is no longer a reason to think that what confirms one must confirm the other. We can, moreover, formulate a confirmation principle for such cases that is sensitive to differences in logical form and captures our basic intuition concerning why pieces of white paper, brown stones, and so forth do not confirm the generalization that all ravens are black; namely, if a particular sentence S_1 confirms a general sentence S_2 directly, S_1 confers the same confirmation on S_3 just in case S_2 and S_3 are about the same thing(s) and make the same assertion.

Fourth, we extended the notion of presupposition beyond the class of assertive propositions to the entire set of propositional types in the language.[55] We did not, however, try to carry out this extension for each of the propositional types, but simply illustrated the extended notion of presupposition for the case of erotetic propositions. Moreover, we did not try to explain why presupposition remains a logical notion after this extension. We do both of these things in the course of this book.

But both require a far more systematic treatment of the way the compositional mechanisms in the language determine presuppositions. Our aim will be to combine the Fregean conception of presupposition with an adaption of Austinian conditions on the use of sentences to perform speech acts. The success of such a combination depends on whether the presuppositional features of corresponding constative and performative sentences are determined in the same way as a function of the meanings of their words and their syntactic structure.

The request for a more systematic treatment of the compositionality of presupposition is equivalent to the request for a solution to what Langendoen and Savin call "the projection problem for presupposition".[56] They state the problem as that of explaining "how the presupposition and assertion of a complex sentence are related to the presuppositions and assertions of the clauses it contains".[57] On the basis certain linguistic data, Langendoen and Savin propose their "cumulative hypothesis" as a solution. This hypothesis says that ". . . the presupposition of subordinate clauses stand as part of the presupposition of the complex sentences containing them".[58]

This hypothesis was falsified on the basis of a number of counter-examples.[59] But I am not concerned with them at present. What is more important

55. Katz, *Semantic Theory*, p. 134f., and Chap. 5.

56. D. T. Langendoen and H. Savin, "The Projection Problem for Presupposition," in *Studies in Linguistic Semantics*, ed. C. J. Fillmore and D. T. Langendoen (New York: Holt, Rinehart, and Winston, 1971), pp. 55–62.

57. Ibid., p. 55.

58. Ibid., p. 58.

59. J. L. Morgan, "On the Treatment of Presupposition in Transformational Grammar," *Papers from the 5th Regional Meeting of the Chicago Linguistics Society* (Chicago: Univer-

here is that the entire discussion of the projection problem has been carried on at the purely descriptive level. Hypotheses take the form of simple empirical generalizations from examples, the criticisms are further examples that do not fit the hypothesis, and the reformulations[60] are amended empirical generalizations. The difficulties in finding revisions of such empirical generalizations that succeed in capturing the relations between presuppositions of clauses and presuppositions of the sentences containing them result from the discussion's not going beyond the descriptive level. In particular, the trouble with the descriptive approach is that, by remaining at this level, no effort is made to find formal explanations of how the presuppositions of sentences derive compositionally from the meaning of their parts. Thus, theoretical constructs necessary to state the relations between presuppositions of clauses and the presuppositions of the sentences containing them are not constructed.

Our discussion of the projection problem departs radically from the descriptive approach and concentrates on the structure of a formal explanation of the compositional basis of presupposition. Contrary to the practice of most of those who have followed the descriptive approach, we shall assume that the projection problem for presupposition is not separable from the general projection problem, and that the solution is a formal model of the compositional process in which readings are assigned to sentences that permit us to predict *all* of their semantic properties and relations.

We begin with some highly important distinctions between the kinds of definitions that can be given of semantic properties and relations in semantic theory. Definitions in semantic theory are of semantic properties and relations in the sense that they explicate a property or relation on the basis of readings of sentences and universals in semantic theory. But the properties and relations themselves may be of linguistic expressions, senses, or objects and states of affairs in the world. Definitions that explicate semantic properties and relations of linguistic expressions or senses, for example, definitions of "semantic anomaly", "ambiguity", "analyticity", and so on, will be called *meaning definitions*; whereas those that explicate semantic properties and relations of objects and states of affairs, for example, definitions of "has a referent", "is true", and so on, will be called *reference definitions*.

sity of Chicago, 1969), pp. 167–177, points out that conditional sentences like "If Jack has children, then all of Jack's children are bald" do not presuppose that Jack has children, although their consequents do. In *Semantic Theory*, I pointed out that opaque constructions block presuppositions.

60. L. Karttunen, "Presuppositions of Compound Sentences," *Linguistic Inquiry* 4 (1973): 169–193, for all of the formalism this paper uses, its account of presupposition remains at the descriptive level, using metaphorical notions like "hole", "plug", and "filter" to refer to the phenomena that should be formally reconstructed. See Katz and Langendoen, "Pragmatics and Presupposition."

Cross-classifying with the categories of meaning definition and reference definition are the categories of structural definition and interpretive definition. A definition is a *structural definition* in case it explicates the structure of a semantic property or relation in a way that permits us to identify instances of it on the basis of their exemplifying the structure. A definition is an *interpretive definition* in case it interprets exemplifications of a semantic property or relation in logical terms.[61] The category of *meaning structural definitions* contains the most familiar definitions from semantic theory, for example, the definition of *semantic anomaly* as the absence of a reading, the definition of *ambiguity* in terms of the assignment of two or more readings, and the definition of *synonymy* in terms of the assignment of the same reading to different linguistic expressions. These definitions characterize a semantic property or relation in terms of a configuration of symbols in the readings of sentences or constituents. They say what formal structure a reading must have for the sentence or constituent to which it is assigned to have the semantic property or relation in question. Meaning structural definitions express generalizations, across the sentences of natural languages, about the common semantic structure underlying the semantic properties and relations so defined.

Reference structural definitions characterize a semantic property or relation in terms of the features of objects and states of affairs that determine the connection between a linguistic expression and some portion of the world. For example, this category of definitions contains the definition of *x is the referent of w* in terms of the condition that, for every semantic marker M in the reading for w (in an optimal grammar), x has the property represented by M. It is important to note here that the referential notions defined in this connection are under the same idealization as the notions dealing with meaning; that is, the notion of a referent of a word is the notion of its referent in the language, not the notion of what some use of the word refers to on that use.[62]

Interpretive definitions, on the other hand, explain the logical significance of the semantic properties and relations characterized in the structural definitions. The interpretive definition of a semantic property or relation expresses the logical features of the sense of a linguistic construction that is attributable to its having that particular semantic property or relation. The interpretive definition of *semantic anomaly* is that such sentences express no proposition and so do not enter into logical (deductive) relations with other sentences; the interpretive definition of *ambiguity* is that sentences express more than one proposition and so enter polymorphously into logical relations; the interpretive definition

61. See the discussion of correspondence principles in J. J. Katz and T. G. Bever, "The Fall and Rise of Empiricism," in *An Integrated Theory of Linguistic Ability*, pp. 24–30.
62. See Katz, "A Proper Theory of Names."

of *synonymy* is that such sentences express the same proposition and so enter into exactly the same logical relations with other sentences (have the same role in arguments).

Cross-classifying with the categories of structural definition and interpretive definition are the categories of *expression definition* and *sense definition*. This dichotomy partitions structural and interpretive definitions into those that characterize semantic properties and relations of *expressions* (that is, sentences and their constituents) and those that characterize semantic properties and relations of *senses* (that is, concepts and propositions expressed by sentences and their constituents). The former category includes the structural and interpretive definitions of "semantic anomaly", "ambiguity", "synonymy", and "translation", whereas the latter includes the structural and interpretive definitions of "analyticity", "contradiction", and "semantic entailment". A definition belongs in the category of expression definitions in case it defines a feature that cannot apply to propositions; for example, it makes no sense to say that a proposition is ambiguous or meaningless. A definition belongs to the category of sense definitions in case it defines a feature that can apply in different respects to the same (ambiguous) expression.[63]

The account of presupposition in semantic theory must take the form of two definitions of the notion "presupposition", one a structural definition and one an interpretive definition. Both will be sense definitions because it makes sense to apply the property of having a presupposition to propositions and because this property applies in different respects to one and the same (ambiguous) sentence. For example, we can apply this notion to (3.59) in different respects.

(3.59)   The bat flew past my ear.

We can say that (3.59) presupposes the existence of a flying mammal and that (3.59) presupposes the existence of a stout stick.

The problem of constructing the interpretive definition is the problem of characterizing the properties corresponding to statementhood in connection with each of the performative propositional types. The problem of constructing the structural definition is to set up the right projection apparatus so that the notions needed in the structural definition of presupposition are available in this apparatus. To attack this problem, we construct a first approximation to a structural definition of presupposition, one that seems to embody the basic idea of Frege's notion, then construct formalizations of the notions employed in the

63. See F. Katz and J. J. Katz, "Is Necessity the Mother of Intension?" *The Philosophical Review* (in press).

first approximation, and finally rework the first approximation and the formalizations until we reach a reasonably satisfactory structural definition.

Our first approximation to a structural definition is (3.60).

(3.60)   (i) A proposition P has a presupposition just in case there is at least one referring term in P.

(ii) The presupposition of a proposition P is the requirement that each referring term in P has its appropriate designatum (that is, the use of a sentence expressing P to make the assertion the sentence makes in the null context presupposes that the referring terms in P have appropriate designata on that use).

We shall make no attempt to actually explain what the term "appropriate designatum" means. The notion that we require for (3.60) is the notion of the designatum of a referring term in a null context. This designatum can be taken as whatever in that context has all those features represented in the meaning of the term in question. The term is a reading, the reading represents certain concepts, and the designatum is every object in a null context that falls under just those concepts. Actual designata are not considered in our approach because they are not determined solely by the grammatical structure of sentences but are influenced, by and sometimes fully determined, by contextual factors. Actual designata, what the use of expressions refer to on the occasion of their use, are matters of performance, whereas the designatum of an expression in a null context is a matter of competence.[64]

The structural definition of presupposition tells us what condition has to be fulfilled to satisfy the presupposition of a proposition; the interpretive definition tells us what it means to satisfy the presupposition. Frege's conception of presupposition can be seen as the proposal that the interpretive definition for this notion be given in terms of statementhood. Frege's view is that the existence of "appropriate designata" for the referring terms in a sentence is a necessary and sufficient condition for it to state a truth or falsehood. The underlying idea is that if there are appropriate designata, there is something for the assertion of the sentence to be about, and the sentence is either true or false. However, if the designation requirement is not met, there is nothing that the assertion is about, and consequently, the sentence can be neither true nor false (on the proper senses of these terms). Given that a proposition's making a statement is its having a truth value and that the truth values are true and false,

64. The designatum of an expression in the null context is what I call the referent of the expression. See the more complete discussion of this point in Katz, "A Proper Theory of Names."

Frege's conception of presupposition suggests the interpretive definition (3.61) for the presupposition of assertive propositions.

(3.61) The presupposition of an assertive proposition P is the condition under which P makes a statement, that is, under which P is a truth or a falsehood.

Now, it might be supposed that this definition is simply not general enough: performative sentences also have presuppositions, but they do not come under (3.61), and we therefore need to construct a more abstract interpretive definition of presupposition, which covers not only sentences like (3.62)-(3.64) but also sentences like (3.65)-(3.67).

(3.62) I baptized you "Throckmorton" yesterday.
(3.63) He promised them riches.
(3.64) She will authorize your release.
(3.65) I now baptize you "Throckmorton".
(3.66) I promise you riches.
(3.67) I hereby authorize your release.

Since a general way of categorizing uses of sentences is in terms of their success in producing the illocutionary act for which their semantic structure qualifies them, we might say that the *illocutionary success condition* of a sentence (on a sense) is the necessary and sufficient condition for it to perform the illocutionary acts (in the null context) for which its propositional type qualifies it. Therefore, (3.60) expresses the illocutionary success condition for constative sentences, and (3.61) provides the interpretation of illocutionary success for such sentences. It would be natural now to try to encompass both constatives and performatives under a general interpretive definition, such as (3.68):

(3.68) The presupposition of the proposition P is the condition under which a sentence expressing P succeeds in performing (in the null context) the illocutionary act of the kind for which its propositional type qualifies it.

This, however, cannot be done: although in the case of assertives the presupposition of a proposition is the illocutionary success condition, in non-assertives the presupposition is not the whole illocutionary success condition. For example, the statement making of (3.62)-(3.64) depends only on the existence of appropriate designata for the referring expressions—that is, the existence of a speaker, addressee(s), riches, and perhaps a confined addressee, but the baptizing, promising, and authorizing of (3.65)–(3.67) depend on more than this. These are necessary but not sufficient conditions for the performance of these illocutionary acts with these sentences. This difference between assertive propositions and nonassertives is, of course, another aspect of the constative/performative distinction. Not only do performatives not state anything, so that they are not true or false, *their presupposition is, though necessary, not a sufficient condition for their illocutionary success.*

These considerations indicate that we should define illocutionary success condition rather than presupposition, constructing the definition of the former so that the illocutionary success condition is the presupposition in the case of an assertive proposition. But insofar as these notions coincide in the case of assertive propositions, and more important, (3.60) will be a necessary condition for the illocutionary success of a performative proposition (that is, a clause in the definition of illocutionary success condition), we require a formalization of "referring term" in (3.60), even though we have downgraded the overall role of presupposition in the theory of performative type.

We have to formalize "referring term" on the basis of the structure of readings. This is what the projection problem for presupposition boils down to in semantic theory. This problem will occupy us in the remainder of the present section. We first motivate taking the notion of a referring term to be that of a term that contributes a clause to the presupposition of the proposition. We then set up lexical readings in which referring terms are represented in the notation of enclosure in heavy parentheses, and introduce projection apparatus that generates readings of sentences with heavy parentheses at just the right places to predict the facts about presupposition in connection with constative sentences.

We interpret the notion of a referring term (or referential position) on the basis of presupposition rather than on the basis of the standard notion of a term for which coreferential terms may be substituted preserving truth. The theory we are developing construes presupposition as a condition guaranteeing a nonempty domain for a predication. What it means to say that a term is a referring term is that the predicates associated with the position the term occupies make assertions about its referent. Correspondingly, what it means to say that a position is referential is that readings occurring in it determine the objects about which the predicates associated with the position make assertions. This notion of a referential position can be distinguished from the notion of a position that permits substitutivity of coextensive terms on the basis of examples like (3.69) and (3.70).

(3.69) Honest politicians actually exist.
(3.70) Toadstools are real things.

On the latter notion, the positions occupied by "honest politicians" and "toadstools" are referential positions, but they are not on the former notion. For suppose that "toadstools" is coextensive with "poisonous mushrooms".

(3.71) Poisonous mushrooms are real things.

Then, we can validly infer (3.71) from (3.70), and so the context "_ is a real thing" is referential in the substitutivity sense. But such contexts cannot be taken as referential in our sense of contributing to the presupposition of the sentence, for then a sentence like (3.70) would be marked as analytic rather than synthetic. If the term occupying such a position were to contribute a clause that makes statementhood depend on its having an appropriate designatum, the presupposition of such sentences would include their truth conditions. For example, the presupposition of (3.69) would be that there is appropriate designata of "honest politicians", but insofar as the truth conditions of (3.69) is that there are honest politicians,[65] these would be included in the presupposition, and therefore, we would be forced to make the false prediction that (3.69) is an analytic sentence (and could, accordingly, not be false).[66] Hence, we have to reject the substitutivity notion of referentiality as appropriate.

It is important to note in this connection, and this, I think, constitutes another strong argument for presupposition, that our theory will provide a very natural solution to the traditional puzzle about negative existential sentences, namely, how can a sentence of the form "X does not exist" ever be true if to assert that X does not exist requires us to refer to X and we can refer to something only if it exists. Previous solutions all seem inadequate because they do not explain what the problematic assumption is and why it should not be made.[67] Our theory offers the following solution. As we have seen in footnote 66, we must avoid saying that the position marked by "X" in sentences of the form "X does not exist" is referential, or else we must mischaracterize such

65. On a presuppositional theory of logical form, (3.69) is not synonymous with "Some politicians are honest". The latter can be either false or not true. It is false when there are politicians but none is honest, and it is not true when there are no politicians. But in both these cases (3.69) is false. Note also that we are not saying that sentences like (3.69) and (3.70) carry no presupposition. They could conceivably be analyzed as presupposing the existence of an appropriate universe, say of material objects in space-time, and asserting the presence of honest politicians and toadstools therein.

66. In connection with sentences like "There are no poisonous mushrooms", "Santa Claus does not exist", and other negative existentials, we would falsely predict that the sentence is contradictory, since their alleged presupposition conflicts with the truth conditions. See Katz, *Semantic Theory*, pp. 178-181.

67. See K. Donnellan, "Speaking of Nothing," *Philosophical Review* 83 (1974):3-31, and E. Erwin, L. Kleiman, and E. Zemach, "The Historical Theory of Reference" (to appear).

sentences as contradictory. But if "X" does not have to refer to something in order for the negative existential to assert that X does not exist, then the first of our two assumptions is false and the puzzle disappears. This solution says that the assumption should not be made because it assigns the wrong logical form to negative existential sentences. It is not wholly clear what logical form should be assigned to them, but we may conjecture that it presupposes a world of things and asserts that X's are not among them.

One further matter before we turn to the formalization. The core of our conception of presupposition is the idea that the use of an assertive proposition to make a statement depends on the successful reference of its referring terms because the existence of the object(s) to which these terms refer is the condition on which the predicate(s) are truly or falsely asserted. Failure to make a statement is thus that some predicate(s) in the proposition fail to be about something. Hence, our conception implies that each and every referring term in an assertive proposition contributes a necessary condition to the necessary and sufficient condition for its statementhood. Each referential term in the proposition is treated on a par with every other.

This is the simplest and most coherent development of the Fregean notion of presupposition, which is why we have adopted (3.60). But it is clearly not the only one. It is possible to imagine alternatives to (3.60) that maintain the requirement that some referring terms must refer but drop the requirement that they all must refer. Such alternatives would be more complex because they would have to specify the further properties of referring terms that qualify them as contributing a condition to the presupposition of the proposition. It would also be necessary to explain why the absence of these further properties should block the contribution of a referring term's presupposition.

One such alternative is this. Someone might hold that successful reference of the agent term is not a necessary condition for statementhood except when it is the only term in the proposition (or perhaps just when there is no recipient term), and that when there is a recipient term, its successful reference is the condition of statementhood. Thus, it might be argued that (3.72) makes a false statement even though its agent term fails to refer.[68]

(3.72)   Santa Claus visited your children last night.

Such an argument lacks an explanation of why the failure of the agent reading to contribute to the presupposition is consistent with the general notion that

68. I am indebted to Robert Fiengo and Janet D. Fodor for suggesting this kind of case. The latter's unpublished paper "Presupposition and Cross-World Relations" takes something like the position I am arguing against here.

the object(s) to which the referring terms refer are the object(s) the assertion is about. It is also hard to see how it might be supplied. But the argument we are considering can be taken simply as an empirical argument to establish the need for both an alternative and such an explanation. Nevertheless, the argument is unconvincing because the plausibility of the claim that the use of a sentence like (3.72) makes a false statement comes from a confusion of falsehood with nontruth, and this is a distinction that our hypothetical critic, in subscribing to some version of the Fregean notion of presupposition, is committed to drawing. What the critic wants to say is that it cannot be the case that Santa Claus visited the children since there is no Santa Claus or we know that nobody visited them. It is possible, however, to express this sort of denial by saying that the assertion in question is not or could not be true. There is no reason to go further and make the strong claim that the assertion is false. We shall look more closely at this fallacy in the next section in connection with the arguments of Harnish and Wilson against factive presupposition.

I shall assume on the basis of these considerations that there is no serious obstacle to our using the simplest structural definition for the notion "presupposition of an assertive proposition", and turn directly to the question of how to state the referential requirement in (3.60) as a condition on the formal structure of readings. The solution we obtain will be needed even if this assumption ultimately proves false, since any alternative to (3.60) will employ the notion of a referring term.

Technically, we ought to speak of a *referring occurrence of a term* rather than of a *referring term*, insofar as the notion of a referring term is a relative one; that is, no term in and of itself is a referring term (or a nonreferring one), but it is so when it occurs in a referential context (or in a nonreferential one). But the looser usage does no harm so long as it is understood that we are speaking relative to referential positions. On this understanding, the formalization of the referential requirement in (3.60) requires (1) apparatus for distinguishing referential and nonreferential positions, (2) a notation for representing a term occurring in a position, and (3) an account of the referentiality of a term on the basis of (1) and (2).

The notation for representing the occurrence of a term in a position consists of the reading expressing the term written slightly below the semantic marker(s) representing the predicate concept(s) associated with the position. The notation thus consists of the reading occupying the place of the categorized variable in figures (3.3) and (3.4). Some occurrences of categorized variables do not mark positions in the present sense, that is, positions corresponding to argument places, but simply points at which the projection rule embeds readings to flesh out terms and predicates, so that we cannot define the notion of a term occurring in a position directly in terms of its being the value of a categorized variable.

As mentioned the section on predicate structure (pp. 63-69), we shall use the apparatus of heavy parentheses to distinguish referential positions from nonreferential ones.[69] Referential and nonreferential positions are differentiated in that the former are categorized variables enclosed within heavy parentheses and the latter are categorized variables not enclosed within heavy parentheses. Accordingly, the referentiality of a term is formally determined when the projection rule puts it inside heavy parentheses in substituting the term for an occurrence of a categorized variable. We could, therefore, restate (3.60) more formally using the notion of a reading enclosed within heavy parentheses to do the work of "referring term".

In order to so restate (3.60), however, we have to use the notion of a reading of a sense of a sentence in place of the informal notion of a proposition. This, then, nicely expresses the condition of adequacy on a solution to the projection problem for presupposition—namely, that it provide a satisfactory account of how the dictionary and projection rule can be formulated so that a semantic component generates readings for senses of sentences such that their subreadings enclosed in heavy parentheses predict their presuppositions. The solution therefore starts at the lexical level. What must be determined there is where heavy parentheses appear around occurrences of categorized variables and where categorized variables in lexical readings are free of them. Then the formulation of the solution moves to the level of complex constituents. What must be determined there is what applications of the projection rule can do by way of removing or introducing heavy parentheses.

We have already found one example of an argument place that must be represented as a nonreferential position, namely, that associated with the constructions "exists" and "there is".[70] Another is the class of opaque verbs of propositional attitude, such as "believe", "want", "hope", "imagine". Although (3.73) presupposes the existence of Santa Claus, (3.74) does not.

(3.73) Santa Claus is sick with the flu.
(3.74) Billy believes Santa Claus is sick with flu.

69. Katz, *Semantic Theory*, pp. 167f.

70. The Kantian objection that "exists" is not a predicate (*The Critique of Pure Reason*, trans., N. K. Smith (London: Macmillan, 1958), pp. 504-505) does not apply here. We are not saying that "exists" is a delimiting predicate of the kind that can figure in definitions.

Thus, the lexical reading of such a verb must contain categorized variables not enclosed in heavy parentheses in order to receive the readings of constituents of the complement sentence such as the reading of the subject of the complement sentence in (3.74), that is, the readings representing the terms occurring in the argument places of the principal relation of the propositional object of the attitude.

Without attempting to offer a lexical reading for "believe", we might indicate the form of the reading in a sentence like (3.74). In doing so, we distinguish two propositions the agent is represented as thinking true. On the one hand, since (3.74) entails (3.75), there is the proposition that the referent of the reading of the subject of the complement sentence exists, and on the other, there is a proposition asserting that the referent has the property attributed to it in the proposition expressed by the complement sentence.

(3.75)   Billy believes that Santa Claus exists.

Thus, the form of the reading for "believe" in (3.74) is something like (3.76).[71]

(3.76)

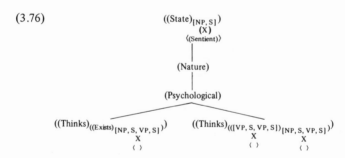

(3.76) represents the "opaque sense" of "believe". It says that the only presupposition of (3.74) is that the reading of its subject has an appropriate designatum. The statementhood of an assertive use of this sentence depends solely on the existence of a believer. (3.76) says also that the truth conditions are the following. The believer is in a state, which implies that the believer is not an agent, since the definition of agent-reading (3.50) contains semantic markers like (Act) or (Activity) but not (State). Also, the state is psycho-

71. We do not yet have the apparatus to explicate the concept of thinking something true or to specify all the components of the propositions thought to be true in terms of the reading of the complement.

logical, contrasting "believe" with "frozen" (where the state is physical) and with "drunk" (where it is partly physical and partly psychological). Also, the psychological state is that of thinking that the person the belief is about exists. Here, the formulation of a lexical reading requires the formalization of the generalization that the believer thinks that there exists a referent of each of the *referential* terms in the proposition functioning as the object of belief.[72] Finally, the psychological state is also one of thinking that the person the belief is about has the property he is attributed in the proposition functioning as the object of the belief.

Verbs like "visit", "chase", and "kill" contrast with verbs of propositional attitude because all the argument places of the relation expressed by the former are referential positions. As in (3.2) and (3.17), we have to write their lexical readings with categorized variables enclosed in heavy parentheses in order to reflect the semantic fact that each term of such relations contributes to the presupposition of sentences in which these verbs appear as main verbs.

There is no general answer to the question of when to represent an argument place in a lexical item as referential, though often there are generalizations like the one above about verbs of propositional attitude. This aspect of lexical readings has to be determined, more or less on a case-by-case basis, by comparing a heavy parentheses treatment with one that makes no use of them to discover which provides the best predictions about the semantic properties and relations of the complex constituents and sentences in which the lexical item appears. Our treatment of the question of whether "exists" and "there is" have nonreferential positions can be taken as paradigmatic. We decided that their positions are nonreferential on the grounds that this better predicts semantic properties and relations: the opposite decision would mistakenly predict that sentences like (3.69) and (3.70) are analytic.[73]

Although there is no general answer to such empirical questions, there are formal constraints that govern the use of heavy parentheses. These may be thought of as well formedness constraints on lexical readings. I shall mention one such constraint, which may be referred to as the "conformity constraint".[74] It is this: *No lexical reading is well formed if it contains two occurrences of the same categorized variable one of which is enclosed in heavy parentheses and the other of which is not.* Either every occurrence of a particular categorized variable is enclosed within heavy parentheses or none is.

72. The nonreferential terms in this proposition (that expressed by the complement sentence) do not give rise to a clause of the truth condition about what the believer thinks exists. Note that in the sentence "John believes that Sam believes that Santa Claus is sick with the flu" there is no clause of the truth condition that John thinks Santa Claus exists.

73. See above.

74. I wish to thank Manfred Bierwisch for suggesting this constraint.

Without this constraint, interpreting lexical readings becomes more complex. In its absence, nothing prevents us from writing a lexical reading that is identical to (3.17) except that one occurrence of the variable categorized for readings of the direct object has heavy parentheses whereas the other does not. But such a reading would say that the recipient's existence is presupposed with respect to the intention of the act but not with respect to the achievement of causing a death (or vice versa).

We have said everything of a general nature that needs to be said in connection with the projection problem for presupposition at the lexical level. The rest concerns the projection process from the lexical level to sentence readings. We need to explain how the apparatus of heavy parentheses interacts with other semantic apparatus as a result of projection rule applications that supply readings for a whole sentence on the basis of its lexical readings. We also need to explain how the derived readings that represent terms are built up out of lexical readings and how such derived readings are routed into their proper positions in the readings of sentences.

There is nothing about term formation that requires special comment in connection with the projection problem for presupposition. The readings representing terms are formed from lexical readings in the standard way. There is also nothing about term routing that requires special comment here. The readings representing terms are routed into positions in the readings of sentences on the basis of the grammatical function that determines the constituents to which the readings of terms are assigned and on the basis of the grammatical functions that categorize the variables in the lexical readings of other constituents. The projection rule thus relates terms to positions representing argument places by substituting readings representing terms for occurrences of categorized variables having the proper categorizations. Thus, terms may be put into referential positions or nonreferential positions. Terms in referential positions may stay there or be moved out. A term that is moved out may be moved into a referential position or a nonreferential position, and so on. The process terminates in a finite number of steps with a term ending up either in a referential position or in a nonreferential one, and each step is determined by the grammatical functions of constituents and the categorizations of variables.[75]

75. Attention to what happens in such reading plug-ins explains why the cumulative hypothesis of Langendoen and Savin fails in the case of sentences with opaque contexts. Suppose the lexical reading of "believe" is of the form (3.76). In the semantic interpretation of (3.74), the reading of the subject of the complement sentence will be lifted out of a position enclosed within heavy parentheses [it occupies such a position in (3.73) and so does in the complement of (3.74)] and plugged into a position in the reading of the verb "believes" that is not enclosed in heavy parentheses. Thus, (3.60) predicts that (3.74) does not presuppose the existence of a Santa Claus, even though its complement sentence does.

What requires special comment in connection with the projection problem for presupposition is the interaction of categorized variables, both enclosed in heavy parentheses and not, with other semantic devices from the lexical readings. It is logically possible for there to be operations that remove heavy parentheses, thereby transforming a referential position into a nonreferential one, and that install heavy parentheses, thereby transforming a nonreferential position into a referential one. Within the framework of semantic theory, each such transformation would be accomplished by an operator belonging to the same category of readings as the antonymy operator,[76] an operator that makes some fixed change in the readings that fall in its scope.

Since in the absence of this kind of interaction categorized variables enclosed in heavy parentheses and categorized variables not so enclosed in them remain as they are throughout the projection process, we have reduced the projection problem for presupposition to determining whether these logical possibilities are empirically realized in natural language and if so, in what forms. We claim that both possibilities exist, and we shall provide examples of each that will describe the kind of operators that remove and install heavy parentheses.

The first possibility is the transformation of a categorized variable enclosed in heavy parentheses into one not so enclosed. The phenomenon of genericness is an example of an otherwise referential context dereferentialized. The verb "eats" is clearly like "chase", "kill", or "visit", which express a relation all of whose argument places are referential positions. An ordinary sentence like (3.77) presupposes the existence of a cow.

(3.77)   The cow is eating the grass.

When the argument place of "eats" that takes agent readings falls in the scope of a generic element in the sentence, the argument place turns into a nonreferential position. This is the case with (3.78).

(3.78)   Cows eat grass (The cow eats grass).

(3.78) has no presupposition about the existence of cows, since it would be true even if no such animals exist. Similarly, the sentence (3.79) is known to be true even though black holes are not known to exist.

(3.79)   A black hole exerts tremendous gravity.

Or, (3.80) is clearly false even though chances are that no man is perfectly virtuous.

76. Katz, *Semantic Theory*, pp. 160–171.

(3.80)   The man of perfect virtue is deceitful when it is to his advantage.

The truth of these sentences does not depend on the existence of referential relations because they are not about particular objects in the world.

Generic sentences are not the only presuppositionless sentences in natural languages. Hypotheticals like (3.81)–(3.83) also lack referential conditions on their statementhood.

(3.81)   If something is a cow, it eats grass.
(3.82)   If something is a black hole, then it exerts tremendous gravity.
(3.83)   If anyone is a man of perfect virtue, he is deceitful when it is to his advantage.

These types of sentence fill a definite need in languages used for both scientific and ordinary purposes. Such languages are required to express assertions about possibilities that can be true or false independently of whether existential conjectures about them prove true. Scientific investigation of controversial entities like black holes, the unconscious, ether, and so on, requires the formulation of true sentences about their properties that we use to decide whether some things in the world are cases of such entities. If we could not formulate truths about the properties of such entities without first knowing whether they exist, we would never find out whether they do.

I suspect that in other respects[77] genericness and hypotheticality are different, although this is not part of my argument here. Generic sentences express a claim about the essential nature of some kind of entity (which may vary with whether the sentence is about a role such as president, an artifact such as chair, or a natural kind such as cows). Hypotheticals express a claim about how things are, should a certain assumption be true. So it seems that the hypothetical sentences (3.81)–(3.83) are not direct paraphrases of the generic sentences (3.78)–(3.80).

To represent the absence of referential condition on the statementhood of both generics and hypotheticals, we need an operator that serves as part of the lexical reading of the syntactic representation of genericness and of some aspect of the conditional construction. Such an operator does not enter into the semantic interpretation of syntactic structures such as the abstract/concrete distinction or the tensed/untensed distinction, insofar as mathematical sentences like (3.84) with abstract noun phrases and a timeless sense nonetheless carry presuppositions.

(3.84)   The least convergent series contains infinitely many primes.

77. Ibid., pp. 178f.

But the operator requires that the structures it interprets define an appropriate notion of scope for its application

We represent the operator in the form (3.85).

$$(3.85) \quad (M_1), \ldots, (\ldots (M_i)_{[\ \ ]} \ldots), \ldots, (M_n) \longrightarrow (M_1), \ldots,$$
$$(\mathbf{x})$$
$$\langle\ \rangle$$
$$(\ldots (M_i)_{[\ \ ]} \ldots), \ldots, (M_n)$$
$$\mathbf{X}$$
$$\langle\ \rangle$$

(3.85) operates on any reading of a constituent in its scope by simply erasing the heavy parentheses in the reading. Such an operator accounts for the argument places of "eats" being referential positions without denying that sentences like (3.78) do not have presuppositions. We need only assume that the scope of the operator includes the argument place in which the agent reading occurs.

The question of characterizing the proper notion of scope here is both complex and important. Normally, the scope of a syntactic symbol is the entire constituent it labels, but in this case scope has to be defined so as also to include other constituents that are anaphoric to the one it labels. As an example, consider (3.86).

$$(3.86) \quad \text{If Jack has children, then all of } \left\{ \begin{array}{c} \text{Jacks's children} \\ \text{them} \end{array} \right\} \text{ are bald.}$$

This kind of sentence was first presented by Morgan[78] as a counter-example to the Langendoen–Savin solution to the projection problem for presupposition. Morgan argued that the sentence in the consequent presupposed that there are children one of whose parents is Jack, but that, contrary to the Langendoen–Savin solution, the entire conditional sentence does not presuppose their existence. The counter-example is of course sound, but the interesting question is *why* does it work. Which step in the compositional process by which the meaning of (3.86) is obtained from the meaning of its words is responsible for blocking the presupposition of a subordinate clause from becoming a presupposition of the sentence?[79]

The explanation we propose is that it is blocked by an application of (3.85) to the heavy parentheses in the reading of the consequent sentence. First, consider the conditional formulations used in (3.81)–(3.83). Such forms express what would be the case were some possibility to be an actuality. This is accom-

78. See Morgan, "On the Treatment of Presupposition in Transformational Grammar," pp. 170f.

79. A version of this explanation appears in Katz and Langendoen, "Pragmatics and Presupposition," pp. 6–8 and 15–16.

plished by taking the sentence appearing in the antecedent of a conditional to state the hypothesis we are asked to assume in the assertion. Thus, (3.81) asks us to assume the existence of cows and (3.86) asks us to assume the existence of Jack's children. It is just this hypothetical element in the meaning of conditionals in natural language that is lost when such sentences are represented in quantification theory using the truth-functional notion of material implication. The proof of this is an old philosophical chestnut. Suppose someone were to claim that if God exists then so does the devil, and you wished to argue against this consequence of the hypothesis. If the claim were translated on the basis of the notion of material implication, that is, "(God exists) $\supset$ (the devil exists)", your denial would take the form "$\sim$((God exists) $\supset$ (the devil exists))" and since this implies that God exists, you would be committed to God's existence. That such an absurdity results from ignoring the hypothetical element in the meaning of a conditional demonstrates its presence.

We might express the effect of this hypothetical element by saying that it acts as a block for truth conditions of the component clauses of conditionals in just the way that opacity acts as a block for presuppositions of component clauses of complex sentences like (3.74). Without trying to say how this hypothetical element blocks such truth conditions, we can observe that conditionals are the inverse of generics. Whereas in generics the presupposition is wiped out but the truth conditions remain, in the antecedent of a conditional the truth condition is wiped out but the presupposition remains (for example, that the noun "Jack" refers in a use of (3.86)).

Second, note that the subject of the consequent sentence in (3.86) bears some kind of anaphoric or inclusional semantic relation to a component of the truth conditions that have been wiped out. It is not quite right to say that the subject of the consequent sentence of (3.86) is syntactically anaphoric to the predicate nominal in the antecedent of this sentence, since, aside from the syntactic questions that arise, sentences like (3.87) would seem to be exactly parallel to sentences like (3.86).

(3.87) If Jack is the father of spinsters, then all of Jack's unmarried adult daughters are bald.

This semantic relation, if it can be specified properly, will provide an extension of the scope of (3.85) that explains why sentences like (3.86) do not presuppose the existence of the designata of referring terms in their consequent sentences. We can make the existence of such a semantic relation the condition under which (3.85) applies to the reading representing such terms and removes the heavy parentheses enclosing them.[80] The reading of "Jack's children" in the reading of the consequent of (3.86) has its heavy parentheses removed, and we predict that (3.86) will be a counter-example to the Langendoen–Savin hypothesis that the presupposition of a complex sentence includes the presuppositions of its clauses.

The complexities to be encountered in attempting to complete the statement of (3.85) include at least the further consideration that this operator might well have to be stated as a context-sensitive rule. We want to supplement (3.61) with a clause that allows generic sentences to make statements, that is, to be either true or false, independently of having a satisfied presupposition. Suppose we were to reformulate (3.61) so that it says that the presupposition is the condition under which nongenerics make a statement, and we characterize statementhood as obtaining in cases where the presupposition is satisfied or the proposition has no presupposition. What would we then say about the propositions, in their generic sense, expressed by sentences like (3.88)?

(3.88) A married bachelor is a bachelor, A round square is round,....

Semantically, they are both analytic and contradictory: If they have a truth value, they are both true and false. Since they are generic, they have a truth value, and therefore, our reformulation of (3.61) and our characterization of statementhood commits us to claiming that such sentences are true and false.

A simple way out of this difficulty, and moreover, one that ties in with other notions in semantic theory, is to make (3.85) context-sensitive by restricting its application to heavy parentheses that enclose only readings representing consistent terms. That is, we prevent (3.85) from applying to readings appearing in term positions that contain two semantic markers from the same antonymous n-tuple.[81] The fact that the heavy parentheses remain in the reading of sentences like (3.88) provides a solution to the difficulty, since, on the basis of them, the propositions of such sentences will be marked *indeterminable*, that is, logically incapable of making a statement. This automatically avoids the problem in our supplement to (3.68).[82]

Introducing this context restriction also has important consequences for other aspects of semantic theory. If we were to spell out the lexical reading for

80. This might be done as a universal condition on semantic components, which says that if some rule wipes out a subreading r_i of a sentence reading R, and there is another subreading of R, R_j, which bears the appropriate inclusional semantic relation to r_i, then any erasure operation of the semantic component that can apply to r_j does.

81. Katz, *Semantic Theory*, pp. 157–171.

82. Ibid., pp. 144–148.

"believe" given in (3.76), it would be necessary to write it with a schema that moves each reading R inside heavy parentheses within the reading of the complement sentence into a distinct component reading of the full sentence, where such a component reading represents the predication that the referent of the subject of "believe" thinks that there is something that is the appropriate designatum of R. In (3.89)(i), the schema would introduce one such component reading, whereas in (3.89)(ii) it would introduce two such component readings.

(3.89) (i)   John believes that Sue wants a unicorn.
       (ii) John believes that Sue phoned Ralph.
       (iii) John believes that a cow eats grass.

Now, in terms of the treatment of generics above, (3.89)(iii) (taking the complement in its generic sense) would have no such component reading, which is clearly right. But on the basis of our context restriction on the rule (3.85), a belief sentence in which (3.88) appears as the complement of the verb is represented as reporting someone's "impossible belief", namely, that a proposition that can neither be true or false (for logical reasons) is true. In such cases it seems right to take the belief sentence as entailing that the referent of its subject thinks that the impossible object exists, and this provides further justification for the context restriction discussed above. With this restriction, the heavy parentheses are not removed from around readings representing contradictory concepts, so that the schema referred to above will provide a component reading in the reading of the full sentence that represents the belief of the referent of its subject that the (contradictory) concept has a non-null extension.[83]

We now turn to the possibility of introducing heavy parentheses that enclose a categorized variable that had no heavy parentheses in its lexical reading. This case represents the last possibility to be considered in formally characterizing the projection problem for presupposition. Once we have determined whether there are rules of heavy-parentheses introduction parallel to rules like (3.85) for heavy-parentheses elimination, the formal characterization of the projection problem then is what other rules are there in one or both of these categories and what are their formal constraints.

Although the reading of the subject of the complement sentence in (3.90) is a nonreferential term and (3.90) does not presuppose the existence of a king of

83. I am indebted to D. T. Langendoen and Robert Fiengo for their help in working out the context restriction and applications discussed here. It is worth noting that this interpretation of belief sentences with contradictory concepts appearing as terms in the propositional object of belief is an example of the ordering of semantic rules, *viz.*, that these rules operate where applicable in a projection process that proceeds from bottom to top of phrase markers.

France, the reading of the subject of the complement sentence in (3.91) is referential and (3.91) does presuppose the existence of a king of France.

(3.90) Sue believes that the king of France is a philosopher.

(3.91) Sue believes of the king of France that the king of France is a philosopher.

Sentence (3.91) is the kind of sentence that philosophers and logicians use to express what they allege to be a transparent sense of "believes".[84]

We can account for such referentialization of the subject of the complement of "believes" and similar opaque verbs by making the rule (3.92)[85] the reading of phrases like "of NP" where the NP is the subject of the complement sentence.[86]

$$(3.92) \quad (M_1), \ldots, (\ldots (M_i)_{[\ ]} \ldots), \ldots, (M_n) \longrightarrow (M_1), \ldots,$$
$$\overset{X}{\underset{\langle\ \rangle}{}}$$
$$(\ldots (M_i)_{[\ ]} \ldots), \ldots, (M_n)$$
$$\overset{(X)}{\underset{\langle\ \rangle}{}}$$

There seems to be good independent reason to treat (3.92) as the semantic representation of an important component of the meaning of the preposition in "of the so-and-so" phrases, since such phrases mean the same, or very close to the same, as phrases like "about the so-and-so", "concerning the so-and-so", and so on, which function to specify the object(s) that some predication will be made of.[87] Evidence for taking the scope of the lexical reading of such phrases to be the verb is that their free occurrence at different positions in a sentence like (3.93) makes it reasonable to treat them as adverbial phrases.

(3.93) (of Sue) Mary believes the worst things (of Sue).

Moreover, since the noun phrase of such prepositional phrases is syntactically identified with the subject of the embedded sentence, as shown by (3.94),

---

84. Or, "The king of France is such that Sue believes that the king of France is a philosopher". See W. V. O. Quine, *Word and Object* (Cambridge, Mass.: M.I.T. Press, 1960), p. 147.

85. Similar remarks as were made about the status of (3.85) apply to this rule.

86. Note that the conformity constraint offers us no basis for handling such referentialization and that (3.13) does not apply. Thus, something like (3.92) is required. Note also that (3.92) enters into the semantic interpretation of constructions like 'NP is such that . . .' in sentences like the example in footnote 84.

87. I owe this observation to D. T. Langendoen.

(3.94) *Sue believes of them that he is a philosopher.

the operation of heavy parentheses introduction can be restricted to the categorized variable whose values are readings of the subject of the embedded sentence.

FACTIVE PRESUPPOSITION

Factive presuppositions are usually associated with sentences like (3.95).

(3.95) Boris regrets (remembers, realizes, knows, etc.) that he made an appointment with the dentist.

They arise from "factive verbs" and take the form of a requirement that the sentence appearing as the complement of a factive verb be true. Our interest in factive presupposition stems from whether it can be brought under the treatment of Fregean presupposition outlined in the previous section.

The formulation of factive presupposition proposed in *Semantic Theory*[88] was that a proposition P is presupposed by a sentence S just in case P follows from both S and its denial $\sim S$. This formulation was thought to be an acceptable test for presupposition in general, so that, insofar as both (3.95) and its denial imply that Boris made an appointment with the dentist, the formulation entails that (3.95) presupposes that Boris made an appointment with the dentist. But it no longer seems to be true that this formulation is an acceptable general test for presupposition,[89] and consequently, the fact that both (3.95) and its denial imply that Boris made an appointment with the dentist is no longer grounds for the claim that there are factive presuppositions. Thus, one argument for the existence of this kind of presupposition disappears. But many people still have the intuition that the truth of the complement sentence in a case like (3.95) is the condition under which the sentence makes a statement (asserts something true or false). This is a *prima facie* reason for thinking that factive presuppositions are the same sort of things as Fregean presuppositions. It seems reasonable to say that just as there has to be a king of France for some assertion about the king of France to be true or false, so there has to be a state of affairs in which Boris made an appointment with the dentist for some assertion about it to be true or false.

Recently, however, Harnish and Wilson have raised doubts about the notion

88. Katz, *Semantic Theory*, pp. 135–136.
89. Katz, "On Defining the Notion of "Presupposition.""

of factive presupposition by constructing two arguments against it.[90] We could not simply accept their arguments and restrict the notion of presupposition to Fregean presupposition because, to the degree that it is reasonable to think that factive presupposition can be brought under Fregean presupposition, it is also reasonable to think that if factive presupposition has to be abandoned, then so does Fregean presupposition.

We should thus attempt to save factive presupposition. Therefore, I will try to show that both the arguments to eliminate factive presupposition are fallacious, and I will try to show how factive presupposition can be treated together with the standard Fregean presupposition.

The first attack on factive presupposition is Harnish's argument that the notion leads to absurd consequences. He argues as follows. Assume that the relation between the sentences (3.96) and (3.97) is that the former is the logical presupposition of the latter.

(3.96)   Snails exceed the speed of light.
(3.97)   Einstein knew that snails exceed the speed of light.

Since it is false that snails exceed the speed of light, (3.97) must be neither true nor false. But, by the same token, (3.98), the denial of (3.97), is also neither true nor false.

(3.98)   Einstein did not know that snails exceed the speed of light.

We may thus infer that (3.99) is neither true nor false.

(3.99)   Einstein knew and Einstein did not know that snails exceed the speed of light.

Sentence (3.99) is a contradiction and hence false, and therefore, we arrive at the absurdity that (3.99) is false and not false. We must therefore reject the notion of factive presupposition.

This argument seems convincing until we realize that its plausibility rests entirely on not adopting a consistent presuppositionalist stance. Harnish is arguing against a view of presupposition that explicitly denies his assumption that (3.99) is a contradiction in the sense of a logically false statement. Presup-

90. R. M. Harnish, "Studies in Logic and Language," Ph.D. dissertation, Massachusetts Institute of Technology, Cambridge, Mass., 1972; D. Wilson, "Presuppositions and Non-Truth-Conditional Semantics," Ph.D. dissertation, Massachusetts Institute of Technology (Cambridge, Mass.: Cambridge University Press, 1975).

positionalists ought to say that (3.99) is not a statement at all because its pre-supposition, (3.96), is false. There is no absurdity, then, because (3.99) is not a contradiction any more than is an assertion that the present king of France is both bald and not bald.[91]

The second argument (due originally to Harnish, but found in essentially the same form in Wilson) runs as follows. It is clearly the case that (3.100) implies (3.101).

(3.100) Richard III did not commit murder.
(3.101) Historians do not (cannot) know that Richard III committed murder.

Now, assume that Richard III did not commit murder. It follows that (3.101). But, then, the falsity of the presupposition of (3.101) is compatible with the truth of the sentence (3.101), contrary to the presuppositionalist position.

This argument commits a fallacy by equivocating between external and internal negation.[92] The interpretation of the premise of the argument under which the premise is true is not the one under which it implies the conclusion, and the interpretation under which the premise implies the conclusion is not the one under which the premise is true. The premise of the argument that is the conditional "If (3.100), then (3.101)" can be accepted as true only when the occurrence of negation in the consequent is external negation. This is to say, the sentence (3.102) cannot be true unless Richard III committed murder, but there is no reason to concede that (3.102) is false if Richard III did not commit murder.

(3.102) Historians know (can know) that Richard III committed murder.

(Presuppositionalists take the assertion of (3.101) to be that the relation "be-lieves on adequate evidential grounds" (or something like it) holds between historians and the state of affairs, so that (3.102) is false in case the state of affairs of Richard III having committed murder obtains and historians either do not believe that it does or fail to have adequate evidence for thinking it does.) But reading the negation as external negation makes the argument irrelevant to

91. I am indebted to Yuji Nishiyama for pointing out this fallacy. See Y. Nishiyama, *The Structure of Propositions* (Tokyo: Keio University, 1975), pp. 55–93.

92. External negation is paraphrasable as "It is not the case that S", which is true in case S is false or S has no truth value. The external negation of S says that S is in the complement of the true sentences. Internal negation is paraphrasable as "It is false that S". A sentence of the form "X is not (= internal negation) Y" is thus true just in case "X is Y" is false.

the controversy about factive presupposition, because presuppositionalists can accept the truth of (3.101) in the form (3.103).

> (3.103)   It is not the case that historians know (can know) that Richard III committed murder [that is, (3.102) is either false or has no truth value].

On the other hand, if the negation in (3.101) is internal negation, that is, (3.101) says that it is false that (3.102), then there is no reason for us to grant the truth of the premise of the argument that is the conditional "If (3.100), then (3.101)". The point is again the same. Therefore, either the premise is true but the troublesome conclusion does not follow, or the conclusion follows but from a premise that begs the question by assuming the falsehood of the position Harnish's argument is intended to refute.

To treat factive and nonfactive presupposition within a common framework, it is necessary to be clear that factive verbs do not form a natural class in semantics but are defined in contrast to nonfactive verbs. Standard examples of nonfactive verbs include "suppose", "assert", "allege", "claim", "believe", "conjecture", "intimate", and so on.[93] Sentences with these verbs as the main verb *never* have presuppositions clauses of which are determined by aspects of the meaning of the complement sentence. Standard examples of factive verbs include "regret", "know", "remember", "realize", "be aware of", "resent", "surprise", "deplore", and so on. Factives are thus definable as verbs such that sentences with them as main verbs have presuppositions *some* clauses of which are determined by aspects of the meaning of the complement sentence. Neither the class of factives nor that of nonfactives is a natural semantic class whose members belong to the class because of a common semantic structure. We have already explained the structure underlying the nonfactivity of "believe"; later we shall provide an explanation of the different structure underlying the nonfactivity of "assert", "claim", and so on, in terms of the performative nature of these verbs.

We now turn to factive verbs, one kind being illustrated by "regret". Here the statementhood requirement is the existence of some particular state of affairs, roughly, that the proposition expressed by the complement sentence describe an actual state of affairs. The propositional content of the complement sentence functions as a referential term in essentially the manner of ordinary Fregean presuppositions, where the referential terms of the proposition are required to designate appropriate objects. The "regret sentence" expresses a

93. The term *factive* comes from P. Kirparsky and C. Kirparsky, "Fact," in *Progress in Linguistics* (The Hague: Mouton, 1970), pp. 143–173.

relation between this term and the term representing the agent. These terms pick out the things that the sentence is about, and the assertion made in the use of such a sentence is true just in case these things bear the relation to one another.

Given that the notation of heavy parentheses is not restricted to readings of concepts, it is natural to use the notation to represent the regret type of factive. The use of this notation is illustrated with the highly simplified lexical reading (3.104) for the verb "regret".

(3.104)

$$((State)_{[NP, S]})$$
$$(X)$$
$$\langle\langle Sentient\rangle\rangle$$

$$(Nature)$$

$$(Psychological)$$

$$((Wishes)_{[S, VP, S]}) \qquad ((Sad\ about)_{[S, VP, S]})$$
$$A/\ (X) \qquad\qquad\qquad (X)$$
$$(\ ) \qquad\qquad\qquad\qquad (\ )$$

Another kind of factive verb is "know".

(3.105)   John knows that the child laughed.

A sentence like (3.105) does not (on the standard analysis) presuppose that the complement sentence describes some state of affairs about which the sentence as a whole predicates something (in the sense in which a regret sentence predicates that the agent is sad about that state of affairs). This is supported by the observation of Kirparsky and Kirparsky:

> There are some exceptions to this second half of our generalization. Verbs like *know*, *realize*, though semantically factive, are syntactically non-factive, so that we cannot say **I know the fact that John is here*, **I know John's being here*, whereas the propositional constructions are acceptable: *I know him to be here.*[94]

Rather, in the case of sentences like (3.105), there is a truth condition to the effect that the proposition expressed by the complement sentence is true. Accordingly, the only contribution that the meaning of the complement sentence

94. Ibid., p. 348.

makes to the presupposition of the whole sentence is a clause requiring that each referring term in the proposition expressed by the complement sentence designate. This can be represented by constructing the lexical reading of "know" so that heavy parentheses in the reading of the complement sentence are not removed in the projection process. Thus, we can restate the structural definition of presupposition in the form (3.106).

(3.106) The presupposition of a proposition P is the requirement that every reading enclosed in heavy parentheses appearing in the reading of P have its appropriate referent.

We note that factive sentences generally may have generic complement sentences, for example, (3.107)-(3.109).

(3.107) Biologists know that the owl is nocturnal.
(3.108) Bill is surprised that the owl is nocturnal.
(3.109) May regrets that the owl is nocturnal.

In the "know"-type case, this is handled automatically, since the absence of referential terms in generic propositions means that they contribute nothing to the presupposition of the whole sentence. Hence, (3.107) presupposes only the existence of some non-null set of biologists. On the other hand, the "regret" case is different, insofar as the lexical reading for "regret" contains categorized variables enclosed with heavy parentheses for which readings from the complement sentence will be substituted. I think the simplest way of handling this situation is to promote (3.85) from its present status as a lexical reading for a syntactic feature to the status of a clause of the projection rule. To do this, we shall have to specify conditions for its application in the semantic interpretation of sentences, one of which will be the occurrence of the feature [+Generic], where the rule will apply as it did when it was a lexical reading of this feature. Another condition for the application of this rule will be the occurrence of pairs consisting of a categorized variable and a generic constituent satisfying its categorization. In such cases, (3.85) operates to wipe out heavy parentheses enclosing the categorized variable.[95] This rule will account for "regret"-type cases such as (3.109) because it wipes out the heavy parentheses enclosing the variables categorized for readings of the embedded sentence in the lexical reading for the main verb.

---

95. This rule is referred to as the "heavy parenthesis wipe out rule" in Katz and Langendoen, p. 6.

4
THE CONSTATIVE SIDE: THE CONCEPT OF ASSERTIVE TYPE

INTRODUCTION

Propositional type is the subject of the remaining chapters. The present chapter concerns assertive propositional type, that is, the aspect of propositional structure that determines that assertion is the illocutionary act performed in the null context. The next chapter concerns the concept of performative type and the division of propositional types into constative and performative. The final chapter examines the range of performative types and sets up a classification of performative subtypes. It considers the implications of this classification for theories about the nature of logic and the relation of logic to natural language.

There are two kinds of truth conditions, extensional and nonextensional. Both are truth conditions in the sense that they specify what an assertive proposition asserts to be the case, but only extensional truth conditions involve an assertion about objects in the extension of the referring terms in the proposition. Propositions with exclusively extensional truth conditions have a presupposition requiring each of their referring terms to designate, and the statements they make are straightforwardly *about* the objects whose existence satisfies their presuppositions. Extensional truth conditions are thus conditions that such objects are as they are asserted to be. Propositions with nonextensional truth conditions, on the other hand, have no referring terms and presupposition. The propositions expressed by generic sentences like (3.78)–(3.80) make statements regardless of whether or not there are cows, black holes, or men of perfect virtue. Moreover, even if there are such things, these sentences do not make assertions about them. Their truth conditions, accordingly, cannot be of the same kind as that of propositions with presuppositions.

What kind of truth conditions they have, however, is an extremely hard question. We shall make no effort to answer it here. The matters that concern us are such that we can reasonably restrict ourselves to the study of assertive propositions with extensional truth conditions.

CONVERSION

We characterized propositional type in (1.30) as that part of the structure of a proposition that determines the illocutionary act performed by sentences expressing it in the null context. The propositional type of (4.1) equips it to make assertions, that of (4.2) to ask questions, that of (4.3) to issue requests, and that of (4.4) to make promises.

>   (4.1)   Someone will drink the wine.
>   (4.2)   Who will drink the wine?
>   (4.3)   Drink the wine!
>   (4.4)   I promise to drink the wine.

The propositional type determines illocutionary potential by converting the condition of the propositional content into what we shall call a "converted condition". The converted condition in the case of (4.1) is a *truth condition*, in the case of (4.2) an *answerhood condition*, in the case of (4.3) a *compliance condition*, and in the case of (4.4) a *fulfillment condition*. The notion of a converted condition is an abstraction covering such particular conditions. An illocutionary success condition tells us what must be the case for there to be a statement, a question, a request, a promise, and so on; a truth condition tells us what must obtain for a statement to be true, an answerhood condition tells us what features a response must have to be an answer to a question, a compliance condition tells us what features an act must have to comply with a request, a fulfillment condition tells us what features an act must have to fulfill a promise, and so on. Every proposition has both an illocutionary success condition and a converted condition.

The structural definition of the illocutionary success condition for the assertive propositions is (4.5).

>   (4.5)   The illocutionary success condition for a use of an assertive proposition P is that either P has no presupposition at all (that is, the reading of P contains no occurrences of heavy parentheses) or else the presupposition of P [in the sense of (3.106)], is satisfied on that use of P.

The illocutionary success condition for other propositional types cannot be given in terms of the defining condition in (4.5). As we have already noted in our discussion of (3.68), the illocutionary success condition for performative propositions requires something beyond satisfaction of the presupposition.

Although we shall not be able to formulate this further condition until we have made progress in explicating the concept of performativeness, we may observe here that the further condition will be, roughly, that the "unconverted condition", as we shall henceforth refer to the condition in propositional content, characterizes the speaker's use of the sentence. We can, however, provide a general interpretive definition of the notion "illocutionary success condition", namely, (4.6).

> (4.6) An illocutionary success condition is a necessary and sufficient condition for the use of a sentence (in the null context) to perform the speech act for which its propositional type qualifies it.

The notion of a converted condition can be explained at this stage in terms of examples like (4.1)-(4.4). The part of the propositional content that corresponds to Frege's notion of content,[1] namely, the relation common to the senses of (4.1)-(4.4) of someone drinking some wine at some time following the moment of speech, plays a comparable role in determining converted conditions to the role that the uncoverted conditions play in determining illocutionary success conditions. The structural definitions for the various converted conditions will be the requirement that the relation determined in the content holds together with certain other requirements that will be developed later. Thus, the interpretive definitions for the various converted conditions will specify the central logical property for the particular type of proposition in each case. For example, in the case of an assertive proposition like (4.1), the truth condition tells us what must be the case for a statement made in the use of such a proposition to be true; in the case of the performative proposition expressed by (4.2), the answerhood condition tells us what is required for a sentence to be a correct answer to the question; in the case of the performative proposition expressed by (4.3), the compliance condition tells us what actions count as complying with the request made; in the case of the performative proposition expressed by (4.4), the fulfillment condition tells us what actions count as fulfilling the promise. Each distinct type of proposition will have a distinct converted condition. Our theory explicates propositional type as what is responsible for the conversion of (the content in) unconverted conditions into converted conditions. We think of propositional type as that part of the structure of a proposition that brings about the conversion of the condition in its propositional content. We shall try to explicate propositional type so that these four above-mentioned conversions and the others fall out naturally as a consequence of the interaction of propositional type and propositional content.

1. See Chapter 1, p. 10-12.

The present chapter explicates the notion "assertive type" and thus the notion "truth condition". Although these explications contain some new concepts and new ways of treating old ones, they basically rely on familiar concepts from semantics and philosophical logic. Our aim is to formulate a conception of assertiveness from which we can go on to explicate performativeness, and accordingly, the development of new notions and the adaptation of old ones are means to this end.

We want our explication of assertive type to embody all the information required to convert the unconverted condition of sentences like (4.1) into a truth condition. We take this information to constitute the form that the assertive component of the meaning of sentences takes.[2]

The core meaning of the concept of assertiveness in simple propositions is, roughly, the attributing of something to something. We take this core meaning as it is and try to develop it to obtain a concept suitable for semantic interpretation. We have already carried this development one step further by taking the thing(s) to which the attribution is made to be the thing(s) that satisfy the presupposition of the proposition. The next step is to take the unconverted condition to express what is attributed in an assertion. The notion of assertion can then be understood as the assertion that the object(s) satisfying the presupposition of the proposition also satisfy the unconverted condition.

THE TERM-PLACE
CORRELATION

The unconverted condition of a proposition is typically a predicate of complex internal logical structure. The semantic marker notation represents predicates in a way that enables us mechanically to unpack that logical structure into component predicates and associate the referring terms with their proper argument places. For example, we can unpack the complex logical structure of the chase relation on the basis of a semantic marker like (3.2) into, *inter alia*, the two component predicates of "engages in an attempt to catch something" and "moves in a manner that determines the direction of the chaser's movement in the course of the chase", where the former is associated with the agent place and the latter with the recipient place.[3] We can associate the referring terms in a proposition like that expressed by (4.7) with these argument places.

2. The formalization of this component of the meaning of a sentence would, in line with the discussion in Chapter 2, be a reading for a declarative sentence-type symbol or feature (similar to "Q", "I", and so on) or perhaps a reading for the syntactic representation of indicative sentence intonation contour.

3. Argument places can, of course, be individuated in terms of semantic roles (just as terms have been above). The definitions for the semantic roles agent, recipient, and so on, determine the agent-place, recipient-place, and so on.

(4.7)   The cat chased the mouse.

That is, we can associate the meaning of the subject with the agent-place and the meaning of the object with the recipient-place. The result of such unpacking and association is called a "term-place correlation". A term-place correlation is a sequence of pairs, one member of which is a subreading of the reading of a proposition that represents a component predicate of the unconverted condition, and the other member is a sequence of subreadings of the reading of the proposition whose elements are the terms to which the predicate applies, where the order of a term-reading in the sequence correlates it with its proper place in the predicate (with which the sequence as a whole is paired).

The term-place correlation expresses the speaker-hearer's knowledge of the relation between the unconverted condition in the sense of a sentence and the objects satisfying its presupposition. Assuming the referential relations to these objects to have been determined, this knowledge determines the assertion that the sentence makes about them.

Three principles are required for these correlations. First, there is the principle discussed in Chapter 3 in the section on predicate structures[4] for specifying how the formal structure of semantic markers is interpreted as predicate functions and how the component predicates are related to occurrences of categorized variables.

Second, there is the principle (3.9). This principle determines which occurrences of categorized variables in a semantic marker map into the same argument place. Together this principle and the previous one determine which component predicates go with which argument places of the unconverted condition. Therefore, when (3.9) collapses occurrences of the same categorized variable into one argument place, the component predicates associated with each of these occurrences are related to that argument place.

Third, there is the projection rule. It not only forms the readings that appear as the terms, but it substitutes these readings for occurrences of categorized variables, thereby providing the terms for the correlation. The actual terms, $t_1, \ldots, t_n$, result from the collapsing of occurrences of categorized variables into argument places: each of the readings that substitutes for occurrences of categorized variables that collapse into the same place collapse into the same term t_i of the sequence. Thus, in the semantic interpretation of (4.7), these principles will represent the reading of "the cat" and the reading of "the mouse" as the terms correlated, respectively, with the argument place associated, *inter alia*, with the component predicate "engages in a physical activity taking the form of movement", and the argument place associated, *inter alia*, with the component predicate "moves in a manner that determines the direction of the chaser's movement".

4. See pp. 59–77.

We may represent this correlation process schematically in (4.8) and (4.9).

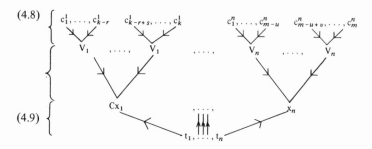

The first stage in (4.8) depicts the association of component predicates in the unconverted condition $Cx_1, \ldots, x_n$, represented by "c" with superscript and subscript, with occurrences of categorized variables, represented by "V". The second stage depicts the collapsing of occurrences of these variables into argument places, represented by "$x_1, \ldots, x_n$", which is effected by (3.9). (4.9) depicts the correlation of terms, represented by "t", with places of the unconverted condition and each of its component predicates, which is accomplished by the projection rule's substitution of readings for occurrences of categorized variables.

The core concept of assertiveness can now be reconstructed in a way that reflects the fact that assertions are composed of subassertions, each of which coincides with an entailment of the proposition. Given that the presupposition of an assertive proposition P is satisfied, there is for each t_i $(1 \leqslant i \leqslant n)$ a non-null set of things, the appropriate designata of t_i. Each of the component predicates of P's unconverted condition correlated with t_i, namely, $c_1^i, \ldots, c_q^i$, are both attributions of a property or relation to the members of this set and the semantic structures that determine the entailments of P relative to the definition of semantic entailment.[5]

TEMPORAL AND QUANTIFICATIONAL PARAMETERS OF ASSERTION

There are two further aspects of the assertions that sentences make: how many objects in the extension of a term are attributed the property or relation correlated with the term; when it is attributed that property or relation. If we add

5. See Katz, *Semantic Theory*, pp. 188–189.

quantificational and temporal parameters to our explication of assertiveness, the assertion relative to a particular term t_i is represented as the claim that some quantity of the designata of t_i satisfies $c_1^i, \ldots, c_k^i$ at some specific time. We may formalize this in (4.10), where "Q_n" is the grammatical function that determines constituents that contain the quantifier information, "DES(t_i)" stands for the designata of t_i, and "T" is the grammatical function that determines constituents that contain the temporal information.

$$(4.10) \quad ((\text{Satisfies})_{\substack{[Q_n] \\ X \\ \langle \ \rangle}} \text{ of DES } (t_i), c_1^i, \ldots, c_k^i, \substack{[T] \\ X \\ \langle \ \rangle})$$

We can be brief about the temporal parameter because the formalization of temporal designations has already received rather extensive treatment.[6] Sentences like (4.11), (4.12), and (4.13) attribute sobriety to John at different times.

(4.11) John is sober.
(4.12) John was sober.
(4.13) John will be sober.

Sentence (4.11) attributes the property to him at the speech point, sentence (4.12) at some time antecedent to the speech point, and sentence (4.13) at some time to follow the speech point. In each case, the reading of the tense constituent is the value of the categorized variable $\substack{[T] \\ X \\ \langle \ \rangle}$ in (4.10). Thus, for the sentences (4.11)–(4.13), the values of this categorized variable are, respectively, $(t^{(o)})$, $(t^{(-n)})$, and $(t^{(+n)})$. Sentences like (4.14) and (4.15) place tighter temporal constraints on their attribution and involve more complex temporal designations but pose no special problem.

(4.14) John is sober every other day.
(4.15) John will be sober at noon tomorrow.

The quantificational parameter cannot be so briefly treated. Nor, however, can it be treated with anything like the detail that its prominence in recent linguistic discussions would suggest. Our compromise is to present some general ideas about the treatment of quantification that convey enough detail for our account of truth conditions. For this, we have to provide some conception of

6. See J. J. Katz, *Semantic Theory* (New York: Harper & Row, 1972). pp. 306–346, and also A. Janda, "An Interpretive Analysis of English Temporal Relations" in *CUNY Forum*, no. 1, ed. R. M. Vago (New York: Queens College and The Graduate Center, C.U.N.Y., 1976), pp. 38–63.

the semantic markers that comprise the lexical readings of quantifier words, indicate how such readings combine to form readings that replace the categorized variable $\overset{[Q_n]}{\underset{\langle\ \rangle}{X}}$ in occurrences of (4.10), and describe how these readings determine the truth conditions of sentences.

(4.16) are examples of quantifier words.

(4.16) a(n), the, all, some, each, every, any, most, few, several, many, seven, twelve, half, . . .

But not all occurrences of quantifier words are quantifiers. A quantifier is a word that, by virtue of its grammatical role in the determiner, informs us about how many of $DES(t_i)$ is asserted to be $c_1^i, \ldots, c_k^i$.

Thus, the semantic information carried by the quantifier words "six" and "many" in (4.17) and (4.18) is not quantificational information, whereas the semantic information carried by these words in (4.19) and (4.20) is.

(4.17) All (of the) six people on the raft drowned.
(4.18) Some of the many gamblers won.
(4.19) Six people on the raft drowned.
(4.20) Many people gamble.

The occurrences of "six" and "many" in (4.17) and (4.18) provide information not about how many of $DES(t_i)$ are asserted to be $c_1^i, \ldots, c_k^i$ but about the nature of the condition that determines $DES(t_i)$. This information tells us something about the number of the objects that a referential noun phrase presupposes. It thus functions semantically in the same way as constituents of the nominal part of the noun phrase. This is confirmed from the fact that the occurrences of "six" and "many" in (4.17) and (4.18) can be glossed as in (4.21) and (4.22), but the quantifier occurrences cannot.

(4.21) All of the group of six people on the raft drowned.
(4.22) Some of the gamblers who were many in number won.

Thus, the meaning of "six" in (4.17) informs us of the cardinality of the set $DES(t_i)$, and the presupposition of (4.17) is that there be six people on the raft in question. The quantifier in (4.17) tells us that each and every one of these six is asserted to have met a watery grave.[7]

7. The question arises of how to define Q_n, that is, how to specify the grammatical relation to the determiner that accords a quantifier word the status as a quantifier. On the basis of N. Chomsky, *Aspects of the Theory of Syntax* (Cambridge, Mass.: M.I.T. Press, 1965), p. 107, we might conjecture Q_n = Pre-Article of, Det, NP.

Quantifier information is about *grouping* and *quantity*. The former tells us how the objects in $DES(t_i)$ are taken as *units of attribution*, that is, what the n-tuples of objects from $DES(t_i)$ are to which $c_1^i, \ldots, c_k^i$ is applied. The quantity information tells us how many of such units or n-tuples is claimed to have $c_1^i, \ldots, c_k^i$. Thus, the semantic markers that will be required in the lexical readings of quantifier words include (Grouping), and (Quantity).

The units of attribution can be individuals, pairs, triplets, and so on, up to the entire membership of the set $DES(t_i)$. The frequently discussed notions of the *distributive* and *collective* features of quantifiers[8] represent the two extremes of this range of possible units. Information about the units of attribution is also provided by constituents that determine the unconverted condition, very often the main verb. The semantic structure of the verb "solo", as in (4.23), determines that the units of attribution with respect to the agent place of the relation are the individuals in $DES(t_i)$.[9]

(4.23) All the men soloed the plane.

The quantifiers that have agent terms in their scope apply distributively. Thus, (4.23) means that each of the men flew the plane individually. In contrast, the agent place of the relation expressed by "mob" is inherently collective. Thus, (4.24) means that the men as a group took the action.

(4.24) The men mobbed the crooked politician.

Most verbs do not determine a particular unit of attribution for their argument places. Verbs like "chase", "hunt", "visit", and "lift" are examples. A sentence like (4.25) contrasts with sentences like both (4.23) and (4.24) in having neither unit determination.

(4.25) The children chased the animals.

But (4.25) is *not* ambiguous. It does not have two senses, one involving distributivity and one not. The assertion leaves it open whether the children chased the animals in a group (or groups of varying size) or singly, and is true as long as they did it in any of these ways. To narrow the assertion so that just one of these ways is allowed requires the introduction of an adverbial that specifies the unit of attribution, as in (4.26), (4.27), and (4.28).

8. Z. Vendler, "Each and Every, Any and All," in *Linguistics in Philosophy* (Ithaca, N.Y.: Cornell University Press, 1967), p. 74.

9. See J. J. Katz, "Recent Issues in Semantic Theory," *Foundations of Language* 3, (1967), p. 169.

(4.26) The children hunted in pairs.
(4.27) The children individually visited the animals.
(4.28) The children together lifted the box.

The quantifiers "each" and "every" determine individual units of attribution. Sentence (4.29) is similar in meaning to (4.23) in that it says that the action is individually performed, and likewise with (4.30).

(4.29) Each of the children lifted the box.
(4.30) Every child lifted the box.

Further evidence for the distributive nature of "each" and "every" is that sentences like (4.31) and (4.32) are contradictory in saying both that the men acted individually and that they acted as a group.

(4.31) Each of the men mobbed the movie star.
(4.32) Every man mobbed the movie star.

It is questionable whether, as Vendler claims,[10] "all" is collective. A sentence like (4.33) seems no more collective in sense than (4.25).

(4.33) All the children chased the animals.

In fact, when the collective sense is wanted, we create it as we do in (4.28) by adverbial modification, as in (4.34).

(4.34) All the children together chased the animals.

If "all" were collective, moreover, we would expect that (4.34) would be redundundant, as is (4.35), and that (4.36) would be contradictory, as are (4.31) and (4.32).

(4.35) Each of the men lifted the box individually.
(4.36) All the men soloed the plane.

Neither, of course, is confirmed. Hence, some quantifiers, like most verbs, appear to leave the unit of attribution unspecified.[11]

10. Vendler, "Each and Every, Any and All," p. 74.
11. It may be that Vendler uses the term "collective" differently from what we have assumed, but his examples indicate otherwise. Rather, what seems to have misled him is his choice of predicate expressions like "is similar" and his use of determiner elements like "the number of", which introduce collectivity themselves. "The number of", like "equi-

It is clear that, for reasons of the kind just given in connection with "all", other quantifiers like "some", "two", "many", and so on, also do not specify a unit of attribution. This means that the alleged quantifier ambiguities in sentences like (4.37), between a sense on which the action is collective and a sense on which it is individual (and perhaps others on which it is partly one and partly the other), is another example of the confusion of meaning and reference.

(4.37)   Some (two, many) children lifted a chair.

Such alleged ambiguities are nothing more than different situations in the world that would satisfy the truth conditions of the proposition. Ambiguities are cases of a many-one mapping of propositions onto sentences, whereas these cases are cases of a proposition related to many different states of affairs, all of which are equivalent with respect to its truth conditions.[12]

Quantity information tells us how many of the units of attribution are asserted to be satisfied by the appropriate clause of the unconverted condition in order for this clause of the truth condition to be fulfilled. Quantity information can take as wide a variety of forms as there are ways to express number in natural languages. Hence the question of how to formulate the readings for this aspect of semantic structure is nothing less than the question of how to represent the full range of numerical expressions in natural languages. Since we obviously cannot attempt to tackle this problem in the present context, we shall assume that readings representing number concepts can ultimately be constructed in a way that satisfies the constraints of semantic theory, and we shall try to indicate some important distinctions such readings must reflect in order to provide appropriate quantity information.[13]

---

numerous", applies to whole groups when it can, that is, when the multiplicity referred to can be taken as a whole. Thus, Vendler's example "The number of all those blocks is 17" involves collectivity, but for the wrong reasons. His example, "The number of each (every one) of those blocks is 17" does not, but because of the inherent distributivity of "each" and "every".

12. This kind of confusion is found in McCawley's discussion of distributivity and collectivity, in J. D. McCawley, "The Role of Semantics in a Grammar," in *Universals in Linguistic Theory*, ed. E. Bach and R. T. Harms (New York: Holt, Rinehart, & Winston, 1968), pp. 152–169. The confusion is also the basis of the pseudo-controversy between Partee and Lakoff. See section II A of B. Hall Partee, "Linguistic Metatheory," in *A Survey of Linguistic Science*, ed. W. O. Dingwall (University of Maryland, 1971), pp. 650–681, and B. Hall Partee, "On the Requirement that Transformations Preserve Meaning," in *Studies in Linguistic Semantics*, eds. C. J. Fillmore and D. T. Langendoen (New York: Holt, Rinehart, & Winston, 1971), pp. 14–16.

13. There is a philosophical issue connected with this assumption. Quincans will take the question of the representation of numerical expressions as a paradigm case of indeterminacy. [See W. V. Quine, *Ontological Relativity and Other Essays* (New York: Columbia University Press, 1969), pp. 43ff.] The kind of considerations that militates against the indeter-

In the standard quantification theory, quantifier information is expressed in terms of universality, negation, and existential import. There are two quantifiers. The universal quantifier is defined in terms of universality and nonexistential import, and the existential quantifier is defined in terms of nonuniversality and existential import. Our conception of quantifier information differs from standard quantification theory in various ways. One is that there is no information about existential import in our quantifier system. The distinction between existential and nonexistential import is handled as part of the presuppositional structure of propositions. This treatment of existential import provides an automatic explanation of why the inference rule of existential generalization fails in connection with both opaque and generic contexts, namely, existential generalization can take place only in connection with terms whose non-null extension is guaranteed by the presupposition of the proposition to which the rule is applied.

Another difference from standard quantification theory is that we do not restrict quantity information to universality and nonuniversality and existential import. We think of the universal and existential quantifiers as end points of a hierarchy of quantifiers with a highly complex system of intermediate levels, at which are found quantifiers corresponding to the quantity information in the meanings of "some", "a", "five", "half", "several", "fifty-seven percent", "many", and the rest. Our treatment of quantity agrees with standard quantification theory in taking the meaning of "all", "every", "each", "any", "one hundred percent of", and such to determine the truth condition that the members of the set of objects (for us, satisfying the appropriate clause of the presupposition) universally satisfy the appropriate predicates from the term-place correlation. But our treatment differs from standard ones in not restricting the other quantity information to that expressed in the existential quantifier. At the present stage of our investigations, we cannot say what the set of primitive quantity markers will be.

These two differences raise doubts whether standard quantificational treatments of the meaning of quantifier words in sentences of natural languages are adequate. Standard quantification theory represents numerical quantifier words in sentences like (4.37) in terms of existentially quantified assertions appearing as clauses of the logical translation. The technique for such translation is illustrated in the translation of (4.38)(i) as (4.38)(ii) for transparent contexts, and (4.38)(iii) as (4.38)(iv) for opaque contexts.

(4.38) (i) Harry has two apples.

---

minacy thesis in this particular case can be found in J. J. Katz, "Where Things Now Stand with the Analytic-Synthetic Distinction," *Synthese* 28 (1974):294–295.

(ii)   There is an x and there is a y, such that x is an apple and y is an apple, x is not identical to y, and Harry has x and Harry has y.

(iii) Harry wants two apples.

(iv)   Harry wants it to be true (the case) that (4.38)(ii).

Since the at-least-one quantifier required in such translation automatically expresses existential import (instead of existential import being independent of the quantifier system, as it is on our treatment), some such special account of the numerical quantifiers associated with terms in opaque contexts is necessary. Otherwise, the interpretation of the existential quantifiers will conflict with the interpretation of opacity. But this makes for an implausible treatment of the quantifier words in the sentences under translation, since (4.38)(iv) and similar translations are not in fact synonymous with the sentences of which they are supposed to be the translations. (4.38)(ii) is not synonymous with (4.38)(i) because the former but not the latter entails such things as that Harry has something not identical to a particular apple. (4.38)(iv) entails that Harry wants it to be true (the case) that he has something not identical to a particular apple [assuming, as I assume the defender of such translations must, that someone who wants some proposition to be true (the case) *ipso facto* wants each of its conjunctions to be true (the case)], whereas (4.38)(iii) does not entail this. It is, of course, important that our claim is about an entailment, that is, about an implication that turns exclusively on the meanings of the words in the sentences. Thus, we can support these counter-examples to the supposition that these quantificational translations are synonymous with the sentences (4.38)(i) and (4.38)(iii) by noticing that a sentence like (4.39) is not a contradiction.[14]

(4.39) Harry wants two apples but he does not want it to be true (the case) that he have something not identical to something he has.

A number of other distinctions cross-classify with the distinctions of quantity that determine the level at which the condition in an assertive proposition has to be satisfied in order for the proposition to be true. One distinction is that between *definiteness of number* (indicating a particular number is in question) and *indefiniteness of number*. Examples of the former are "a", "one", "both", "three", and "the", and examples of the latter are "some", "all", "any", and "several". We have no account of this and the remaining distinctions.

Another distinction cross-classifying with the above divides *proportion quantifiers* from *nonproportion quantifiers*. Examples of the former are "one

---

14. See J. J. Katz, "The Real Status of Semantic Representations," *Linguistic Inquiry*, in press, footnote 21.

hundred percent", "half", "a small fraction of", and so on. Among the non-proportion quantifiers are *interval quantifiers* and *noninterval quantifiers*, with examples of the former including "between five and ten", "between a dozen and two dozen", and so on. The empirical issues that can arise here can be illustrated by the question of whether "most" belongs among the proportion quantifiers or among the interval quantifiers; that is, does "most" mean just the same as "at least one more than half" or does it mean "at least one more than half but not all".

We may mention the one further distinction between *absolute quantifiers* and *relative quantifiers*. Examples of absolute quantifiers include "all", "some", "half", "seven", "most", and so on, and examples of relative quantifiers are "few" and "many". These latter quantifiers are, roughly, paraphrasable as "a small indefinite number of" and "a large indefinite number of", respectively. They thus determine a level of satisfaction similar to how a relative adjective like "tall" determines the meaning of constructions like "tall Martian".[15] That is, "few" in expressions like "few people on this earth" is a proportion quantifier that determines the number of people in the domain of predication in relation to the size of the earth's population. It is not at all clear, however, how such determination works and what such expressions mean.

ASSERTIVE TYPE

We can now use the notation illustrated in (4.10) to sketch the formalization of the concept of assertiveness for simple propositions. Since (4.10) represents the clause of the truth condition just for an arbitrary term of the term sequence in a proposition, we require an expansion of (4.10) such as (4.40), where the term sequence consists of the n terms of the propositional content.

$$(4.40) \quad (((\text{Satisfies})_{[Q_{n1}]}^{X} \text{ of DES}(t_1), c_1^1, \ldots, c_k^1, {}_{X}^{[T^1]}) \ \& \ldots \&$$
$$((\text{Satisfies})_{[Q_{nn}]}^{X} \text{ of DES}(t_n), c_1^n, \ldots, c_m^n, {}_{X}^{[T^n]}))$$

The symbol "&" is logical conjunction. Thus, the truth conditions for a proposition is the logical sum of the truth condition associated with each of its terms. The truth condition associated with a term t_i is the satisfaction of

15. Katz, *Semantic Theory*, pp. 254–261.

the predicates $c_1^i, \ldots, c_j^i$ by the objects in $\mathrm{DES}(t_i)$ for the particular choices of the quantificational and temporal parameters. If a c_{j-r}^i, $r \leqslant j$, is a one-place predicate, $\mathrm{DES}(t_i)$ satisfies c_{j-r}^i in case the proper number of units of attribution in $\mathrm{DES}(t_i)$ have the property expressed by c_{j-r}^i at the time fixed by the temporal parameter. If a c_{j-r}^i is a two-or-more-place predicate, $\mathrm{DES}(t_i)$ satisfies c_{j-r}^i in case, for each of the terms $t_{i_1}, \ldots, t_{i_s}$ correlated with the other places of c_{j-r}^i, $\mathrm{DES}(t_i), \mathrm{DES}(t_{i_1}), \ldots, \mathrm{DES}(t_{i_s})$ sequentially satisfies c_{j-r}^i.

Given (4.40), we can provide (4.41) as a first approximation to a structural definition of the notion *assertive proposition*.

(4.41) A proposition P is assertive in type just in case one of the members of the reading of P is an instance of (4.40) in which each of the variables is replaced by appropriate readings.

Definition (4.41) says that the reading of an assertive proposition is a set of semantic markers, one of which is an instance of (4.40) that meets the condition in the definiens of (4.41). The readings of nonassertive propositions will also contain instances of (4.40), but, of course, ones in which the values of the variables do not meet the condition in the definiens of (4.41). The completion of (4.41) awaits the characterization of the notion of performativeness in (5.41). There we characterize the values of the variables required for a proposition to be performative, and thus the notion of appropriateness in (4.41) is simply any n-tuple of values that fail this requirement.

The definitions (4.42) and (4.43) indicate how the account above of the semantic structure of assertive propositions fits into the standard Aristotelian conception of truth, on which truth consists in correspondence with reality.

(4.42) The proposition P is true just in case P is assertive, the presupposition of P is satisfied, and the objects satisfying the presupposition have the properties and bear the relations expressed in the condition of P at the time and in the numbers indicated.

(4.43) The proposition P is false just in case P is assertive, the presupposition of P is satisfied, and the objects satisfying the presupposition do not have all the properties or bear all the relations expressed in the condition of P at the time and in the numbers indicated.

It goes without saying that (4.42) and (4.43) are incomplete both in themselves and in the constructions they depend on. In themselves, note that they deal only with propositions having what we referred to earlier as extensional truth conditions. Regarding the constructions they depend on, note that the theory of presupposition on which (4.42) and (4.43) depend is unfinished in many ways, and in particular, in the area where presuppositions make reference to linguistic objects.[16]

Later, after characterizing the notion of performativeness, we shall employ these definitions to explain why performatives, unlike constatives, can be neither true nor false.

Two ideas guided our theorizing about the notion of assertiveness in the meaning of propositions. Assertiveness determines the type of assertive propositions; that is, it is the grammatical basis for their potential to be used to make statements in accord with their propositional content, and it relates the two components of the propositional content in that it converts the presupposition into a statementhood condition and the unconverted condition into a truth condition. The general principles about type and conversion embodied in these ideas will guide our theorizing about nonassertive propositions in the next two chapters.

16. I hope at some later time to contrast the conception of truth sketched in these definitions with that of A. Tarski, "The Semantic Conception of Truth," in *Semantics and the Philosophy of Language*, ed. L. Linsky (Urbana, Ill.: University of Illinois Press, 1952), pp. 13–47. The chief difference, of course, is that my conception supposes that natural languages are not incoherent, to be replaced, stepwise, by an unending sequence of artificial languages, each of which is the meta-language for its predecessor. Thus, my conception of the logical form of sentences is presuppositional and the truth antinomies are avoided by making the laws of logic applicable only to propositions whose presupposition is satisfied and constructing the presuppositions of Epimenedian sentences to require their reference to be grounded in a statement, so that their presupposition is not satisfied. H. Herzberger and I tried to work out a way of doing this without sacrificing the expressive power of natural languages. S. Kripke, "Outline of a Theory of Truth," *The Journal of Philosophy* 72, no. 19, languages in "The Concept of Truth in Natural Language," unpublished manuscript, Cambridge, 1967. S. Kripke, "Outline of a Theory of Truth," *The Journal of Philosophy* 72, no. 19, (November 1975): 690–716, offers an account of groundedness for an artificial language, obtaining highly interesting logical results; but there is no obvious way to apply his account to natural languages, to determine what class of sentences in them is subject to the groundedness condition.

5
THE PERFORMATIVE SIDE: THE DISTINCTION AND THE CONCEPT OF REQUESTIVE PROPOSITIONAL TYPE

INTRODUCTION

Our approach to explicating the constative/performative distinction will be first to characterize one particular performative propositional type in detail and then to compare it with our characterization of assertive propositional type, in order to find the differences that can be plausibly taken as constituting the general distinction between constative and performative propositions. Once having obtained a hypothesis about the nature of the distinction, we shall try to show that, because the hypothesis is part of a theory of competence, it avoids the difficulties Austin's hypothesis ran into. In the next chapter, we shall consider several other performative propositional types to establish that no feature of our hypothesis about performativeness is peculiar to the particular performative type considered here.

That type is the requestive. To arrive at a characterization of requestive propositional type, we shall employ a strategy suggested by our criticism of Searle's claim that illocutionary force information is outside the grammar. We argued in Chapter 1 that the various predicates expressing the illocutionary force information in performative sentences appear in the truth conditions of corresponding constatives, and that it is therefore necessary, in a compositional theory of sentence meaning, to accord these predicates the same linguistic status in both cases. We argued further that, insofar as the occurrence of these predicates in the truth conditions of constatives determines the semantic properties and relations of these sentences, and as the semantic component of the grammar is admittedly the proper place to account for semantic properties and relations, it follows that Searle is wrong in claiming that the grammar is not the place to account for the illocutionary force information of performatives.

For example, the illocutionary force information that the speaker of (5.1) undertakes an obligation to perform an act and that the act is future relative

to the time at which the promise is made figures in the truth conditions of
(5.2).

(5.1) I promise you to do it.
(5.2) I promised you to do it.

Since the difference in tense between (5.1) and (5.2) cannot be responsible for
a difference in linguistic status between extragrammatical and grammatical
information, the predicates 'undertakes an obligation to perform an act' and
'act is future relative to speech point' are to be accounted for as aspects of the
lexical meaning of the verb "promise".

Given this compositional origin of illocutionary information, our strategy is
to characterize the structure of requestive propositions by first looking at the
grammatical meaning of corresponding assertive propositions to determine the
compositional structure of their statementhood and truth conditions and then
"unconverting" these conditions to reveal what brought about their conversion,
namely, the requestive type.

THE MEANING OF "REQUEST"
AND ITS FORMALIZATION

The sentences (5.3) and (5.4) correspond, respectively, to (5.1) and (5.2).

(5.3) I request that you chase the dog.
(5.4) I (Sally, they, and so on) requested (will request, and so on) that
       you chase the dog.

To implement our strategy, we first provide a hypothesis about the truth conditions for sentences like (5.4), some motivation for the account of the meaning
of "request" embodied in the hypothesis, and a formalization of this account
as a lexical reading for this verb.

We may assume that the meaning of the embedded sentence "you chase
the dog" is obtained from (3.2) for the verb "chase" and the lexical readings for
its subject, object, and tense constituents. We take the meaning of this embedded
sentence to describe an action (or inaction) rather than an assertion by virtue of
its being the meaning of a subordinate clause. We term the action (or inaction) in
question "A". The hypothesis about the truth conditions of sentences like (5.4)
is (5.5).

(5.5) (i) That the agent (the speaker, Sally, and so on) produced an event
            having the form of a communication.

(ii) That the agent produced this event with the intention of communicating to someone (the addressee).

(iii) That the utterance meaning of the event is a proposition.

(iv) That the propositional content of this proposition, in part, describes the action A.

(v) That the agent of A is the requestee (the person of whom the request is made).

(vi) That the temporal specification for A puts it after the speech point specification for the request.

(vii) That the purpose of the agent's producing the event was to get the requestee to perform A.

(viii) That the addressee (the recipient of the agent's action in producing the communication) and the requestee are not necessarily the same.

(5.5)(i) has an obvious and a subtle aspect. It is obvious that "request" is semantically similar to communicative verbs like "tell", "ask", "inform", and so on. Everyone who has written on the subject has noticed that such a verb describes communicative acts. Not so obvious is the fact that the meaning of "request" does not require the act of communication to be successful. The event referred to in (5.5)(i) is in every way like a communication except (possibly) for its message failing to be received, just as a law-like statement is in every way like a law except (possibly) for failing to be true.[1]

The communication may fail in two ways. There may be no addressee, as when a hunter takes the movement of branches caused by a gust of wind to be caused by a poacher and shouts an order to get off the property or a warning to watch out. And there may be an addressee, but he, she, or it may not "get the message", as with a deaf poacher.

There are strong arguments for claiming that production of the appropriate event can be a request even if it does not succeed in communicating anything to anyone. For example, a sinking ship does not fail to request help just because its SOS messages were not picked up. Moreover, it seems correct to say that Smith asked Boris for a cigarette in a case where Smith mistakes Boris for Jones and asks in English, which Boris does not understand. It seems clear that Smith asked Boris for a cigarette but that Boris did not understand him. Note that Smith could truly say, "Maybe you didn't understand me, but I just requested that you give me a cigarette". Again, if someone uses (5.6) to make a request that someone else open the window, but the other person does not understand the utterance in this way and takes the speaker to have simply stated

1. I wish to thank Richard Mendelsohn for helpful discussions on this point.

a fact, it still seems right to say that the speaker made a request (which was not understood).[2]

(5.6)   The room is awfully stuffy.

Finally, consider the following case. You and I are at the beach and we see a bottle floating up to the shore. Inside is a note from people stranded on a desert island requesting help. You bet me fifty dollars that there is a request for help in the bottle. Now, can I win this bet simply by throwing a stone and smashing the bottle so that the message is never received? This seems clearly not even an unethical way of winning.

Does there have to be an addressee? It seems clear that there does not as long as the requestor does not know that there is no one to receive the message. In the sinking ship case, it does not seem to matter whether the people on the ship are the last humans alive. Their SOS signals are still requests for help. Futile requests, but requests nonetheless. Further, suppose that we are in a helicopter, observing through a telescope a myopic cripple. The cripple is at a street corner, and his or her lips move. Even though there is no one around, it might still be true to say that the cripple is requesting help in crossing the street. It should be noted that the situation is different if there is an explicit second-person subject of the complement sentence, as in (5.3), and it is construed referentially, that is, as addressing some particular individual rather than anyone who may be, as it were, within earshot. We shall shortly mention a theoretical reason for not requiring the existence of an addressee.

(5.5)(ii) says, however, that the notion of an addressee is part of the meaning of "request" as a component of the speaker's intention. That is, although one can speak without intending to do so and request without there being someone to be addressed, one cannot request without intending to communicate something to someone in expressing the request. If the intention of the agent in producing an utterance of (5.3) is not to get someone to understand the proposition expressed by this sentence (or some message that can be obtained from this proposition by pragmatic principles and knowledge of the context), then the utterance cannot be an act of requesting.[3] A child who sneaks up on his younger brother stealing cookies and, simply to scare him, roars "Don't eat those cookies!" has not ordered him not to eat the cookies. The intention to have the request complied with is, of course, another matter, which, as we shall soon see, is undetermined by the meaning of "request".

2. This example was suggested to me by William Stewart (in conversation).
3. The exact statement of such intentions is complicated. See J. Searle's discussion in *Speech Acts* (Cambridge: Cambridge University Press, 1969), pp. 42–50.

(5.5)(iii) requires that the information conveyed by the communicative event have the semantic structure of a proposition (rather than a concept). This is the point Vendler mistakenly put as the syntactic condition that performative verbs are "container verbs". (5.5)(iii) does not say that we do not sometimes make requests in saying such things as "Stop!", but only that we do so on the basis of pragmatic principles that determine that the utterance meaning of this exclamation has the semantic structure of a proposition.

(5.5)(iv) requires that the propositional content of the communicated proposition describe what the requestee is asked to do as something that belongs to the category of things do-able. No stronger requirement that the action be logically or actually do-able is imposed, so that requests to square the circle or fly faster than the speed of light count as (impossible) requests. Moreover, sentences like (5.7) and (5.8), in which the complement sentence of the performative verb does not express an action, are, as sentence types, semantically anomalous.

(5.7) I request that you believe that two is the only even prime.
(5.8) I order you to understand the Gödel theorem.

This does not mean that they are not often used to make perfectly meaningful requests in certain contexts. But the requests they make in such contexts are normally for the requestee to *do* what is necessary to put him or herself in the desired mental state. These considerations indicate that the lexical reading for "request" should contain a selection restriction under the variable categorized for readings of the verb phrase of the embedded sentence that allows as values only readings that represent meanings involving the concept of action or of the absence thereof.

(5.5)(v) links the requestee and the act or action requested. It is the basis for our definition of the semantic role of requestee below. It explains why it is not possible to request one person to do something that only another person can do. Thus, it accounts for the semantic anomaly of sentences like (5.9).

(5.9) I request that you carry out your brother's suicide.

Statement (5.5)(vi) is equally obvious. It is impossible to request an action that has already taken place or one that is taking place at the moment the request itself is being uttered. (One can, of course, request that the act or action continue or that some other action of the same kind occur.) Thus, the verbs "request" and "thank" are antonymous in respect to the time of the action in question.

Statement (5.5)(vii) is formulated in terms of the purpose of the agent's act of communication rather than the agent's intention, because the requester need not intend to get the requestee to perform the requested action. An example of this is the henpecked husband who asks his obnoxious in-laws to visit not with the intention of bringing about the visit (the manner in which he makes the request might show he has no such intention) but simply to obey his wife's order that he ask them. Also, sophisticated parents sometimes request their negativistic young children not to eat their spinach with the intention of thereby getting them to eat it. The point is that getting the requestee to perform the action is a purpose of the requester's communicative act in much the same way that check-mating the king is the purpose of the activity of playing chess. Just as a chess player might not intend to check-mate his or her opponent in playing the game (but to be checkmated, say, in order to make the opponent feel good), so a requester might not intend to get the requestee to perform the act in making the request.[4]

Statement (5.5)(viii) leaves it open whether the intended recipient of the communication is the person to whom the request is directed. Usually, of course, they are one and the same, and when there is a specified second person object of the performative verbs, is in (5.10), they must be.

(5.10)   I request that you stand here beside me.

But there are examples of cases in which they are different. One is the case of the sergeant who orders (assuming this to be a kind of request) a private to do K.P. in reading the daily orders to a formation from which the private is absent. The fact that the private is not there to hear the order does not mean that the sergeant has failed to order him to do K.P. Moreover, it is clear that the addressees are the soldiers present at the formation. They are the soldiers whom the sergeant is actually addressing. It is quite natural for the absent private, on returning, to ask the other soldiers what the sergeant ordered him to do that day.

Further evidence in favor of allowing the possibility that the addressee and the requestee are not the same individual comes from the meaning of the contrasting expressions "direct request" and "indirect request", "direct order" and "indirect order", and so on. Since a direct request (order, and so on) is one in which the addressee is the requestee and an indirect request (order, and so on) is one in which the addressee is not, being instead the intermediary in the con-

4. The notion of getting the requestee to do the act is understood in causal terms. The communicative act is conceived of as the cause in roughly the sense in which "cause" is used in sentences like "What he said to her caused her to leave the party". We shall handle it in the same way we treated the notion of cause in the meaning of "kill" in the representation (3.17).

veyance of the message (hence the qualification "indirect"), the simplest account of the compositional meaning of these expressions has to be based on the hypothesis that the meaning of "request", "order", and so on, leaves it open whether or not the addressee and the requestee are identical.

The formalization of (5.5)(i)-(viii) as a lexical reading for "request" will be a semantic marker of the same type as (3.2). The major difference is that the component semantic marker standing for the base predicate represents the concept of an act rather than that of an activity. The distinction between these concepts is that an act is the smaller behavioral unit and an activity is made up of a number of acts related in time and having a unique overall character. This distinction is exemplified in a sentence like (5.11).

(5.11) Smith was killed in the act of cutting a wire while engaging in the activity of laying mines.

Roughly, act concepts are to activity concepts as state concepts are to process concepts.[5] Act concepts and activity concepts fall under the category of action concepts, and our general approach to the study of action concepts would be to work out their structure on the basis of the invariants found in the readings of the act concepts and activity concepts.

Another important difference is that, being a communicative act, requesting, unlike chasing, is not just physical in nature. It is in part psychological; in part it is like running, chasing, or hitting, and in part it is like thinking or remembering. In its physical aspect, the act proceeds by means of the agent producing an event in space and time. There can be no further specificity about this event insofar as a wide range of types is possible, for example, spoken communications, written communications, gestural communications, and so on. In its psychological aspect, the act involves the agent's intention to have the addressee understand the message through the production of the event. It is this dual nature of communicative acts that precludes our using antonymous semantic markers like (5.12)(i) and (5.12)(ii) to represent the fact that the concept of a communicative act involves both the concept of having a psychological nature, as in the meaning of verbs like "think" or "remember", and the concept of having a physical nature, as in the meaning of verbs like "run", "chase", or "hit".

(5.12) (i) $((\text{Nature})^{(\text{Physical})})$
        (ii) $((\text{Nature})^{(\text{Psychological})})$

5. J. J. Katz, *Semantic Theory* (New York: Harper & Row, 1972), pp. 293-362. Note the contrast when the concepts of act and activity in (5.11) are switched around, *viz.*, "Smith was killed in the activity of cutting a wire while engaging in the act of laying mines".

If we did so, we would be unable to say that the meaning of a verb like "request" contains both these concepts without saying that it is internally inconsistent, in the manner of the meaning of expressions like "male aunt".[6] Therefore, we shall represent the dual nature of communicative acts in the form (5.13).

(5.13)

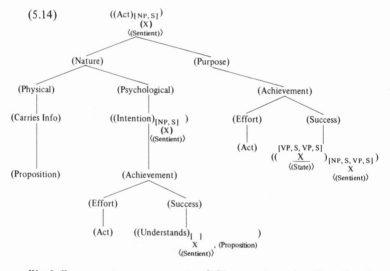

The lexical reading for "request" can be formulated as (5.14).

(5.14)

We shall comment on some aspects of this semantic marker. First, the selection restrictions. In all cases but one, categorized variables in (5.14) have the selection restriction that the readings that can be their values must contain the semantic marker (Sentient). This seems straightforwardly implied by the fact that the agent has intentions and the addressee can understand propositions. In the other case (the categorized variable whose values describe what is requested of the requestee), the selection restriction is that the readings that can be values must not contain the semantic marker (State). We express this restriction negatively because requiring such readings to contain the semantic marker (Action) is overly restrictive, insofar as we can make negative requests and promises. That is, we can request that someone not punch us or we can promise not to

---

6. This is a typical example of the general constraint on the use of antonymy apparatus.

speak to someone. Since such things are not actions in the ordinary sense, but rather the refraining from action of a certain kind, we would preclude genuine requests and promises if we stated the selection restriction positively.

Note that, although the selection restriction as stated will account for the semantic anomaly of sentences like (5.7) and (5.8), it may require further clauses to rule out all other things outside the class of things that are do-able. I leave this matter for further investigation.

Second, the repetition of the component semantic markers (Act) and (Proposition) is different from the repetition of the semantic marker (Achievement), but, as (5.14) stands, this difference is unstated. The three occurrences of (Act) have to be understood as marking the same act and the two occurrences of (Proposition) as marking the same proposition. On the other hand, the two occurrences of (Achievement) have to be understood as marking different achievements, one having to do with comprehension and the other compliance. The simplest way to represent this difference is to add a new interpretive convention for semantic markers. Since the two occurrences of (Achievement) in (5.14) have different subtrees under them, we may introduce the *coincidence convention:*

(5.15) Whenever a semantic marker (M) contains two or more occurrences of the same component semantic marker, these occurrences are to be taken as standing for the same concept in the sense represented by (M) just in case no two of these occurrences have different subtrees.

Without the coincidence convention, trees like (5.14) would have to be replaced by lattices having just one occurrence of each of the iterated semantic markers and having branches connecting the one occurrence of the semantic marker to the semantic markers that dominate the iteration. Not only would such a lattice notation be more complex than our tree notation, but a lattice formalism would require a new interpretive convention to prevent the principles interpreting branching in terms of predicate functions from applying to these many-one semantic marker connections and to provide them with the proper interpretation. Furthermore, introducing some kind of indexing to mark sameness and difference is more complex still. Moreover, the coincidence convention is more natural because distinct subtrees such as those under the occurrences of (Achievement) in (5.14) represent the difference in the two achievement concepts. If the other repetitions were not to be interpreted as standing for the same thing, the whole semantic marker would be an incomplete semantic representation because it fails to represent this difference (surely part of the meaning of the linguistic constituent).

Third, the distinction that we made in connection with (5.5)(vii) between the purpose of an act and the purpose or intention of its agent can be formalized in the difference between the position of (Purpose) in (5.14) and in (5.16).

$$(5.16) \quad (((\text{Purpose}) \, (\text{Act}))_{[\text{NP, S}]})$$
$$(\text{X})$$
$$\langle(\text{Sentient})\rangle$$

In (5.16), (Purpose) and (Act) are both associated with the reading that will replace the categorized variable, as indicated in (3.6), whereas in (5.14), (Purpose) applies to (Act) and (Act) is associated with this reading. We might point out here that the formal structure of (5.16), obtained by a rule similar to (3.18), will be the basis for most adverbial modification in connection with performative verbs. The representation of sentences like (5.17) will contain such formal structures expressing the concept of the agent having hope (confidence, and so on) that the request will be complied with.

(5.17)   Mary hopefully (confidently) requested Joe to leave.

An adverb like "quickly" is different, since in construction with performatives like "request", "promise", "warn", and so on, it simply means that the agent lost no time in performing the illocutionary act. But in both kinds of adverbial the addition, by the projection rule,[7] of the reading of an adverb to the reading of the performative verb leaves the branches under the highest occurrence of (Act) in its lexical reading unchanged. This is important in order that we may construct simple and natural definitions like (5.41) below.

Fourth, the square brackets above the categorized variable in the position of the first argument place of the understand relation (the variable whose values are addressee readings) were left blank because at present syntactic theory offers us no characterization of the grammatical function we need. In an ordinary sentence like (5.3), where the addressee and the requestee are the same, the value of this variable can be picked out by the function [NP, S, VP, S] . But in sentences like (5.18) and (5.19), where the addressee [the person(s) referred to by the italicized constituents] is not the same as the requestee, syntax offers us no characterization of the required function.

7. The lexical reading of an adverbial is an operator that attaches branches representing the sense of the adverbial to the semantic marker representing the sense of the constituent with which it is in construction. The sense of the modifier-head construction is thus that of a new predicate (rather than the old predicate with plugged up argument places, as in the case of sense combinations with subjects, objects, and so on.). See (3.18).

(5.18) John requested through *George* that Bill return his watch.

(5.19) In reading the orders to *the formation*, the sergeant ordered every absent private to do K.P.

Indeed, at present, syntactic theory does little more than characterize a few simple grammatical functions (and hence relations) like "subject of", "object of", and so on. This failure of syntactic theory to meet the needs of compositional semantics also harms the construction of syntactic theory by ignoring the range of constraints on its rules that would be imposed by characterizations of each grammatical function (and relation). Be this as it may, the unavailability of such characterizations is a chronic problem for interpretive semantics. Often, in order to get on with research in semantics, it is necessary to use the best available grammatical function even though it may be less than fully adequate.

We are now in a position to provide structural definitions for a number of semantic roles. We can formally define "requester reading", "addressee reading", "requestee reading", and a sufficient condition for the structural definition of "goal reading". The first two of these notions ought to be special cases of the notions of "agent reading" and "recipient reading", respectively. To achieve this, we construct the structural definition of "requester reading" in terms of the structural definition for "agent reading" in (3.50), and the structural definition of "addressee reading" in terms of the structural definition for "recipient reading" in (3.51). Thus, we give the structural definitions (5.20) and (5.21):

(5.20) R is the *requester reading* in the sentence reading R_s = df. (1) R meets the conditions (3.50a), (3.50b), and (3.50c), and (2) the part of R_s that represents the propositional content has the form (5.14).

(5.21) R is the *addressee reading* in the sentence reading R_s = df. (1) R meets the conditions (3.51a) and (3.51b), (2) the part of R_s that represents the propositional content has the form (5.14) with or without the substructure under (Purpose), and (3) R is the value of the categorized variable $((\text{Understands})_{[\ ]}\ \ \ \ \ )$
$$X, (\text{Proposition})$$
$$\langle(\text{Sentient})\rangle$$

We can draw the distinction between addressees and requestees by adding (5.22).

(5.22) R is the *requestee reading* in the sentence reading R_s = df. (1) the part of R_s that represents the propositional content has

the form (5.14) and (2) R is the value of the categorized variable
$$\underset{\langle(\text{Sentient})\rangle}{\overset{[\text{NP, S, VP, S}]}{X}}$$ in the rightmost branch.

Definitions (5.21), (5.22), and (3.51) have the desirable consequence that addressees but not requestees are recipients. Finally, we can now provide a sufficient condition for the definition of the semantic role of "Goal", namely, (5.23).

(5.23) R is the *goal reading* in the sentence reading R_s if (1) the part of R_s that represents the propositional content has a branch (M_1)–(M_2)–$\ldots$–(M_n) such that there is an R' in (M_1) that satisfies (3.50), (2) the part of R_s that represents the propositional content also has a branch of the form (M_1)–(Purpose)–(M_h), and (3) R is the structure (M_h).

Eventually, we hope to incorporate (5.23) into a necessary and sufficient condition for the notion "goal reading".

The semantic marker (5.14) is adequate as part of the basis for predicting the compositional meaning of sentences like (5.3) and (5.4) only if we add a further condition extending the application of the heavy parentheses wipe-out rule introduced at the end of Chapter 3. As things now stand, the reading of an embedded sentence enters (5.14) assigned to the main verb of the matrix sentence and proceeds throughout the rest of the semantic interpretation of the full sentence without losing the heavy parentheses enclosing its term positions. Accordingly, the reading of the full sentence fails to indicate any change in the nature of the action requested, that is, any change reflecting the interaction of the meaning of the main verb and the meaning of the embedded sentence. Hence, it wrongly predicts that (5.24) presupposes the existence of a king of France.

(5.24) John requested that you introduce him to the king of France.

Since someone can request an introduction to someone who does not exist,[8] a report to this effect like (5.24) (say, as an illustration of how stupid John is—"he's so stupid he requested an introduction to the king of France") cannot presuppose the existence of the party to whom the agent wishes to be introduced. It must be true or false even if there is no such party. One cannot comply with such requests, of course, but this is another matter.

8. Note that monarchs have commanded their alchemists to find the philosopher's stone.

To prevent the heavy parentheses around the readings of constituents like "the king of France" in (5.24) from entering the reading of the full sentence, we add the further condition (5.25) to the heavy parenthesis wipe-out rule.

(5.25) (3.85) applies to any heavy parentheses in a reading dominated a semantic marker such as (Purpose) and (Intention) .[9]

Thus, in the semantic interpretation of a sentence like (5.24), the reading of the noun phrase and verb phrase of the embedded sentence are first substituted for the variables in (5.14) categorized by [NP, S, VP, S] and [VP, S, VP, S], respectively, and then the projection rule applies (3.85) to these readings (since they are now dominated by (Purpose)) to remove the heavy parentheses around the reading of the indirect object of the embedded sentence, "the king of France". Consequently, the reading of the full sentence (5.24) does not make the prediction that successful reference of the indirect object of the embedded sentence is a necessary condition for the statementhood of a use of (5.24).

Furthermore, if, as we shall argue below, the lexical reading of every performative verb is similar to "request" in containing such an occurrence of (Purpose), (5.25) automatically provides an explanation of the frequently noted fact that the meaning of the complement of a performative verb in a sentence like (5.24) does not contribute to the presupposition of the sentence.

Above we remarked that we would mention a theoretical reason for not requiring the existence of an addressee. The reason is simply that the concept represented by (Intention) , like that represented by (Purpose) , seems to suspend referentiality in connection with the term positions of any predicate functions that specify the particular intention in question; if we capture the right class in (5.25), we automatically rule out a presuppositional requirement of the existence of an addressee. We might also mention that we have not indicated what other semantic markers besides (Purpose) and (Intention) belong in (5.25) because we have not yet determined them.

To complete the formalization of (5.5), we have to indicate how condition (vi) will be formally represented. What we want to represent, then, is the basis for explaining the semantic contrast between "request" and "thank". As yet, we have indicated nothing about where the notion of the futurity of the action A comes from. Now, it seems clear that this notion does not come from temporal information in the meaning of the embedded sentence—that is, the complement sentence that characterizes the action A—since such clauses are tenseless. For example, sentences like (5.26)(i)-(iii) have embedded sentences that are tense-

9. Note that the semantic marker (Psychological) in (5.14) and later in (5.54) will not appear in (5.25).

less, but still determine an appropriate future time for A as a function of their tense constituent.

(5.26) (i) Sally requests that you be a voter.
    (ii) Sally requested you to chase it.
    (iii) I request you to have a swim.

We are thus free to go ahead with our supposition that this notion of futurity comes from the meaning of the verb "request" together with the meaning of the tense constituent in the matrix sentence. The simplest and most natural way to represent this aspect of the meaning of "request" (and using the treatment of "request" as a paradigm, to represent this aspect of the meaning of "promise", and so on) is to take advantage of the fact that the concepts of effort and success, which are part of the concept of the purpose of a request, are a species of cause and effect and as such inherently ordered in time. We may thus hypothesize that the semantic markers (Effort) and (Success) are of the form (5.27)(i) and (5.27)(ii), respectively, where the categorization picks out the tense constituent of the matrix sentence.[10]

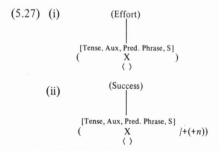

(5.27) (i)   (Effort)

        [Tense, Aux, Pred. Phrase, S]
        (X   )
             ⟨ ⟩

    (ii)   (Success)

        [Tense, Aux, Pred. Phrase, S]
        (X $/+(+n))$
             ⟨ ⟩

Let us consider an example, such as (5.28).

(5.28) I request that you do it.

The tense constituent of the matrix sentence is simple present and its reading is the semantic marker $(t^{(o)})$. Thus, the instances of (5.27)(i) and (5.27)(ii)

10. For discussion of the formalism of temporal designation, see Katz, *Semantic Theory*, pp. 306–332. Note that the grammatical function [T] in (4.40) will be defined so that, when (β) in a branch of the form (α)–(β) is a temporal designation and there is an instance
$$[T^i]$$
of (4.40) in which a $c_j^i = (\alpha)$, the value of X in that instance of (4.40) is (β).
⟨ ⟩

in the reading of (5.28) will be (5.29)(i) and (5.29)(ii), respectively, which locates the illocutionary act's occurrence at the speech point and the success-ful completion of the action requested at some unspecified number of units beyond the speech point.

(5.29) (i)   (Effort)
              |
              $(t^{(o)})$

        (ii) (Success)
              |
              $(t^{(+n)})$

Accordingly, the desired futurity of the requestee's carrying out of the action requested can be obtained as a consequence of the fact that the causal relation locates effects in the future relative to their causes, and the two actions, the requestee's carrying out of the action requested and the requester's communica-tion of the request, are, respectively, categorized as a species of effect and cause in the reading of "request".

There is a slight complication introduced by the fact that the semantic marker (5.14) represents two successes of the illocutionary act, one the under-standing of the message by the addressee and the other compliance by the requestee. [There is no problem about the effort, since it must be represented in the form (5.27)(i) in both instances.] The complication is that it might be supposed that (5.27)(ii) is not the proper temporal specification for the re-questee's compliance because it does not indicate that this action must follow the understanding of the message. Thus, it might be supposed that (5.27)(i) is the proper temporal specification for the understanding of the message, and that the proper temporal specification for the requestee's compliance requires a superscript in which $(+n) + (+m)$ is added to the reading of the tense constit-uent. It would, of course, be no trouble to revise the formalization of futurity in accord with this supposition, but it may be wrong to do so. It is perhaps possible for the compliance to occur at the same time or prior to the comprehen-sion. For example, consider the case in which a sergeant is issuing orders to members of a company in addressing a formation from which a private is absent. Suppose that one order is for the private to put on his hat, but, because this order is formulated in militarese and the soldiers in the formation are unfamiliar with it, it takes a while for the order to be understood. Suppose further that the private who is familiar with militarese happens to overhear and acts immediately.

It could be that he puts his hat on before the soldiers to whom the orders are addressed understand them.

We now explain why certain often-cited conditions are absent from our account of the meaning of "request". One such condition is that we cannot request someone to do something if we know that the requestee is sure to do it anyway. Searle's preparatory rule for requesting, which says that a necessary condition on requesting is that it is not obvious to both the speaker and the addressee (assumed to be the requestee) that the latter will do the action "in the normal course of events of his own accord",[11] is an example of this kind of condition. Its absence from our account reflects our view that speech act theory does not constitute an autonomous theory but is a hybrid of semantics and pragmatics and as such runs pragmatic conditions such as Searle's "non-obviousness condition" together with genuinely semantic conditions.

It is not hard to see how Searle and others might have come to the view that such pragmatic conditions are actually necessary conditions on the performance of the speech act of requesting with an appropriate performative sentence. Within a framework that makes no distinction between semantics and pragmatics, oddities cannot be separated into conceptual anomaly, on the one hand, and situational inappropriateness, on the other. Thus, cases of oddity, such as requesting a child to buy itself some candy when that child is poised, drooling, over a candy counter, coin in hand, ready to make its selection, are explained as violations of conditions on the performance of the speech act. The principle in such a framework would be that something is a condition on the performance of a speech act if there is some nonsyntactic deviance in the use of language that might be treated as the violation of that condition.

That it is a mistake to take such conditions to be necessary conditions on the performance of a speech act is obvious once we note that such oddity disappears when the requestor is attempting to influence the requestee's reasons for performing the action. For example, a student might be sure to visit some friends in New York over the Christmas vacation and this may be obvious to both the student and the host (both know the student cannot stand staying around the empty campus during holidays, both know the student makes a practice of such visits, and so on) but nonetheless this knowledge does not make the host's asking the student to visit for the holidays an odd request. The difference between this case and that of the child at the candy counter has nothing to do with how obvious it is to the parties concerned that the requestee will do the act anyway, but with the fact that in the child but not the student case the request is pointless. The request to the child is odd because it is clear ahead of time that it can have no effect whatever on the character of the child's act. The

11. Searle, *Speech Acts*, p. 63, pp. 66–67.

request to the lonely student is issued in order that a request can be part of the student's real or apparent reason for acting, and this provides encouragement of the sort that makes the requestee feel wanted and not feel he or she is imposing. This is the point of the request.

Such "nonobviousness conditions" are given in the case of other illocutionary acts like promising. The same kind of counter-examples are found in them, too: if there is a point to the request, there will be no oddity no matter how obvious it is to everyone that the act will be done anyway. It may be perfectly obvious that I shall send your books to you—they are cluttering up my house; I can't stand to look at so many theological books; and moreover, the university has offered to pay the postage. Nonetheless, there is nothing odd about my promising you that I shall send them. I may do this because I know you wish to have a formal commitment on my part (because, say, you have sold some of them on the condition that you would get my promise).

Our criticism is not simply that Searle and others confuse obviousness with pointlessness,[12] but that no such condition can be a necessary condition on the performance of illocutionary acts like requesting or promising,[13] and therefore, none can be part of the meaning of such performative verbs. Evidence is readily available. Sentences like (5.30)(i) and (5.30)(ii) would both be inconsistent if nonpointlessness were a necessary condition, but they are clearly consistent.

> (5.30) (i) The man requested that the child buy the candy but his request was completely pointless.
>
> (ii) I made a pointless promise in promising to send the books.

Also, sentences like (5.31)(i) are not anomalous, as they should be if Searle were right. Further, a sentence like (5.31)(ii) is not analytic.

> (5.31) (i) It is not that I don't believe you will do it, but, just for the record, I request that you do it.
>
> (ii) John's request was not something that the requestee would do anyway in the normal course of events.

12. Searle (*Speech Acts*, p. 59) mentions pointlessness but does no more with it than to use the notion as a way of paraphrasing his "nonobviousness condition".

13. It is clear that Searle intends his "nonobviousness condition" to be a necessary condition on the performance of speech acts. He says this on p. 57, and also makes it doubly clear by ordering his rules so that the essential rule does not apply unless this preparatory rule has applied (see p. 63).

Thus, pointlessness is better regarded as a pragmatic factor. This is confirmed by the analogy of pointless promises to insincere promises, which Searle rightly counts as genuine promises,[14] and also by theories of pragmatic interpretation like Grice's that make the prohibition against pointless remarks a matter of working out the implications of an utterance on the basis of features of its context.[15] In the sequence of stages that Grice's theory postulates in the working out of such implications, the stage at which the meaning of a sentence type is computed is ordered prior to that at which the "conversational maxims" come into play to determine the implications that are part of what a token of the type "conversationally implicates" in the context. The "maxim of relation", which enjoins speakers to make relevant contributions to conversations, is essentially a prohibition against pointlessness, and its position in these stages precludes it from determining any facet of the meaning of a sentence type. Thus, pragmatic theory of this kind explains the oddity of the request to the child at the candy counter quite differently from Searle's theory. This oddity would be explained after the account of the meaning of the sentence type, as a case of failure to conform to the maxim of relation, thereby leading listeners astray because they will be set to find a point to an utterance that has none. Thus, we obtain distinct notions of situational inappropriateness and conceptual anomaly.

REQUESTIVE PROPOSITIONAL TYPE
AND COMPLIANCE CONDITIONS

Relative to an account of the notion "performative proposition", which will be presented in the next section, we can define "requestive proposition" by the structural definition (5.32), where the definition of performativeness will specify *inter alia* the sort of readings that must replace the categorized variables in (5.14).

(5.32) A proposition P is *requestive* just in case P is performative and the propositional content of P has the form (5.14) except that the categorized variables are replaced by their values.

Since an assertive proposition like (5.4) differs from the corresponding requestive like (5.3) only in the nonperformativeness of the former, we easily explain why the state of affairs under which it would be true to assert (5.4) are just

14. Searle, *Speech Acts*, p. 62.

15. H. P. Grice, "Logic and Conversation," in *Syntax and Semantics*, vol. 3, ed. P. Cole and J. L. Morgan (New York: Academic Press, 1975), pp. 41–58.

those under which a speaker of (5.3) would make a request using this sentence. Since (5.5) can be taken (together with appropriate readings of the subject, embedded sentence, and so on) as the illocutionary success condition of a sentence expressing a requestive proposition, it follows that the illocutionary success condition for requestive propositions (and, as we shall see below, for other propositions of other types, too) is significantly different from the condition under which assertive propositions succeed in making a statement. In the case of the assertive proposition expressed by (5.4), the illocutionary success condition is simply the satisfaction of its presupposition, the existence of appropriate objects for the readings of its subject and of the subject of its complement sentence to designate.[16] In the case of the requestive proposition expressed by (5.3), however, the illocutionary success condition is both the satisfaction of its presupposition and the satisfaction of its unconverted condition by the objects that satisfy its presupposition. This is to say that the illocutionary success condition of the proposition expressed by (5.3) requires, beyond the existence of a speaker and an addressee who is also the requestee, that the speaker communicate something, that the communication have the form of a proposition, that the proposition describes a future act in which the addressee is the agent, and so forth. The argument for such an expansion of the illocutionary success condition is straightforward. Suppose that the speaker of (5.3) is the person referred to as Sally in a use of (5.4), and suppose, furthermore, that that use of (5.4) is a true report of what happened in the use of (5.3). Then, since the truth of this report depends on Sally's speech behavior at the time she uttered the token of (5.3) being an instance of requesting the requestee to chase the dog, the condition under which Sally succeeds in making this request by using (5.3) must include all the conditions necessary to guarantee that her speech behavior at the speech point of (5.3) is an instance of the act of requesting the requestee to chase the dog.

The illocutionary success conditions for assertive propositions are given in (4.5); the illocutionary success conditions for requestive propositions in (5.33).

(5.33) The illocutionary success condition for a requestive proposition P is that P's presupposition be satisfied,[17] and the sequence of objects that satisfies this presupposition also satisfies the unconverted condition of P.

16. We use the term "illocutionary success condition" in connection with both constatives and performatives. The important differences will turn out to depend on which kind of proposition such conditions are for.

17. Since the propositions in question here cannot be generic, there is no need for the further clause in (4.5).

Now, (4.5) and (5.33) together with (4.6) give us the principles (5.34) and (5.35).

> (5.34) A sentence expressing an assertive proposition P performs (in the null context) the illocutionary act of stating if its presupposition in the sense of (3.106) is satisfied.
>
> (5.35) A sentence expressing a requestive proposition [one whose reading meets (5.32)] P performs (in the null context) the illocutionary act of requesting if its presupposition in the sense of (3.106) is satisfied and the objects satisfying it also satisfy the unconverted condition of P.

(5.33) is misleading in one sense; namely, it is not necessary, as its statement might suggest, to formulate a separate definition for each kind of performative proposition. This can be seen from the fact that the illocutionary success conditions for each of the other kinds of performative propositions bears the same relation to the truth conditions of the corresponding assertive proposition as does the illocutionary success condition of requestives. For example, the relation found in (5.3) and (5.4) is also found in the pairs in (i)-(iii) of (5.36).

> (5.36) (i) I promise you to go; Sally promised you to go.
> (ii) I warn you to go; Sally warned you to go.
> (iii) I apologize to you for going; Sally apologized to you for going.

Hence, we may provide the general definition (5.37). Together with (4.6), we get (5.38).

> (5.37) The illocutionary success condition for a performative proposition P is that P's presupposition be satisfied, and that the sequence of objects that satisfies this presupposition also satisfies the unconverted condition of P.
>
> (5.38) A sentence expressing a performative proposition P performs (in the null context) the illocutionary act for which its propositional type qualifies it if its presupposition in the sense of (3.106) is satisfied and the sequence of objects that satisfies the presupposition also satisfies the unconverted condition of P.

To complete this treatment of requestives, we have to characterize the conversion of the unconverted condition of such propositions. That is, we have to say what a compliance condition is.

The first point to make is that satisfaction of the illocutionary success condition in the case of requestive propositions gives rise to a kind of bivalence. Just as the truth condition of an assertive proposition has a companion falsehood condition, so the compliance condition has a companion noncompliance condition. If the illocutionary success condition is satisfied, no matter what the requestee does, the request that the proposition makes is either complied with or not (when time is up) so that the compliance condition is satisfied or the noncompliance condition is, whereas if the illocutionary success condition is not satisfied, there is no request either to be complied with or not (just as there is no statement to be true or false when the presupposition of an assertive proposition fails).

What is the condition under which a request is complied with? There are two possible answers. One is that compliance consists in the requestee behaving in a way that counts as a case of the act requested. On this answer, the requestee would comply with the request that he chase the dog just in case he chases the dog at some appropriate time after the time of the request.[18] The other answer is that the requestee performs the appropriate act, at least in part for the reason that the requestor's communication had the purpose of getting the requestee to perform the act. The second answer is preferable because the first misses the critical distinction between behaving in accord with the request and actually complying with it. For example, suppose we request that George move his head several times rapidly. He does this, but not for any reason having to do with our request; he does it only to avoid a bothersome insect. We would not, I think, call this compliance with our request, but call it compatible with the request, that is, in accord with it. Again, suppose that someone pleads with the king to pardon his brother. The king does pardon him, but by mistake. It does not seem in this case that the king has granted the plea.[19]

18. It is perhaps a pragmatic constraint that the requestee's act must occur within a reasonable time. Is it absurd or semantically deviant for someone to claim they are complying with a request when they now do something they were requested to do fifty years ago. My guess is that the context usually involves a tacit temporal limitation. Thus, I will assume that, for a requestive to be an explicit performative, the proposition itself must impose an upper temporal limit on the performance of the act requested, for example, "I request that you leave in one minute".

19. It is easy to see why in most cases requests seem to depend on its not being obvious that the requestee will do the action in the normal course of events but do not really depend on this. If someone is going to do something anyway, and if all the requestor wants is that the action get done—which in most cases *is* all requestors want—then no request needs to be made. A request then is pointless. On the other hand, if for some reason the requestor wants compliance, and as our analysis has it, compliance is more than the act's getting done, then a request is not pointless, even if it is virtually certain the requestee will do it anyway. Another example is the fanatical tyrant who wants obedience to his commands.

We may thus propose the definition of the notion "compliance condition" (5.39).

(5.39) The compliance condition for a requestive proposition P is that (a) there is a requestee (that is, the requestee reading in the reading of P has an appropriate designatum), (b) the requestee's behavior falls under the concept represented by the reading that substitutes for $\dfrac{\underset{}{[\text{VP, S, VP, S}]}{X}}{\langle\langle\overline{\text{State}}\rangle\rangle}$ in the instance of (5.14) in the reading of P, and (c) the requestee behaves this way in part because it was the purpose of the request issued by the use of P to get the requestee to behave this way.

The notion of "noncompliance condition" can be defined as in (5.40).

(5.40) The noncompliance condition for a requestive proposition P is that at least one of the conditions (a)–(c) in (5.39) fail.

THE COMPETENCE CONCEPT
OF PERFORMATIVENESS

The present section draws the distinction between constative (assertive) propositions and performative propositions. Our account of the distinction is an explication of Austin's initial conception before he undermined it in the course of his own attempt at explication. Our diagnosis of why Austin undermined his initial conception is that he did not base his explication on a sharp competence/performance distinction. Questions about the structure of language were never distinguished from questions about use of language, with the consequence that Austin framed the constative/performative distinction as a thesis about performance, thereby making it vulnerable to counter-examples. In the last section of this chapter, we shall defend a competence conception of performativeness. We shall try to show that such counter-examples are beside the point when the distinction is framed as a thesis about competence. We shall argue that the situation here is as if the distinction between grammaticality and ungrammaticality were mistakenly framed as a thesis about the use of language and then challenged on the grounds that some allegedly grammatical sentences are too long or too syntactically complex to be understood or spoken.

The next chapter completes our theory of propositional type. There we indicate the range of performative propositional types and provide a definition parallel to (5.32) for the major types and subtypes and a definition of their converted condition (for example, fulfillment condition for promissory propositions, heeding condition for advisory propositions, and so on) parallel to (5.39). We shall close with a consideration of the significance of this theory for philosophical logic and the philosophy of language.

Austin began his study of how things are done with words with a tentative characterization of the notion of a performative utterance. He said that "they do not 'describe' or 'report' or constate anything at all, are not 'true or false' " and that "the uttering of the sentence is, or is a part of, the doing of an action, which again would not *normally* be described as saying something".[20] Our account of the constative/performative distinction, as a reconstruction of Austin's work along the lines just described, will thus have to provide plausible explanations, in terms of (4.42) and (4.43), of why constatives can be either true or false, while performatives cannot be either (that is, reference to them as true or false is deviant) and of why saying is doing when what is said is performative and the circumstances are appropriate. Moreover, the line we draw between constatives and performatives must coincide with our intuitions about which cases fall on which side of this distinction.

Austin considered the possibility of a purely grammatical criterion for performative utterances, but although he acknowledged that there are good reasons for initially favoring such a criterion, in the end rejected it. When considering the question of "whether there is some *grammatical* (or lexicographical) criterion for distinguishing the performative utterance",[21] Austin took as the natural hypothesis that such utterances are uses of first-person singular, present-indicative, active sentences. But he found "important and obvious exceptions all over the place",[22] and he concluded that the demand for a purely grammatical criterion was mistaken. He was thus led to think that such a grammatical criterion was at best a reflection of certain aspects of speech acts and to center his investigation on acts exclusively. Austin remarked:

We said that the idea of a performative utterance [is] . . . the performance of an action. Actions can only be performed by persons, and obviously in our cases the utterer must be the performer: hence our justifiable feeling—which we wrongly cast into purely grammatical mould—in favor of the "first person", who must come in, being mentioned or referred to; moreover, if the utterer is acting, he must be doing something—hence our

20. J. L. Austin, *How To Do Things with Words* (Oxford: Oxford University Press, 1962), pp. 5f.

21. Ibid., p. 55.

22. Ibid., pp. 57-60. We consider these "exceptions" below.

perhaps ill-expressed favoring of the grammatical present and grammatical active of the verb. There is something which is *at the moment of uttering being done by the person uttering.*[23]

The move Austin makes here in abandoning a purely grammatical criterion for performativeness for one that applies to acts was largely due to the limitations of the grammar which he had to work with and the absence of a competence/performance distinction. It is the conception of traditional, surface structure-oriented grammar rather than the idea of a purely grammatical criterion of performativeness that is mistaken. We agree with Austin that there is no purely grammatical criterion of the kind he sought, but deny that this implies that there is no grammatical criterion for (explicit) performative sentences. We shall therefore show that the shift from actions to sentences, from performatives to explicit performatives, from syntax to semantics, and from traditional taxonomic grammar to contemporary transformational grammar, permits us to construct a version of the "first-person singular, present-tense indicative, active sentence" criterion that is not subject to Austin's exceptions or others like them.

We frame our criterion in terms of features of the representations of sentences at the semantic level of a grammar. Accordingly, instead of using the syntactic notion "first-person singular", we use the semantic notion "agent reading"; instead of using the syntactic notion of "present tense", we use the semantic notion "speech point reading"; and instead of using the syntactic notion "indicative active sentence", we use the semantic notion "action proposition reading". Thus, our definition will have three clauses. The first specifies that the doing required for performance of the act involves nothing more than the proper kind of saying. The second clause specifies that the agent of the illocutionary act described in the performative proposition is the speaker of the sentence that performs the act. The third specifies that the time of the agent's performance of the illocutionary act is the speech point of the utterance of the sentence used to perform it. Thus, the structural definition of performativeness is (5.41).

(5.41) A proposition *P* is *performative* (that is, nonassertive) just in case (i) the reading of *P* contains a semantic marker of the form (4.40) and also a semantic marker representing the propositional content of *P* either having the form shown in (5.14) or one exactly like it except for some other semantic structure under (Purpose), (ii) the agent reading in the reading of *P* represents the concept of the speaker of the use of the sentence expressing *P* at the time specified in the temporal designation associated with the component semantic

23. Ibid., p. 60.

marker (Act), and (iii) the temporal designation associated with (Act) is ($t^{(o)}$), and (iv) each of the other categorized variables are replaced with their values.[24]

Among Austin's objections to the "first-person singular" aspect of the syntactic criterion is his enumeration of first person plural performative utterances, for example, "we promise" and "we consent", and his claim that the features of first person and active voice are not essential because of examples like (5.42)–(5.44).[25]

(5.42) You are hereby authorized to pay. . . .

(5.43) Passengers are warned to cross the track by the bridge only.

(5.44) Notice is hereby given that trespassers will be prosecuted.

There are two further types of counter-example, (5.45) and (5.46).

(5.45) The court declares you to be out of order.

(5.46) $\left\{\begin{array}{l}\text{The speaker of this sentence} \\ \text{The person speaking} \\ \text{The person who is uttering this sentence} \\ \text{The person addressing you at this moment} \\ \text{The person you now hear uttering these words}\end{array}\right\}$ promises to do it.

(The examples in (5.46) and (5.42)–(5.44) rule out any syntactic criterion of the kind Austin considered. The examples (5.46) show that first person form is

24. Just as there is a distinction in syntactic theory between particular rules and types of rules, and between particular definitions and types of definitions, so in semantic theory there is a distinction between a particular definition like (5.41) and the type of definition used for characterizing the notion of performativeness. As with the case of particular syntactic rules, and perhaps even more so than for syntax, we have good general reasons for suspecting that particular theoretical constructions may prove incorrect in one or another way, not the least of which is the fact that (neither) semantic (nor transformational) analysis has been around as long as formal theories of natural languages. Indeed, the point of such particular definitions is not so much to state the whole truth about the semantic structure underlying performativeness, propositional type, and so on, but to illustrate the plausibility of this kind of definition of such semantic structures. The theory being put forth here requires only that the kind of definition introduced for these notions be successful. The significance of the particular definitions for the theory lies in their ability to show us signs of such success. Thus, though it will be a matter of concern if certain aspects of the characterization in (5.41) turn out to be wrong, it will be a matter of far greater concern if no such characterization can be given.

25. Austin, *How To Do Things with Words*, p. 57.

only one possible syntactic means of expressing speakerhood. That these examples can be extended in all sorts of ways, using all sorts of different syntactic forms, shows furthermore that a semantic rather than syntactic characterization of the clause is required. The examples (5.42)–(5.44) not only show that Austin was right about the active voice but, more important, that no criterion framed in terms of surface structure will be adequate. However, these cases can be handled in a transformational grammar. In such grammars, they would be represented as having first-person subjects in their deep syntactic structure that are erased transformationally, producing surface forms with ellipsed subjects.

The remaining examples raise two questions. First, there is the question of a plurality of speakers. If a group of people promise to move my piano by uttering in unison (5.47), does each individual promise to play his or her part in the move, or do they "speak with one voice" and promise as a group?

(5.47)   We promise to move your piano.

This is certainly an interesting question for the theory of action, but it does not matter for us which way it is settled. Since we do not require that the speaker be a single person, we can accommodate the latter alternative, and the former could be handled by taking the utterance meaning of (5.47) (in such a context) to be the grammatical meaning of (5.48).

(5.48)   I promise to do my part to move your piano.

Second, there is the question of proxy cases raised by sentences like (5.45) and (5.49).

(5.49) $\left\{ \begin{array}{l} \text{We, the Better Beer Company, promise} \\ \text{The Better Beer Company promises} \end{array} \right\}$ you a refund for flat beer.

Are these consistent with (5.41)(ii)? The principal thing to note about these cases is that the actual speaker of a sentence like (5.45) and (5.49) is acting as a proxy for somebody like a company or state, so that the speaker is not, in and of himself or herself, the one who makes the charge or promise. When B acts as a proxy for A, say, in voting or taking a vow, A actually votes or vows—by means of B's serving as an authorized substitute for A. If you are my proxy at my marriage ceremony, your verbalizations express my marriages vows, and if you are my proxy at an election, your ballot casts my vote. Thus, in proxy uses of sentences like (5.45), it is not the speaker but the court or the state that charges the defendant with being out of order, and in proxy uses of sentences like (5.49), it is not the speaker but the company or its ruling body that guarantees to refund the purchase price. Furthermore, not only does the proxy not charge, promise, vow or vote, the person(s) the proxy substitutes for, the agent who charges, promises, vows or votes, does not need to utter anything to so act. These acts are done solely by virtue of the proxy's utterance. Hence, it follows that in proxy cases the speaker of the utterance with which the act is performed is not the agent of the act.

This, however, does not contradict (5.41)(ii), for (5.41) is not a criterion for determining speech acts, as Austin sought, but a criterion for determining performative propositions. It says nothing about actual speakers and agents. It addresses itself to whether a semantic marker of a certain kind occurs in certain formal relations to other semantic markers. With this in mind, the apparent inconsistency can be easily explained. The sentences like (5.45) and (5.49) are not explicit performative sentences; they do not express performative propositions. That is, they cannot be used to perform the acts in question *in the null context*. Nonetheless, they commonly do perform a speech act in non-null contexts where there is background information that the speaker is the duly authorized proxy for the agent. But this is because this information makes it possible to use sentences like (5.45) and (5.49) rather than expanded versions in which expressions like "in the name of", "on behalf of", "speaking for", or "as proxy for" appear. There are two hypotheses about the speech acts performed by such explicit proxy forms, and hence, performed by (5.45) and (5.49) in appropriate non-null contexts. One is that they perform acts of charging, promising, vowing, and voting, and the other is that they perform acts of proxy charging, proxy promising, proxy voting, and proxy vowing (that is, the speaker is the agent of the proxying act). Both are consistent with (5.41)(ii). On the first, the proxy relation makes the agent in the act of charging, promising, vowing, or voting the real speaker and the proxy is merely the person who utter his or her words. On the second, the success of a proxying act like proxy promising also issues in a promise, but in much the same way that I can make promises without doing anything whatever at the time the promises are made by arranging with someone that they have my promise to give them a hundred dollars whenever someone else promises to give them this sum. Thus, there is no inconsistency between (5.41)(ii) and the fact that sentences like (5.45) and (5.49) can be used to create charges, promises, vows, and votes, even though the person who literally utters the words is not the charger, promiser, vower, or voter.[26]

26. The first hypothesis, of course, raises the question of how the notion of the real speaker is characterized, but this question arises independently, in connection with many other cases. For example, people say that someone's dead father is speaking to them even though the medium is uttering the sounds; likewise, when the creatures from planet X take over human brains, we say that it is not the mayor who orders us to surrender but Them.

Austin's objections to the "present-tense indicative" component is of a piece with some of his objections to the mood clause.[27] He says:

> Mood will not do, for I may order you to turn right by saing, not "I order you to turn right", but simply "Turn right".... Tense will not do either, for in giving (or calling) you off-side I may say, instead of "I give (or call) you off-side", simply "You were off-side" ... [there are] cases where there is no explicit verb at all, as when I say simply "Guilty" in finding a person guilty, or "out" to give someone out.[28]

Again, we have vivid examples of how inadequacies in the grammatical structure presupposed by Austin and the absence of a competence/performance distinction were responsible for his thinking that the idea of a grammatical criterion is mistaken. In a transformational grammar, the imperative "Turn right!" is not an exception, since imperatives receive an underlying syntactic representation that is semantically interpreted to express the notion of the speaker's requesting a right turn. Furthermore, the simple past-tense sentence (5.50) is not an exception to a competence grammatical criterion for performativeness, insofar as (5.50) can no more perform the act of calling an off-side in the null context than (5.51) can perform the act of promising in such a context.

    (5.50)   You were off-side.
    (5.51)   You will have the money.

In the context that Austin has in mind, where the speaker is an official and this is known to the players, the use of (5.50) has the grammatical meaning of (5.52) as its utterance meaning, just as uses of (5.51) often have the grammatical meaning of (5.53).

    (5.52)   I call you off-side.
    (5.53)   I promise you that you will have the money.

Finally, the fact that we can use forms like "Guilty" and "Out" to perform acts of finding a person guilty or calling someone out does not count against a grammatical criterion. Their ability to function performatively also depends heavily on the context, and our criterion is designed only to pick out explicit performative sentences, sentences that function performatively by virture of their meaning.[29]

27. Austin, *How To Do Things with Words*, p. 58.

28. Ibid., p. 58.

29. Austin says, "Thus what we should feel tempted to say is that any utterance which is in fact a performative should be reducible, or expandable, or analysable into a form with a

The clause (5.41)(i) was obtained in the following way. The semantic marker (5.14) representing the general form of requestive propositions contains two major branches, one characterizing the nature of an illocutionary act and the other its purpose. Note that the characterization of the nature of the act contains nothing to specify the particular illocutionary act of requesting. It is the characterization of the purpose of the act that contains the information uniquely determining the act as one of requesting.[30] Thus, we may conjecture that this feature of the structure of requestive propositions is a general feature of all performative propositions—that is, their semantic representation has the form of such a two-branched tree, one branch characterizing the nature of an illocutionary act and the other the purpose of a particular type of illocutionary act. On this conjecture, then, the definition of performativeness has to be stated in terms of this characterization of an illocutionary act.

The requirement that the reading representing P's propositional content be of the form indicated excludes not only trees without some of the features indicated but also ones with features not indicated. (5.41)(i) is intended to formalize the idea that only the utterance of a sentence with the meaning specified therein can perform an illocutionary act (in the null context), that is, that only appropriate sentences [see (5.41)(ii) and (5.41)(iii)] with such a narrow propositional content can have unconverted conditions that can be satisfied simply by their utterance (in a null context). By ruling out a branch under the semantic marker ((Act)...) containing semantic markers describing a causal (or other empirical) relation of the communication to some future event, this clause of the definition reconstructs Austin's illocutionary/perlocutionary distinction insofar as it is a matter of grammatical structure.[31] This distinction is exhibited in the contrast between performative verbs like "promise" or "request" and causative verbs like "persuade" or "convince". The perlocutionary character of the latter kind of verb is, as it were, written in their meaning, since it involves the notion of the agent causing the recipient to believe something as the effect of the agent's having given the recipient reasons for this belief (though not necessarily with the intention of bringing about this state of belief, since one can persuade unintentionally). Hence, the lexical reading of one sense of "persuade" is something like (5.54)(i) and one for another sense is (5.54)(ii).

---

verb in the first person singular present indicative active (grammatical). This is the sort of test we were in fact using above" (*How To Do Things with Words*, pp. 61-62). He goes on to say, "Thus: 'Out' is equivalent to 'I declare, pronounce, give, or call you out...'". Our point can be put by observing that grammar offers no means of expressing such an equivalence relation, as shown in Chapter 2. A pragmatic theory of the form (1.16) is required.

30. See our discussion of compliance conditions above.

31. Austin, *How To Do Things with Words*, pp. 101f.

(5.54) (i)

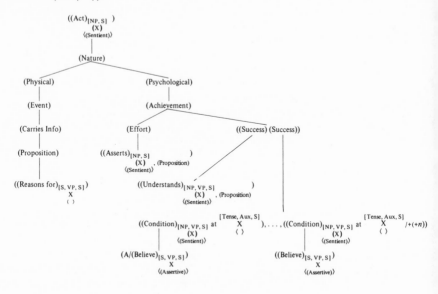

(5.54) (ii)

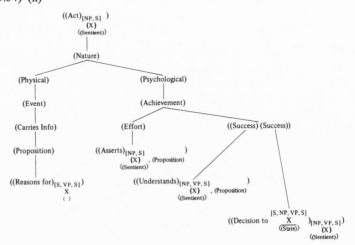

We assume for the sake of convenience that the grammatical functions [S, VP, S] and [S, NP, VP, S] used in (5.54)(i) and (5.54)(ii) pick out *that* complements expressing the object of a belief and infinitival complements expressing courses of action, respectively,[32] that is, complements of "persuade" like "that the earth is round" and ones like "to jump in the lake". Thus, (5.54)(i) represents the sense of "persuade" that describes the getting of someone to believe some proposition and (5.54)(ii) represents the sense that describes the getting of someone to decide to do something. Both these senses of "persuade" are causative like the sense of "kill". Other senses of "persuade" are noncausative, for example, the one that occurs in sentences where the subject of "persuade" is an abstract noun phrase like "the argument".

These lexical readings in (5.54) fail to satisfy the condition (5.41)(i), which requires that the meaning of a performative contain no concept that gives rise to a truth condition that the agent succeed in producing the effect of the communicative act. This requirement is necessary because otherwise it would not be possible for "saying to make it so", since "its being so" must depend solely on the speaker saying the right words under the right conditions. In precluding the meaning of performative sentences from containing anything about the empirical relation between their utterance and subsequent contingent events, (5.41) explains the grammatical side of Austin's distinction between what we do *in* saying something and what we do *by* saying something.

Our formalization of the distinction between verbs that describe illocutionary acts and verbs that describe perlocutionary acts explains why sentences like (5.55) are semantically anomalous.

(5.55) I hereby persuade (convince) you to disperse the crowd.

Such present-tense sentences do not carry any of the nonperformative senses associated with the present tense in English, *viz.*, the sense of habitual action in a sentence like (5.56) or the historical-present sense of sentences like (5.57).

(5.56) I persuade patients with lung trouble not to smoke.
(5.57) I persuade the reader of this in the first chapter.

Sentences like (5.55) also do not carry a performative sense. Although they have both an agent reading that represents the notion of the speaker of the sentence and a tense constituent whose reading represents the speech point, they fail (5.41)(i) because their main verb describes a perlocutionary act. Hence, such

32. The situation is much more complex, for example, *that*-complements can express, a course of action, as with "Joe persuaded Harry that he go", and sentences like "Joe persuaded Harry that he should go" seem to bear both senses.

sentences are semantically anomalous because "hereby" requires that the speaker's utterance of the sentence be the means that brings about the act it describes, that is, that the sentence express a performative proposition.

Sentence (5.58) reports a causal achievement of the speaker's, namely, that the speaker's communication to the crowd, the cause, was efficacious in producing its dispersal, the effect.

(5.58) I persuaded the crowd to disperse.

Being the effect, the dispersal is inherently ordered later than the communication. In the semantically anomalous sentence (5.55), since the communication is assigned to the speech point, its effect, the dispersal, would have to be assigned to some later time. Since the interpretation of performative sentences entails that the event described in their verb phrase occurs when the sentence is uttered [for example, the promising of the money described in the verb phrase of (5.53) occurs when (5.53) is uttered], sentences like (5.55) have to be semantically anomalous because the event described in the verb phrase, that is, the persuading of the crowd, is a causal effect of the utterance and as such cannot occur at the same time as the utterance itself. Because the event is represented as future relative to the speech point, the sentence cannot carry a performative interpretation and, having no other interpretation, is semantically anomalous.

Earlier, we said that our explication of Austin's constative/performative distinction would provide a reconstruction of both of the basic features of his initial characterization: that performative sentences do not assert and so cannot be true or false, whereas constatives do and so can be either; and that the saying of a performative sentence is the doing of something beyond the mere saying of something. Before ending this section, we shall satisfy the fulfillment condition of this promise.

Why is appropriately saying a performative sentence the doing of something, and furthermore, as Austin frequently observed, doing of a sort that is not normally described as saying something? What Austin meant was that statements about what happened on the occasion of the performance of an illocutionary act do not report on the saying of something in the same manner as statements conveyed by sentences like (5.59)–(5.61), that the statement conveyed by a sentence like (5.62) reports the making of a request, which need not involve the saying of anything at all.

(5.59) He shouted for Bill to stop singing.
(5.60) She argued loudly and energetically on their behalf.
(5.61) They reported the news over the radio in rather crude language.
(5.62) Everyone requested that Bill stop singing.

The speaker of (5.62) implies nothing about the form of words used, their loudness, the polemical intent behind them, and so on. The speaker does not even imply that words were used to communicate the request. Unlike shouting, acts of requesting, promising, and so on, fall in a category of actions that impose no requirement concerning verbal or orthographic form as a condition of membership. For example, the request that (5.62) makes might, in the proper circumstances, be made by putting one's fingers in one's ears.

Lexical readings for performative verbs (and semantically equivalent syntactic structures) are written to conform to the generalization embodied in (5.41)(i). Thus, the readings of explicit performative sentences, obtained essentially by term readings substituting for occurrences of categorized variables in such lexical readings, take their form from these lexical readings. Since the illocutionary success condition for explicit performative sentences *viz*., (5.37) can be satisfied by just the use of such a sentence in an appropriate speech context, the utterance of such a sentence constitutes the act that the sentence itself describes. Saying is doing, because uttering a performative sentence in an appropriate speech context produces a speech event with just the properties required to count as a doing of the act. Moreover, because these lexical readings, like (5.14), are written in conformity to (5.41)(i), they embody a full abstraction from the above-mentiond linguistic features of promising, requesting, and so on. Specifying nothing more than the nature of the act as a performative communication, such lexical readings explain why people have so wide a choice of behavior in promising, requesting, and so on, ranging from the use of explicit performative sentences, to the use of sentences that are far from the explicit performative for the act, to nonverbal movements, gestures, and the like.

Why is a performative sentence never true or false? According to (4.42) and (4.43), which define these notions, a proposition can be true or false only if it is assertive. According to (4.40), a proposition is assertive only if its reading contains an instance of (4.40) in which each categorized variable is replaced by an appropriate reading. This condition can be completed in the definition (5.63). The duality of the definitions of "assertive proposition" and "performative proposition" precludes the application of truth and falsehood to performative sentences.[33]

33. We formalized performativeness using an instance of (4.40) because the alternative of precluding instances of (4.40) from the readings of performative sentences is neither required nor simple. This can be seen from consideration of the character of the selection restriction that would be needed for the variable in (4.40) categorized for readings of constituents providing temporal information in order to preclude instances of (4.40) from the readings of performative sentences. The problem is to formulate this selection restriction so that occurrences of the categorized variable receive no values in all and only the cases in which (5.63) obtains.

We want the selection restriction to say that the condition for substitution is that either

(5.63) A proposition P is *assertive* (nonperformative) just in case (i) the reading of P contains a semantic marker of the form (4.40) and also a semantic marker representing the propositional content of P, (ii) no categorized variables occur in the reading of P, and (iii) the reading of P does not satisfy both (5.41)(ii) and (5.41)(iii).

Austin himself felt it unnecessary to argue explicitly for the truth valuelessness of performatives because their being so seemed wholly obvious. Although I agree with his assessment of the facts, the polemical situation has changed because philosophers have since argued that performatives really have truth values; accordingly, it is now necessary to say why a theory that accepts Austin's intuition and tries to explain it is preferable to one that denies the intuition.

The reason for the tendency among certain philosophers to insist on treating performatives as constatives is, I think, the conservatism encountered in science when the only theory available simply will not explain some persistent facts. The attitude is that "the theory is all right, but the facts are misleading." Similarly, philosophers who explain the structure of propositions exclusively on the basis of truth exhibit such conservatism in the face of the facts uncovered

---

the reading to replace the variable is not the temporal designation of the speech point, or if it is then it is not both the case that (5.41)(i) and (5.41)(ii) are satisfied. The problem is that the apparatus of selection restrictions has, thus far, been formulated as what might be called a "context-free" condition—as a condition on the semantic markers in the reading of the constituent that satisfied the categorization of the variable. What is needed is a *context-sensitive condition* that contains a requirement on other aspects of the semantically interpred phrase marker, specifically, the agent reading and the reading representing the unconverted condition, something like the *double-angle* notation in (i),

(i) $\begin{array}{c} \text{[F]} \\ \text{X} \\ \langle\!\langle Z \rangle Y \rangle \end{array}$

where "Z" is the restriction on the reading R of the constituent C that meets the categorization [F] and "Y" is the restriction on the other constituent-reading pairings in the semantically interpreted underlying phrase marker, that is, except for the constituent-reading pairing C;R. If, in (4.40), we use (i) as the form of the occurrences of the variable categorized for readings of temporal constituents, and if the double-angle notation under them is, roughly, (ii),

(ii) $\langle\!\langle (t^{(o)}) \rangle \overline{(5.41)(i) \ \& \ (ii)} \rangle$

where the bar represents an extension of the bar notation for single angles and (ii) expresses the requirement that no value of such a categorized variable can have the form of the semantic marker for the speech point when the context contains pairings that jointly satisfy (5.41)(i) and (5.41)(ii), then every case where (5.41) is satisfied, (4.41) cannot be satisfied. Clearly, this kind of theoretical complication is to be avoided if possible.

by Austin. They prefer to insist that such sentences are really constatives rather than to venture into uncharted conceptual territory without the familiar theory of logical form as a guide.

It is easy to indulge this tendency because two aspects of performatives are sufficiently analogous to constatives to be exploited by someone who wants to claim that performatives are really constatives. One aspect is that the speaker's behavior at the speech point in uttering a performative (and in succeeding to perform the illocutionary act) corresponds to a description of the act, which is part of the meaning of the sentence. This is analogous to the correspondence between some state of affairs in the world and how the truth conditions of a constative describe it. Accordingly, someone who wishes to argue that the speaker's performative utterance is true can exploit this analogy to give a certain *prima facie* plausibility to their conclusion. Thus David Lewis writes:

> If I say to you "Be late!" and you are not late, the embedded sentence is false, but the paraphrased performative is true because I *do* command that you be late. I see no problem in letting non-declaratives have the truth-values of the performatives they paraphrase; after all, we need not ever mention their truth-values if we would rather not.

> Austin says ["I bet you sixpence it will rain tomorrow"] is obviously neither true nor false, apparently because to utter the sentence (in normal circumstances) is to bet. Granted; but why is that a reason to deny that the utterance is true? To utter "I am speaking" is to speak, but it is also to speak the truth.[34]

Lewis's criticism misses Austin's point. Austin did claim that, in using performatives, saying is doing, but he did not think that this is the reason they are neither true nor false. Austin's reason was that a performative makes no assertion about what is the case, so that, unlike (5.64), which asserts that the speaker is speaking, it cannot be true or false.

(5.64)   I am speaking.

Austin makes his point quite clear:

> Bending low before you, I remove my hat, or perhaps I say "Salaam"; then, certainly, I am doing obeisance to you, not just engaging in gymnastics; but the word "Salaam" does not, any more than does the act of removing my hat, in any way *state* that I am doing obeisance to you. It is in this way that

34. D. Lewis, "General Semantics," *Synthese* 22, no. 1/2 (December 1970):58-59.

our formula *makes* the issuing of the utterance that action which it is, but does not *state* that it is that action.[35]

Moreover, Austin clearly distinguishes this consideration from the one that Lewis mistakenly takes as *the* reason:

> [performative utterances] ... A. ... do not "describe" or "report" or constate anything at all, are not "true or false"; and B. the uttering of the sentence is, or is a part of, the doing of an action, which again would not *normally* be descirbed as saying something.[36]

Furthermore, Austin here explicitly excludes the type of consideration that Lewis brings up, since the utterance of (5.64) is different from the utterance of a performative like (5.65) in just the respect that the former is normally described as saying something, *viz.*, that one is speaking, whereas the latter is normally described as a doing, *viz.*, promising (cf. the discussion of (5.59)-(5.62) above).

(5.65) I promise you to do it.

Lewis's mistake is typical of constativist positions that exploit this aspect of the use of performatives: he equates the satisfaction of a condition with the satisfaction of a truth condition. Given that the speaker's behavior in making a bet or a promise corresponds to the description of the action that is part of the meaning of the sentence, and given that this description determines a condition satisfied by the correspondence, it does not follow that the utterance can be called "true". Since not all conditions are truth conditions, and the issue is whether there are felicity or illocutionary success conditions, Lewis begs the question in concluding that there is "no problem" in taking performative utterances of a sentence like "Be late!" to be true when the speaker succeeds in ordering the recipient to be late. Lewis tries to make it appear as if no harm is done in going along with his suggestion to let performatives have truth values ("After all, we need not ever mention their truth-values if we would rather not"). But to an Austinian, this smacks of a cover-up: following Lewis's suggestion would help to conceal the fact that the application of "true" to performative utterances does not carry its literal meaning (roughly, asserts what is the case) but is a metaphorical way of saying that the utterance performs the speech act. The harm—from our viewpoint—is that we may thus never get to properly debate

---

35. J. L. Austin, "Performative-Constative," in *The Philosophy of Language*, ed. J. R. Searle (Oxford: Oxford University Press, 1971), p. 16.
36. Austin, *How To Do Things with Words*, p. 5.

the issue of whether, as Austin thought, the logic of statements must be revised in connection with performatives.

Before turning to the second analogy, and the second kind of constativism, it is worth pointing out that Lewis compounds this mistake with a confusion about the relation between the present tense of performatives and the present tense of progressives. Note that there is an ambiguity about what is said in the *use* of a constative sentence like (5.66).

(5.66) I am requesting you to tell me.

One can reply either "False, you are insulting my intelligence" or "O.K., I'll tell you". It is not possible to make both responses to both propositions or to make either response to the other proposition. This difference between present progressive and performative senses also appears in connection with modifiers. The sense of the present progressive in (5.66) can take extensions of duration as in (5.67), but the simple present of performative sentences cannot.

(5.67) I am requesting you to tell me and I've been doing so for at least an hour.

Sentence (5.68) is thus semantically anomalous, just as (5.67) cannot be taken to mean that the act in question has been going on for at least an hour.

(5.68) I request you to tell me and I've been doing so for at least an hour.

One could, of course, say that the speaker has been "making this request for at least an hour", but this would mean something different, that the speaker had been performing a number of distinct acts during the hour (each with the same compliance conditions). Given this difference between the present progressive form and performatives, it becomes clear that Lewis mistakenly takes the syntactic present tense to be univocal semantically. He then bases his extension of truth conditions to performatives on the appropriateness of such conditions for present tense progressive forms like (5.64) and on the fact that the truth condition of (5.64) is analogous to the illocutionary success conditions of performatives in being satisfiable by the speaker verbalizing the proper sentence.

Second, there is the aspect that (explicit) performative sentences have complement sentences that express assertive propositions, and thus the sense of a performative sentence contains a proposition that bears a truth value.[37] Some-

37. D. W. Stampe, "Meaning and Truth in the Theory of Speech Acts," in *Syntax and Semantics*, vol. 3, ed. P. Cole and J. Morgan (New York: Academic Press, 1975, pp. 1-39, particularly, pp. 25f.

one, therefore, can argue that a speaker who promises in uttering (5.69) makes a claim that is true if he or she does buy the drinks, and false if not.

(5.69) I promise that *I will buy drinks tonight*.

This type of constativist theory makes a different mistake. It confuses the properties of parts with properties of wholes. Saying the italicized part of (5.69) can be the saying of something true or false, but only if said by way of stating something about the future. If said by way of promising [short for the whole of (5.69)], there is no reason to grant that it says anything true or false. But, more to the point, first, there is no reason to think that it is said by way of stating something when it is said in the saying of the whole sentence (5.69), and second, even if said by way of stating something, there is no reason to think that saying the whole sentence is not performing *two* speech acts, one of promising and one of predicting. Moreover, saying the italicized part of (5.69) in isolation is open to both interpretations but these are clearly alternatives, not conflations. A reports B's having said the italicized part of (5.69). C can ask, particularly if B is a notoriously insincere promiser but a perfectly reliable truth teller, "Did B promise to buy our drinks or assert it?" This equivocation—between whether the buying of the drinks is asserted in the making of the promise or whether the making of the promise involves such information in connection with its fulfillment condition—shows that, strictly speaking, the analogy establishes nothing. Moreover, there are cases like (5.70) that lack appropriate complement sentence or underlying propositional structure.

(5.70) I greet you (in the name of the king).

Besides posing counter-examples to the claim that this approach can be a general account of performatives, these examples show that even if this approach could get around the previous difficulties it would be beside the point. The example shows that the approach attaches a truth value to the wrong thing and leaves the performativeness of a sentence unexplained. The fact that in the use of a sentence like (5.69) or (5.70) for performing an illocutionary act the speaker might be asserting something is no explanation of what has to be explained, *viz.*, why it is that such sentences are performative.

The principal reason for insisting on a performative/constative distinction is Austin's observation that it makes no sense to attribute truth or falsehood to performatives. We might put this in terms of grammatical theory by saying that sentences like those in (5.71) contrast with sentences like those in (5.72).

(5.71) (i) "I christen you 'Morris'" is true (false).

    (ii) "I apologize for christening you 'Morris'" is true (false).

    (iii) "Christen the baby 'Morris'!" is true (false).

    (iv) "I thank you for not christening me 'Morris'" is true (false).

    (v) It is true (false) that I christen you 'Morris'.

(5.72) (i) "Kevin thanked me for not christening him 'Morris'" is true.

      (ii) It is true that Kevin thanked me for not christening him 'Morris'.

The former are semantically anomalous whereas the latter are fully meaningful in the language. Framed in this way, the point can be developed by considering the implications of the anomalous structures in sentences like (5.71). Thus, just as (5.71)(iii) is semantically anomalous, (5.73)(i) and (5.73)(ii) are semantically anomalous but (5.74)(i) and (5.74)(ii) are not.

(5.73) (i) A true request is preferable to a false one.

      (ii) John's request (order) is true (false).

(5.74) (i) A true statement is preferable to a false one.

      (ii) John's statement is true (false).

Moreover, expressions like "true promise", "true apology", and so on, are not semantically ambiguous. They have no sense corresponding to the sense of "true statement", but have only a sense in which "true" means "sincere".

Not only have philosophers and linguists constructed theories on which performatives are constatives, they have sometimes argued directly against Austin's observation. One such argument is of special interest because the examples on which it is based turn out to provide further evidence for the performative/constative distinction. In connection with examples like (5.75), Jane Heal has argued that, since we can respond by saying such things as (5.76), "at least some explicit performatives utterances are statements".[38]

(5.75) (i) I gladly promise to help you move.

      (ii) Out of regard for your welfare, I advise you to move.

      (iii) With every confidence in your ability, I appoint you.

      (iv) I order you to leave the room.

(5.76) (i) That's a lie, you aren't at all glad.

      (ii) What he said is quite true; he does have your good at heart.

      (iii) I hope that's true, but if it is you have changed your opinion of him since last week.

      (iv) Very true, you order me to leave the room.

38. J. Heal, "Explicit Performative Utterances and Statements," *Philosophical Quarterly* 24 (April 1974):106–121.

Heal considers the obvious reply to the principle she invokes that

> . . . if in an utterance the proposition that p is expressed and it is possible to assess the utterance as true or false or as a lie that p, then that utterance is a statement,[39]

namely, that the propositions expressed by (5.75) are compounds of a performative and a constative and that only the latter are referred to in responses like (5.76). That is, (5.75)(i) expresses both the proposition expressed by "I promise to help you move" and the proposition expressed by "I am glad about being able to make this promise to help you". Her rejection of this reply is based on the claim that an explanation of such compounding of propositions in terms of the underlying grammatical relations of adverbials like "gladly" would involve "considerable elaboration of grammatical theory". This claim is nothing more than hand-waving. First, many adverbials (for example, "necessary", "probable", and "certain") applied to constatives require just such compounding of propositions, and second, the claim puts the question of economy incorrectly. Considerations of economy make sense only as an argument for a theory that can explain as much as its rivals. The question of whether there is a fact of compounding to be explained is begged by Heal, so an argument that appeals to considerations of economy is illegitimate.

The real question, then, is what do sentences in (5.75) and (5.76) mean. Looked at from this standpoint, Heal's cases actually provide a new source of evidence for Austin's distinction. Note first that the proper gloss of (5.76)(i) is "The speaker of (5.75)(i) is not glad to make the promise to help" and the proper gloss of (5.76)(ii) is "The speaker of (5.76)(ii)'s motive in advising the recipient to move is a regard for the recipient's welfare". Hence, these responses do not address themselves to the performative proposition in the meaning of (5.75)(i) and (5.75)(ii). Such responses "bypass" the performative of the two propositions in the compound propositions (5.75)(i) and (5.75)(ii). Likewise, (5.76)(iii) bypasses the performative proposition in (5.75)(iii) and addresses itself to the assertive proposition expressing the speaker's claim to be confident in the recipient's ability. But when both propositions in a compound proposition are assertive, as in (5.77), the response "That's a lie" or "What you say is false" can be understood as possibly addressing both—that is, as denying that John promised to do such a thing or that John promised to do it gladly.

(5.77)   John gladly promised to jump out of the window.

39. Ibid., p. 114.

The fact that such responses operate selectively, bypassing performative components of compound propositions but not assertive components, can be explained only on a theory that makes the performative/constative distinction. This constitutes strong supporting evidence for Austin's distinction.

One further piece of evidence is the fact that "very true" in (5.76)(iv) does not refer to the performative (5.75)(iv) but to the respondent's assertion that the speaker of (5.75)(iv) ordered the respondent to leave the room. This is shown by the fact that "you order me to leave the room", which is an assertion, spells out what is expressed by the remark "very true".

Finally, I want to examine an interesting recent attempt by K. Bach to show that performatives are statements.[40] Bach takes the utterance of an explicit performative like "I order you to leave" to make a statement and also to count as the performance of an act of ordering someone to leave. He tries to explain the ability of such utterances to perform illocutionary acts as a consequence of the pragmatic reasoning the audience goes through, and is intended by the speaker to go through, in order to square their presumption that the speaker is speaking the truth with the (assumed) fact that a speaker who utters "I order you to go" is *stating* that he or she is ordering them to go. The interest of this attempt of Bach's is that, although it takes a position similar to Lewis's, it allows performative utterances to be treated as the appropriate kind of doings, and that it invokes Gricean principles to try to show how the performative import can be derived without assuming sentences have performative meaning. We shall show that Bach's argument that the ability of such sentences to perform illocutionary acts is not a consequence of the meaning of their subject, tense, and performative main verb is question begging. And, more important, we shall show that his attempt to derive a performative import for utterances of sentences that are not assumed to have a performative meaning fails, and that his attempt fails in a way that discredits any attempt to use Gricean principles for this purpose.

Bach imagines speakers of English who use formulas like "I order . . ." just to make statements about what the speaker is doing at the moment of speech. He points out that the illocutionary force of an utterance of a sentence like "I order you to leave" must thus come from outside the sentence, perhaps from the utterance of another sentence or from an accompanying gesture. He concludes that "no special grammatical feature can account for [the performative] effect," since "there is not reason . . . to hold that for these speakers words like 'order' would differ in meaning from what they mean for us".[41] Now, assuming that, in

40. K. Bach, "Performatives are Statements Too," *Philosophical Studies* 28 (1975): 229–236.
41. Ibid., p. 233.

the idiolects of these speakers, the performative effect of forms like "I order . . ." must come from outside their grammatical structure, if, as Bach supposes, such forms do *not* differ in meaning from their counterparts in English, his conclusion follows. But to suppose this is to suppose just what has to be proved; namely, that the ability of an utterance like "I order you to leave" to issue an order is not a consequence of the meaning of the formula "I order . . ." in English. For if we assume to the contrary that the ability of such an utterance to issue an order derives from the meaning of the formula in English, their word "order" must differ in meaning from the English word "order". *Ex hypothesi*, the latter has a meaning such that an explicit performative sentence in which it appears as the main verb can issue an order without further sentences or accompanying gestures. The meaning of the English performative formula "I order . . ." has the force of such further sentences or accompanying gestures built into its meaning. In contrast, the word "order" in the idiolects of this special group of speakers has a meaning such that an explicit performative sentence in which it appears as the main verb makes a statement with no further sentence or accompanying gesture. We may distinguish these words by designating the English verb "order$_E$" and the verb in the idiolects of these speakers "order$_S$". The semantic condition for calling a use of a sentence of the form "I order$_E$ . . ." an order is just that it be a standard use. The semantic condition for calling a use of a sentence of the form "I order$_S$ . . ." an order is that the speaker use it in a context in which there is an appropriate further sentence or accompanying gesture. The meaning of "I order$_S$ . . ." is something like 'The speaker is stating that he or she is ordering$_E$ . . .'. Therefore, lacking the built-in illocutionary force for ordering, utterances of sentences of the form "I order$_S$ . . ." have to receive a requestive interpretation on the basis of contextual features. Thus, their use to issue an order is no different from the use of "I promise to take care of you" accompanied by an appropriate gesture (like the speaker's shaking a fist at the audience) to issue a threat.

Bach attempts to derive the performative inport of utterances in the following way.

> . . . there is a fundamental 'communicative presumption' among users of a language, to the effect that when they say something, what they are doing in saying it is determinable by their audience. Because this is a matter of mutual belief, the sepaker can reasonably intend his audience to take him as intending his act to be determinable, and it is on this basis, together with the utterance itself and the circumstances surrounding it, that the audience determines what that act is. The act is successful insofar as this determination is made correctly. . . . in the case of performative utterances, . . . nor-

mally the audience reasons, and is intended to reason, as follows:

1. He is saying, 'I order you to leave'.
2. He is stating that he is ordering me to leave.
3. If his statement is true, then he must be ordering me to leave.
4. If he is ordering me to leave, it must be his utterance that constitutes the order (what else could it be?).
5. Presumably, he is speaking the truth.
6. Therefore, in saying 'I order you to leave', he is ordering me to leave.[42]

Sentences like "Do not believe any statements I make because everyone of them is false" are counterexamples to Bach's derivation. On the one hand, they obviously can be used to make requests, and on the other, they cannot be construed as statements of the speaker's where the audience can presume that the speaker is speaking the truth. Indeed, a comparison of this counterexample of the paradoxical sentence "Every statement I make is false" brings out the performativeness of the former: We do not have the intuition that the imperative (or an equivalent declarative like "I request that you do not believe any statement I make because every one of them is false") is self-referential in the manner of "Every statement I make is false", and this can only be because performatives do not make assertions at all.

HOW TO SAVE AUSTIN
FROM AUSTIN

In this concluding section, we survey a range of cases that have been problems or counter-examples for other accounts of performativeness. In particular, some led Austin to abandon the performative/constative distinction in its original form. We shall try to show that a theory such as the one developed above has no trouble with them.

Consider negative sentences like (5.78).

(5.78) (i) I do not request that you go.
    (ii) It is not the case that I request you to go.
    (iii) I make no promise to go.
    (iv) It is not the case that I promise to go.

Searle supposes that they are genuine performatives,[43] but he gives no reason

42. Ibid., p. 234.
43. Searle, *Speech Acts*, p. 33. I agree with Searle that they are not autobiographical but this does not mean that they are performative. They state that the speaker is not doing something.

and insofar as sentences like (5.78) can be true or false, it seems clear that his supposition is wrong. If so, then such sentences are not performatives, and it might be argued that they are not excluded by (5.41) and a further condition is required to make that definition adequate.

But in fact (5.41) already excludes cases in which the performative verb is in the scope of the antonymy operator. The determination of whether a sentence is performative is based on whether or not the projection process assigns it a reading that satisfies (5.41). Since the reading of a sentence like one in (5.78) is partly the result of applying the antonymy operator to the reading of the performative verb (with perhaps other elements of the verb phrase), given the nature of the change in readings that this operator brings about, the reading of such a sentence is guaranteed to fail (5.41). (See Chapter 6, pp. 238–241.)

It might be claimed a similar counter-example arises in connection with modals; sentences like (5.79), which are not explicit performative sentences, would be counted as such by (5.41).

(5.79) I might request you to do it.

Again, the objection fails to pay close attention to the nature of the readings in question. If these readings are in part the product of readings of the modal words, and if the lexical readings for the modal words "might", "can", "could", and so on offer a reasonable account of their logical structure, then sentences like (5.79) will be represented as having essentially the same logical form as sentences like (5.80).

(5.80) It is possible that I would request you to do it.

[Other examples of the parallelism include "I can request (command, order, and so on) you to do it" and "I have the authority (right, and so on) to request (command, order, and so on) you to do it.] Therefore, the word in the sentence that determines its overall logical form is not, as in (5.81), the performative verb "request", but the modal "might".

(5.81) I request that you do it.

Thus, the lexical reading that determines the form of the reading of (5.79) is the lexical reading of the modal. Whatever may be the ultimate explication of a modal notion like possibility, it is clear that the readings of sentences like (5.79) and (5.80) will fail to satisfy (5.41), since such sentences assert that the state of affairs in which the speaker performs the illocutionary act is something that can occur.

We are not at all denying that a sentence of the form "I can promise you. . ."

is a natural or common way of promising under a wide range of circumstances. The claim that they are not performatives says only that the circumstances under which they can be used to promise do not include the null context, although it is clear that non-null contexts exist in which such sentences simply inform the addressee of the speaker's ability to fulfill the promise. Possibly a pragmatic account of these conditions will say that they are ones in which the only question is whether the speaker is in the proper position to make the promise to the addressee.[44]

Austin noted that the "first-person singular, present-indicative, active" criterion is doubtful because some sentences of this form express assertions about habitual action and so-called historical-present time.[45] But here, too, the change from a syntactic to a semantic criterion avoids the difficulty. Although present tense is the common syntactic form for expressing all three times, the meanings of (simple) present, the present of habitual action, and the historical present distinguish them easily. We shall sketch these differences even though, logically speaking, it would not matter to our theory that some sentences whose tense expresses the time of the speech point are nonperformative.

Sentences (5.82)-(5.84) are typical examples of sentences expressing habitual action; sentences (5.85)-(5.87) are examples involving performative verbs.

(5.82) They smoke.
(5.83) He strong-arms people (causing a disturbance).
(5.84) She eats enormous meals.
(5.85) I request the impossible.
(5.86) I warn people about the danger of forest fires.
(5.87) I advise the king.

One difference immediately disqualifies these forms from carrying the illocutionary force of performatives. Sentences that carry a habitual-action sense require verbal complements that express kinds or types of actions (for example, impossible ones, minimal commitments), whereas performative sentences require verbal complements that express a particular action or specific acts. Thus, the complements of (5.82)-(5.87) are similar to stative forms like (5.88) in expressing abstract rather than particular senses.

(5.88) He fears death, They anticipate disaster, We know the rules, Many of us know the truth. . . .

---

44. See B. Fraser, "Hedged Performatives," in *Syntax and Semantics*, vol. 3, ed. P. Cole and J. L. Morgan (New York: Academic Press, 1975), pp. 187–210.
45. Austin, *How To Do Things with Words*, pp. 63–64.

However, the main semantic difference between cases like (5.85)–(5.87) and genuine explicit performative sentences is the semantic difference in the interpretation of their present-tense forms. The meaning of the simple present tense in explicit performative sentences and sentences like (5.89) is the moment bounded by the onset and termination of the utterance of the sentence.

(5.89)   Melvin is angry.

Thus, (5.89) expresses the claim that Melvin is in a state of anger at the time the speaker utters (5.89). The meaning of the present tense in sentences expressing habitual action involves an indefinite number of durations spread over the past and perhaps extending into the future. Furthermore, there are the notions of some regularity in these occurrences and that the repetition is due to some habit of the agent's, an enduring trait, a disposition, a position he or she occupies, or something of the kind. Hence (5.87) differs from (5.90) in that the former implies occurrences of advisings of the king, whereas the latter does not imply any such occurrences.

(5.90)   I am an advisor to the king.

The same point is illustrated by the fact that (5.91) is contradictory but (5.92) is not.

(5.91)   I advise the king but I've never advised him nor will I.
(5.92)   I am an advisor of the king but I've never advised him nor will I.

So-called historical-present forms[46] are references to past events as if they were present, or timeless specifications. Sentence (5.93) is a typical example of a "historical-present" form.

(5.93)   Yesterday I saw someone I knew in childhood. I stepped up to him and nodded. "I think I know you," says I; "you don't," says he.

The third sentence of (5.93) is interpreted as assigning the occurrence of the reported dialogue to the point in the past designated by the temporal reference(s) in the preceding, context-setting, sentences. The conventions governing the historical present in English, whatever their grammatical basis, make us transpose

46. We exclude generic forms, which also employ the present tense. Also, we exclude cases like "The team plays tomorrow", since they are really no different in meaning than "The team will play tomorrow". Although their syntactic tense is present, semantically they are future, as a result of the compositional contribution of the adverb.

the presentness associated with the tense constituent back to this point in the past. Austin's example (5.94) can be understood in this way if taken to be equivalent to (5.95).

(5.94) On page 49, I protest against the verdict.
(5.95) On page 49, I protested against the verdict.

If not, it has to be understood as a timeless specification of location, on a par with (5.96).

(5.96) The pages of the book are between its covers.

In either case, they present no problem for our treatment of performatives.

The next set of possible counter-examples, (5.97)–(5.102), figured prominently in Austin's reasons for retracting his original distinction.

(5.97) I claim that you did it.
(5.98) I state that I hurt a flea.
(5.99) I acknowledge that you were the first.
(5.100) I admit I am responsible.
(5.101) I concede that I am at fault.
(5.102) I insist that you are guilty.

He wrote:

> ... it is not easy to be sure that, even when it is apparently in explicit form, an utterance is performative or that it is not; and typically anyway, we still have utterances beginning "I state that..." which seem to satisfy the requirements of being performative, yet which surely are the making of statements, and surely are essentially true or false.[47]

Earlier Austin expressed the last point, saying:

> ... when we come to pure explicit performatives such as "state" or "maintain", surely the whole thing is true or false even though the uttering of it is the performing of the action of stating or maintaining.[48]

Austin was wrong to take such sentences to be counter-examples to a sharp distinction between performatives and constatives. He was right in thinking that,

47. Austin, *How To Do Things with Words*, p. 91.
48. Ibid., p. 90.

commonly, their use is "the making of statements". Such uses assert the truth of the proposition expressed by the complement sentence. He was also right in thinking that their use performs the illocutionary act of claiming (stating, acknowledging, and so on). But he was in error when he concluded that he had found cases that are both performative and constative. His failure to employ a competence/performance distinction[49] confined his theorizing exclusively to the domain of acts and had as a consequence that questions about the grammatical meaning of sentences were not separated from questions about their utterance meaning on the occasions of their use. Once we separate them, all appearance of their being counter-examples to this dichotomy vanishes: the *sentences* (5.97)–(5.102) are explicit performatives, not constatives, but their uses, their *tokens*, typically make statements.

The case for saying that sentences like (5.97)–(5.102) are performative and not constative is straightforward. Their meaning in the language equips them to perform their semantically specified, common illocutionary act of declaring (in the null context). We take declaration to be the common act-description in the meaning of "declare", "state", "claim", and so on, just as we took requesting to be the common action in the case of verbs like "request", "order", "beg", and so on. Thus, "declare" might be held to differ in meaning from "concede" only in terms of specifying how the assertion is to be taken, namely, as the speaker making known that he or she determines the complement sentence to be a truth, in contrast to the speaker retracting an earlier denial of the truth of this sentence.

As in the case of (5.69)–(5.73), sentences like (5.103) and (5.104) are semantically anomalous.

(5.103) "I $\begin{Bmatrix} \text{claim} \\ \text{state} \\ \text{acknowledge} \\ \text{admit} \\ \text{concede} \end{Bmatrix}$ that these pages are torn" is true (false).

(5.104) It is true (false) that $\begin{Bmatrix} \text{claim} \\ \text{state} \\ \text{acknowledge} \\ \text{admit} \\ \text{concede} \\ \text{insist} \end{Bmatrix}$ that these pages are torn.

49. In fact, it was both this failure and the reliance on traditional grammar that were responsible for the error. Austin continues the second of the two quoted passages, saying, "... we could distinguish the performative opening part (I state that) which makes clear how the utterance is to be taken, that it is a statement (as distinct from a prediction, etc.)

(We are leaving out the sense where they simply affirm the fact of the speaker's going on record with some claim, statement, and so on, which the speaker does not intend to withdraw, in the manner in which "It is true that I promise that I will go" affirms a promise.)

Another set of arguments for the performative nature of sentences like (5.97)–(5.102) are those introduced in Chapter 2 countering Ross's higher performative analysis of declarative sentences. We observed there that such an analysis implied the synonymy of declarative propositions, like the one expressed by (2.4), with assertive ones, like (2.3). We argued that this has to be false insofar as (2.3) semantically entails (2.44) whereas (2.4) does not, and (2.4) semantically entails (2.45) whereas (2.3) does not. And we argued their nonsynonymy on the grounds that a number of their other semantic properties and relations are different. These arguments support our claim that the propositions expressed by sentences like (5.97)–(5.102) are performatives. Ordinary uses of (5.98) that assert something assert the proposition expressed by the complement of (5.98), which entails that the speaker hurt an insect, rather than the proposition expressed by (5.98) as a whole, which entails nothing about the speaker hurting anything. The former proposition can be true or false, but the latter, not being part of the statement made, cannot be either.

Still another type of argument for this conclusion emerges from the contrast of (5.105) and (5.106), understanding "he" to be anaphoric.

$$(5.105) \quad \text{I} \left\{ \begin{array}{l} \text{claim} \\ \text{state} \\ \text{acknowledge} \\ \text{admit} \\ \text{concede} \\ \text{insist} \end{array} \right\} \text{ that George is a spy but he isn't.}$$

(5.106) George is a spy but he isn't.

Sentence (5.106) is a flat contradiction, but (5.105) are not. We have here a contrast between a propositional contradiction and a pragmatic oddity. The user of a sentence like (5.105) performs the illocutionary act of announcing his or her endorsement of the truth of the proposition that George is a spy but then goes on to deny that George is a spy. The speaker thus undercuts the communicative

---

from the bit in the *that*-clause which is required to be true or false" (*How To Do Things with Words*, p. 90). He immediately undermines this point, suggesting that, in the cases "I liken x to y" and "I analyze x as y", "we are not able to split [them] into two parts in this way". Such a suggestion would clearly never have been made within the context of theories of grammar that do not restrict grammatical analysis to surface structure.

purpose of the act (which is something like going on record as backing the truth of the proposition that George is a spy) because in the very communication the speaker compromises this purpose by asserting the denial of the proposition he or she is supposed to be backing.[50] It is clear that the hearer knows that the speaker must know that the second clause of (5.105) implicates that the speaker does not think this proposition is true.

Austin mistakenly thought that cases like (5.97)–(5.102) were counter-examples simply because he restricted himself to talking about utterances and actions, to performance. Had he made the competence/performance distinction, he could have held that an explicit form like (5.98) is performative and, quite consistently, that its use states that something is the case as a consequence of pragmatic considerations. Thus, in our account, cases like (5.97)–(5.102) come out exactly parallel to other propositional types. For example, (5.97) stands in the same relation to its complement sentence as (5.107) stands to its.

(5.107) I promise that I will be home soon.

The sentences (5.97) and (5.107) are explicit performatives, whereas their complements, considered as independent sentences, are not explicit performatives. But, depending on the context, an *utterance* of such nonexplicit performatives (that is, constatives) can perform the same illocutionary act as the explicit performative does in a standard use. Without a sharp competence/performance distinction, which provides us with a conception of how it is possible for semantically different sentences to interact with different contextual features to produce the same illocutionary act, it is easy to take the typical use of a sentence like (5.97) for making assertions as grounds for regarding it as a constative. In the absence of a competence/performance distinction, the natural criterion for distinguishing between performatives and constatives takes the "requirements of being performative" to apply to utterances and judges them as satisfying the requirements on the basis of what is typically done in their production.

The competence/performance distinction provides us with the benefits of idealization. Like the use of idealization in the theory of gases and mechanics, we do not have to state laws in terms of real objects and events—in our case, utterances and the speech acts they perform. Instead, we can state them in terms of idealized objects and events such as sentence types, their meaning in the language, that is, their meaning in the null context, and context types. As a consequence, the classification of sentences into the categories of performative and constative and into subcategories of the former do not depend on the

50. See R. M. Harnish, "The Argument from 'Lurk'," *Linguistic Inquiry* 4, no. 1 (1975): 145–154; reprinted in *An Integrated Theory of Linguistic Ability*, pp. 261–270.

features of utterances and the speech acts they perform any more than the laws of the theory of gases and mechanics depend on the actual behavior of objects. Thus, the fact that, in isolation, the complement of the verb in (5.97) and the sentence (5.97) itself both perform the act of stating is on a par with the fact that, in isolation, the complement of the verb in (5.97) also makes accusations or that, in isolation, the complement of the verb in (5.107) makes predictions and threats. These facts are treated in just the way that mechanics treats the facts that real physical objects with the same gravitational force acting on them fall at different rates, or that real objects with different gravitational attractions fall at the same rate (as consequences of the interaction between gravitational force and other forces such as the friction of that air). Thus, classifying sentences into performatives and constatives can be carried out on the basis of their senses in the language; the kind of speech act that either a performative or constative sentence performs can be taken as a consequence of the structure of its sense and the features of the speech context in which it is used. Since "the requirements of being performative" are now imposed only on sentences in the idealized null context, just as gravitational laws are framed for ideal situations like frictionless planes, cases like (5.97)–(5.102) are not counter-examples to the performative/constative distinction, but only counter-examples to the assumption that such a distinction is to be drawn for utterances on the basis of the illocutionary act performed in their production.

Austin pointed out the existence of an interesting class of nonperformative verbs that describe actions in which saying something is doing something. He remarked:

> Is it always the case that we must have a performative verb for making explicit something we are undoubtedly doing by saying something? For example, I may insult you by saying something but we have not the formula "I insult you".[51]

If I utter (5.108) under ordinary conditions, I shall succeed in insulting but if I utter (5.109), I will fail to insult anyone (except perhaps in the most unusual circumstances).

(5.108) You are a no-good fink, a bum, and your intelligence is less than a dull child's.

(5.109) I insult you.

Why does a sentence like (5.109) not serve as a means of insulting when insulting

51. Austin, *How To Do Things with Words*, p. 65.

is something one can do simply by uttering appropriate words in an appropriate context?

To see why such sentences do not serve as such a means, consider first the meaning of insult sentences in which the subject is not the first-person singular pronoun and the tense is, say, past. Such a sentence asserts that the agent said unflattering things about the recipient which constituted an attack on his or her worth, but of course it need not indicate what these unflattering things are. The meaning of "insult" thus characterizes an act of saying without specifying what is said, although whatever it is it is unflattering. The lexical reading of "insult" might be (5.110), where the function α picks out the addressee.

(5.110)

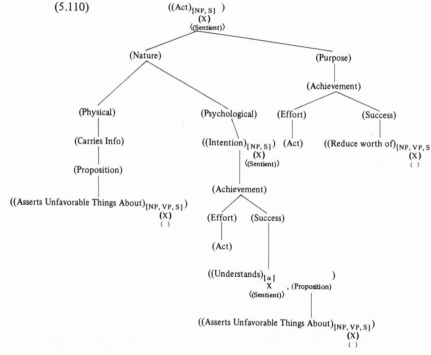

(Before continuing with the question we are trying to answer, note that (5.110) represents insulting as an intentional act. I think this is correct, but there is room for argument. My intuition is that when someone is unintentionally insulted, whether or not the remark is insulting, the agent cannot be properly blamed for having insulted the person. The agent may even say something like "I didn't mean to insult you", but this does not imply that the agent insulted the person. It can be taken as a report of the agent's intention, and so, on our view, a way of saying that the agent did not insult the person and implicating that he or she is sorry for having caused them to feel insulted. But, for present purposes, nothing much hangs on this issue.)

Given that the meaning of (5.109), unlike that of (5.108), contains nothing unflattering about the recipient, but simply contains the assertion that something of that nature is said about the recipient, (5.109) will not have the potential to satisfy its own unconverted condition that a performative sentence has to have. Insofar as the unconverted condition of (5.109) is satisfied just in case the referent of its subject says something unflattering about the referent of its object at the speech point, no use of (5.109) can be sufficient to satisfy the illocutionary success condition of the utterance. Therefore, when first-person present-tense "insult" sentences are not taken constatively, that is, on a habitual-action sense or a historical-present sense, the combination of their having a performative-like grammatical form plus their lacking the unflattering predication(s) required for illocutionary success gives them a distinctive "hollow ring". I do not mean that such sentences are semantically anomalous. Rather, I interpret them in a manner similar to the way that a presuppositionalist theory views the illocutionary success (statement making) of sentences like "This sentence is false" and "This sentence is true". Such a theory would say that the condition under which these sentences satisfy their illocutionary success condition and make a statement is that their subject refers to a statement, and that the meaning of these sentences produces a referential loop back to themselves that prevents their illocutionary success.[52] Similarly, the meaning of a sentence like (5.109) prevents its illocutionary success. Thus, just as we would take Epimenedian sentences to be meaningful but incapable of making a statement, so we would take sentences like (5.109) to be meaningful but incapable of performing the appropriate illocutionary act.

We can predict the nonperformative status of sentences like (5.109) by their failure to meet the condition (5.41)(i). Assume that something like (5.110) is correct. Then, the reading of (5.109) does not satisfy this condition because the leftmost branch of (5.109) is not the left-most branch of (5.14). Just as (5.54) violated this condition for having the terminal semantic marker ((Reasons

---

52. Technically, such sentences are ungrounded. See H. Herzberger, "Paradoxes of Grounding in Semantics," *Journal of Philosophy* 17, no. 6 (1970):145–167, which is based on some of the work in H. Herzberber and J. J. Katz, "The Concept of Truth for Natural Language" (1967, unpublished).

for)$_{[S, VP, S]}$) , so (5.110) violates it for having ((Asserts Unfavorable Things
$\quad$ X
$\quad$ ⟨ ⟩

About)$_{[NP, VP, S]}$).
$\quad$ (X)
$\quad\;$ ⟨ ⟩

What we have just said about "insult" is also true of its near antonym "praise". "Praise", too, gives rise to sentences like (5.109), which describe doings of a kind that only other sentences, essentially different from them, can accomplish. A sentence like (5.111) is the parallel of (5.109).

$\qquad$ (5.111)$\quad$ I praise you.

It is as empty of flattering remarks as (5.109) is of unflattering ones. Nonetheless, it is true that "praise" and "honor" can function in certain cases to perform the act of praising or honoring. They do so, however, because of special features of the context in which they so function. For example, when said by a king in the course of an appropriate ceremony, (5.111) and (5.112) can confer praise and honor.

$\qquad$ (5.112)$\quad$ We honor our young prince.

Saying such things in such circumstances counts as praising and honoring because the entire situation is so highly ritualized. The context supplies the reason for the praise or honor (for example, victories over the barbarians), and the utterances themselves become appropriately flattering statements.

$\quad$ Austin saw "insult" as a case for which the traditional grammatical criterion fails: "Our criterion", he said, "will not get in all cases of the issuing of an utterance being the doing of something, because the 'reduction' to an explicit performative does not seem always possible".[53] From our perspective, the aim of obtaining such a criterion is misguided. This is exactly what Austin's own counter-examples show. Replacing the idea of a performative/constative distinction that properly separates utterances that are the doing of something from utterances that are not, we propose that this distinction be a demarcation between sentences whose grammatical meaning describes the kind of act performed by the utterance of the sentence and sentences whose grammatical meaning does not describe such an act. Our perspective reverses Austin's: instead of beginning with utterances of any form and then trying to reduce those that can "do something" to an explicit performative, we begin with the class of explicit performa-

53. Austin, *How To Do Things with Words*, pp. 68–69.

tive sentences and then try to relate them to utterances that "do something". We thus frame the performative/constative distinction as a division of sentences into explicit performatives and others, and seek to explain how nonexplicit performatives do what they do on the basis of the interaction between their grammatical structure and the context. On our approach, a pragmatic theory will count the use of a nonexplicit performative sentence S as "performative in the context C" just in case $PRAG(D(S), I(C(t)) = R(S')$, where S' is an explicit performative (on a sense). It follows from this that the act of insulting someone in the use of a sentence like (5.108) is not a case of an utterance that is performative in context. But this presents no problem. There is no reason why *every* case of an utterance doing something should be understood in performative terms. It seems natural that cases like the use of (5.108) to insult should be understood simply as ones in which the action falls under the category of an insult.

We come, finally, to the inevitable miscellanea of problematic cases in which performatives can often seem not to be so, and vice versa. I shall give an instance of each kind to illustrate how they might be dealt with. I will not try to go further, first, because there is no serious possibility of making a complete survey of the full range of such problematic cases, and second, because the next chapter will shed light on the proper way to treat some of these instances.

Austin took "threaten" to be a performative, contrasting it with the causative "intimidate".[54] Austin's authority in empirical lexicography is deservedly great, yet one finds it hard to dispel doubts about this judgment. Neither (5.113) nor (5.114) seems to be performative, but our doubts might be explained away.

(5.113) I threaten you.
(5.114) I threaten you that I will murder you (unless you pay up).

If one were to argue that neither is performative, (5.113) would have to be handled in the manner of "insult". But the "hollow ring" here seems to come from the absence of a particular threat and consequence. Trying to handle these cases by analogy with the account for "insult" runs into difficulty in connection with (5.114), where there is no "hollow ring" but just a peculiarity of some sort. Contrast (5.114) with (5.115), which is deviant straightforwardly.

(5.115) I insult you that you have the morals of a reptile.

Thus, instead of assuming that Austin was wrong and trying to concoct some new story to explain "threaten" as nonperformative even though threatening can consist in nothing more than producing an appropriate utterance, let us see

54. Ibid., p. 130.

if we can find reasons to count "threaten" as a genuine performative, and moreover, reasons that explain the peculiarity of a sentence like (5.114).

First, the meaning of sentences like (5.116) is, roughly, that the agent informed the recipient of his intention to do him the particular harm of causing his death.

(5.116)   Ralph threatened Richard with death.

It is reasonable therefore to classify "threaten" with performative verbs like "inform", "warn", and so on. Second, there are clear cases where there is nothing peculiar about sentences with "threaten" as their main verb being performative. These, unlike (5.112), are not cases where the context has to ritualize the utterances, for example, (5.117) and (5.118).

(5.117)   I threaten you and your city with destruction unless you surrender.
(5.118)   I hereby threaten you for the last time.

The fact that the speaker of (5.117) would have to be someone like the general or king of a besieging army is of no more significance than the fact that the speaker of (5.119) would have to be someone like a president.

(5.119)   I promise to grant executive pardons to everyone guilty of a political crime.

Third, there is a ready explanation of the peculiarity of cases like (5.114), which also accounts for why (5.117) does not seem peculiar. It is as follows. Threats promise harm to people as a means of getting them to do the will of the person making the threat. Thus, in the normal case, it is the menacing aspect of this expression of intention to do harm on which the threatener relies, and it is to be expected that the threatener will do nothing to make the threat less menacing (other things being equal). Now, it is also clear that the explicit performative form is a more formal, stylized, ceremonious mode of performing a speech act. Thus, there is a progression from less to more formality, stylization, and ceremony in the examples (5.120)–(5.122).

(5.120)   I will go on Saturday.
(5.121)   I promise that I will go on Saturday.
(5.122)   I hereby promise that I will go on Saturday.

Since in general the more the emphasis on form, the less on content, it follows that, in order not to reduce the menacing aspect of the threat, the threatener will reduce the formal aspect of the sentence used to perform the speech act. This explains the peculiarity of (5.114) as an undercutting of the purpose of the act by the use of a highly formal and stylized sentence when a sentence like (5.123) might equally well have been used.

(5.123)   I will murder you (unless you pay up).

This explanation allows that cases like (5.117), whose speakers are generals of besieging armies, kings, and such, will not sound peculiar, insofar as they can do without the ordinary rhetorical devices for promoting the menacing aspect of a threat, and their station in life calls for formality, style, and ceremony as a matter of course. Hence, sentential forms that reflect this are not self-defeating in their case.

Vendler offers some interesting examples of verbs that look like performatives but are not. He says:

> . . . I can say that he (or I, for that matter) has alleged or insinuated something, or bragged about this or that. What I cannot say, however, nor could anybody else, are things like [(5.124)–(5.126)] .

(5.124)   I insinuate that she was in his bedroom.
(5.125)   I allege that I never saw her before.
(5.126)   I brag that I am the best in the class.

> The reason is obvious: the implications of these verbs (implying doubt, deviousness, or lack of due modesty) are such that by using them in the performative way the speaker would undercut his own word. If, for instance, I were to say *I insinuate*. . . , then I could not possibly be insinuating, for by saying this I would reveal my intentions, which is incompatible with the nature of an insinuation. Similarly, if I were to say *I allege*. . . , I could not be alleging, for by thus casting doubt upon what I was going to say, I could not claim credence for it, which is essential to alleging. For these verbs the performative use would be self-destroying, amounting to an "illocutionary suicide" The situation is not quite so bad for *brag*. . . .[55]

Although Vendler has brought up important examples and invented an interesting form of explanation for a class of linguistic peculiarities, this explanation does not really handle these examples of failure of performativeness. First, note

55. Z. Vendler, *Res Cogitans* (Ithaca, N.Y.: Cornell University Press, 1972), pp. 207–208; Ibid., Appendix, "Shadow Performatices", pp. 207–209.

that this form of explanation has nothing especially to do with performative-ness. Harnish, who discovered it independently, employed it against Ross's "*lurk* argument".[56] Harnish pointed out that Ross's syntactic explanation of the oddity of sentences like (5.127) is unnecessary because it can be explained pragmatically without complicating the grammar at the syntactic or the semantic levels.

> (5.127)   I am lurking below your bedroom window.

According to Harnish, the oddity of (5.127) arises because the meaning of "lurk" involves the condition that the agent takes his or her whereabouts to be relevantly secret at the time of the lurking, and the utterance of (5.117) is incompatible with such secrecy. As Harnish says:

> . . . the interval of secrecy that I am committed to believing, by what I say, includes the point in time at which I compromise that secret by seriously uttering that sentence. In this way the speech act defeats itself in the present progressive.[57]

Second, this form of explanation does not really apply to "insinuate", "allege", and "brag". Vendler sees something of the trouble in connection with the last of these verbs. In fact, "brag" is clearly not assimilable to this paradigm of pragmatic explanation. As Vendler suggests, the relevant semantic condition for "brag" is that the agent exhibits lack of due modesty. Bragging, by definition, is asserting something of a self-flattering nature (directly or indirectly) that is beyond the bounds of modesty.[58] Therefore, there is no self-defeating incom-patibility here. The "conflict" is not even on the dimension of truth. I may say (5.128), whereas on Vendler's account this should be impossible in the way that (5.126) is.

> (5.128)   I assert, and I certainly admit I am bragging, that my son is the smartest kid in the class.

Moreover, the same trouble arises with "allege". Here the semantic condition is somewhat different from what Vendler suggests, for there is no invariant connec-tion with casting doubt upon what is said. Alleging something is merely assert-

56. Harnish, "The Argument from 'Lurk'".
57. Harnish, "The Argument from 'Lurk,'" p. 150.
58. An example of indirect self-flattery is where the speaker of (5.128), through his rela-tionship, basks in reflected glory.

ing without appropriate evidence or proof.[59] Vendler's explanation for the self-defeating nature of (5.125) is:

> ["allege" is in the dimension of truth]. Yet, at the same time, it casts doubt upon the truth of the allegation. These opposite forces operate harmlessly in the nonperformative use. . . . In the performative use, however, these forces would clash: I would claim belief for something, adding that it is unworthy of belief.[60]

This explanation does not hold up because doubt about the unworthiness is only sometimes and in some circumstances a consequence of asserting without appropriate evidence or proof. Note that (5.129) has none of the oddity of (5.125), and further that (5.130) involves no sense of clashing logical forces.

(5.129) I assert, though what I am asserting is open to doubt (is doubtful, highly dubious, etc.), that Bill is guilty.

(5.130) What I am asserting now in hereby saying that Bill is guilty is no more than an allegation but I nonetheless believe it and assert it to be true.

What is really involved is that we generally assume that we shall be asked to believe things on rational grounds, so that there is a *prima facie* oddity about being asked to believe something for which appropriate evidence or proof is explicitly denied. Finally, in Vendler's account, "insinuate" would involve a semantic condition that the agent deviously "has something up his sleeve", and the clash arises because, although the act must thus hide the agent's true intention, the utterance of a sentence like (5.124) reveals it (or too much of it). But Vendler is wrong on each point. There is nothing about a sentence like (5.124) that reveals the true intention of the agent. Furthermore, hiding the agent's intentions is no part of insinuation. Lyndon Johnson's insinuation that Gerald Ford was stupid by saying Ford had too often played football without a helmet left no one in doubt about Johnson's intentions. This did not undercut his successful act of insinuating. "Insinuate" means only that the communication works by oblique reference. The agent does not want to say the thing openly and straightforwardly, but there is no way to specify a general rule about the reason for this. It may be the desire to hide something, but, then again, it may be just the desire to say the thing artfully, subtly, or humorously.

59. Vendler, *Res Cogitans*, p. 208. Note that the nonredundancy of an expression like "unsupported allegation" does not undermine our claim, since such allegations are ones for which their author has offered no support.

60. Ibid., p. 208

Since Vendler's explanations collapse, we return to the question of why "brag", "allege", and "insinuate" are not performatives. My answer is that the unconverted conditions of these verbs do not represent three kinds of speech act whose performance is undercut when the speaker tries to use one of these verbs, but represent three ways of performing one kind of speech act. All three of these verbs describe how an assertion is made. "Brag" describes the manner of an assertion as going beyond the bounds of due modesty; "allege" describes it as based on no appropriate evidence, as delivered without proof; and "insinuate" describes it as made obliquely. Since these verbs describe the special manner of asserting in bragging, alleging, and insinuating, they do not express a condition that can be satisfied simply by their use in an appropriate present-tense sentence, and hence, they cannot count as performatives. The oddity of sentences like (5.124)–(5.126) is a consequence of this failure.

6
PROSPECTS FOR A THEORY OF PROPOSITIONAL TYPE

INTRODUCTION

Having an account of the constative/performative distinction based on the analysis of a single performative propositional type, we turn now to the other performative propositional types. A complete theory of propositional structure in natural language obviously requires a specification of every propositional type, an appropriate definition (analysis) for each, and an account of the subcategories within these types. We cannot undertake so large a job as this here, but we can discuss a number of propositional types other than the requestive and consider some important subcategories of requestive and other performative propositional types. Our primary interest is to develop a classificational principle for performative propositional types that can direct further investigation. Our secondary interest will be in the philosophical significance of such a principle and the classification it yields.

CLASSIFYING PERFORMATIVE TYPES

Earlier investigations have sought a principle for classifying illocutionary types in one or the other of the areas of speech or language. Austin, consistent with the general character of his approach, sought it in speech. In setting the stage for his classification, he wrote:

> What will *not* survive the transition [from an account based on the distinction between constative and performative sentences to an account based on the character of the behavior exhibited in performing speech acts], unless perhaps as a marginal limiting case, and hardly surprisingly because it gave trouble from the start, is the notion of the purity of performatives: this was es-

sentially based upon a belief in the dichotomy of performatives and constatives, which we see has to be abandoned in favor of more general *families*
of related and overlapping speech acts, which are just what we have now to
attempt to classify.[1]

Our principle, then, will differ from Austin's by being based on "the purity of
performatives" and "the dichotomy of performatives and constatives". Instead
of concerning speech behavior, as does Austin's classification of acts into *Ver-
dictives*, *Exercitives*, *Commissives*, *Behabitives* and *Expositives*, our classification
concerns the grammatical structure of sentences.

Searle's recent attempt to revise Austin's classification not only accepts
Austin's view that the principle(s) that yield the categories primarily concern
themselves with illocutionary acts, but seeks to make revisions in Austin's scheme
where it departs from this view.[2] Searle writes:

The first thing to notice about [Austin's categories] is that they are not
classifications of illocutionary acts but of English illocutionary verbs. Austin
seems to assume that a classification of different verbs is *eo ipso* a classification of kinds of illocutionary acts, that any two nonsynonymous verbs must
mark different illocutionary acts.[3]

Searle has the following six criticisms of Austin's classification:

In ascending order of importance, there is a persistent confusion between
verbs and acts; not all the verbs are illocutionary verbs; there is too much
overlap of the categories; there is too much heterogeneity within the categories; many of the verbs listed in the categories don't satisfy the definition
given for the category; and, most important, there is no consistent principle
of classification.[4]

Searle is, I think, by and large right in what he says under each of these headings,
particularly in their common assumption about the classification of illocutionary
types. However, Searle's revision turns out to be an only slightly modified version of his own previous analysis of types of illocutionary acts in *Speech Acts*;

1. J. L. Austin, *How To Do Things with Words* (Oxford: Oxford University Press, 1962),
p. 149.

2. J. Searle, "A Taxonomy of Illocutionary Acts," in *Language, Mind, and Knowledge*,
Minnesota Studies in the Philosophy of Science, vol. VII, ed. K. Gunderson (Minneapolis:
University of Minnesota Press, 1975), pp. 344–369.

3. Ibid., p. 351.

4. Ibid., p. 354.

and accordingly, it also fails to satisfy the requirement, whose importance Searle rightly stresses, that an adequate classification of illocutionary types be based on principles.

Searle's revision can be summarized in the accompanying chart, where the symbols under the "Illocutionary Point" slot stand, respectively, for the notions of telling people how things are, trying to get them to do things, committing ourselves to doing things, expressing our feelings, and bringing about changes through our utterances; the symbols under the "Direction of Fit" slot stand either for the downward, words-to-world direction, or the upward, world-to-words direction, or both; the symbol "(P)" is a variable ranging over the different possible psychological states expressed in the performance of the illocutionary acts in this class; "p" stands for the propositional content in Searle's sense, "H" stands for the hearer, "S" the speaker, and the notation "S/H + Property" ascribes some property (not necessarily an action) to either S or H.[5] Compared

Illocutionary Type	Classification			
	ILLOCUTIONARY POINT	DIRECTION OF FIT	PSYCHOLOGICAL STATE	PROPOSITIONAL CONTENT
Representatives	⊢	↓	Believe	p
Directives	!	↑	Want	H does A
Commissives	C	↑	Intend	S does A
Expressives	E		(P)	S/H + property
Declarations	D	↕		p

to the analysis of types of illocutionary act in *Speech Acts*,[6] the slots here, with the possible exception of the Direction of Fit slot, correspond to the types of rule there. The Illocutionary Point slot, the Psychological State slot, and the Propositional Content slot correspond to the Essential Rule, the Sincerity Rule, and the Propositional Content Rule, respectively. We also find that, except for one new type, there is only the collecting of Thank, Greet, and Congratulate under *Expressives*, the inclusion of Question under *Directives*, and the inclusion of Advise and Warn under *Representatives* and *Directives*. The basic types remain Assert/*Representative*, Request/*Directive*, Promise/*Commissive*, and Thank/*Expressive*.

Actually, Direction of Fit is not an innovation. Direction of Fit says how the

5. Ibid., pp. 354–361.
6. J. Searle, *Speech Acts* (Cambridge: Cambridge University Press, 1969), pp. 57–71.

propositional content is supposed to relate to the world.[7] In the case of *Representatives*, the fit is word-to-world; in the case of *Directives* and *Commissives*, it is the other way around. But this is nothing more than the fact, found in Essential and Propositional Content Rules of these types, that acts in the former category count as undertakings to the effect that the content represents an actual state of affairs whereas acts in the latter two categories make reference to a future act. The case of *Commissives* is somewhat unclear because Searle is inconsistent in the revision. In his discussion of *Commissives*,[8] he explicitly rejects an account on which these acts are attempts to get the speaker to do something, but in his discussion of *Expressives*, he withholds a Direction of Fit marking in these cases on the grounds that "In performing an expressive, the speaker is neither trying to get the world to match the words nor the words to match the world".[9] Thus, Searle implies that in *Commissives*, too, there is no direction of fit. Furthermore, this incoherence affects the new category of *Declarations*: these acts are supposed to embody both relations, but they do not try to get the words to match the world (like *Representatives*), and though they do attempt to get the world to match words, they are not *Directives*.[10] Although *Declarations* are a new and important illocutionary type, it seems as if they are not, after all, definable without some special comment under *Illocutionary Point* about their being attempts to bring about some change in the world solely by virtue of their occurrence.[11]

Be this as it may, the problems with Searle's revision are not my primary interest. Rather, the point here is that what Searle has presented is essentially the classification familiar from *Speech Acts*, improved in many details, but with no more of a principled basis than the unrevised version. I am not claiming that these classifications do not use important conceptual distinctions to characterize types (this is true of Austin's classification, too), but that there is no comprehensive doctrine that determines in general the kind of conceptual distinctions that can be used to characterize illocutionary types and the kind that can be used to characterize their subtypes. There is nothing to prevent Searle from introducing any new conceptual distinction that may seem to describe a difference among illocutionary acts. Searle's classification can thus be criticized on exactly the basis he criticized Austin's, namely, having no consistent principle of classification.

Vendler's extension of Austin's classification seeks a principle concerned with grammatical structure, as we do, but his approach, we have already seen,

7. Searle, "A Taxonomy of Illocutionary Acts," pp. 346–347.

8. Ibid., p. 356.

9. Ibid., pp. 356–357.

10. Ibid., p. 360.

11. Ibid., p. 358.

concentrates on syntactic structure.[12] Our approach differs from his in basing its classificational principle in semantic structure. We may expect two advantages. First, we can overcome the limitations of syntactic analysis in dealing with semantic phenomena that we found in Vendler's treatment of performative structure. Second, we can eliminate the further limitation of syntactic analysis that, even where it may succeed in a syntactic analysis of certain performative structures, the analysis employs constructs from the theory of English syntax that are at least partly language-specific. A semantic approach stands a far better chance of characterizing the language-universal propositional types.[13]

To obtain a principle or principles for classifying types of performative propositions, moreover one statable in terms of the formal structure of semantic representations, let us return to the case of the requestive propositional type. We characterized this type in terms of the semantic marker (5.14). Now, from the definition of performativeness (5.41), we can see that the performative nature of a requestive proposition consists in its unconverted condition having the semantic structure represented in the first of the two major branches in (5.14), that is, everything in the tree except perhaps for another substructure under (Purpose). This suggests a very narrow constraint on the set of distinctions that can be used to classify performative types. Assuming that the reading of the unconverted condition of every other performative proposition is like the reading for "request" in having two major branches, one of which describes the nature of the act and the other its purpose, we conjecture that, as in the case of (5.32), the information that determines the type of a performative proposition is that represented in the second major branch. Informally, the principle is that the purposes of illocutionary acts and these alone determine the types of illocutionary acts. Formally, the principle is (6.1). The obvious corollary is (6.2).

(6.1) The second of the two major branches in the reading whose first major branch marks a proposition P as performative, that is, the branch of the form $((\text{Act}) . . .) - (\text{Purpose}) - . . .$, specifies the type of P. The full set of such semantic structures determines the categories in the classification of performative types.[14]

(6.2) The subtypes of a particular performative type T are specified by the semantic markers occurring as the predicate functions applied to the semantic markers in the structure determining T.

12. Z. Vendler, *Res Cogitans* (Ithaca, N.Y.: Cornell University Press, 1972), pp. 16-26.

13. This is a version of the criticism in J. J. Katz, *The Underlying Reality of Language and Its Philosophical Import* (New York: Harper & Row, 1969), pp. 187-188.

14. Note that our definitions are in terms of semantic representations and therefore no criticism such as that Searle raises against Austin in "A Taxonomy of Illocutionary Acts" (p. 351) applies to us.

This corollary makes the determination of the subtypes under a performative type T a matter of the conceptual qualifications of the purpose concept that determines T. This is, of course, natural. But within our framework, (6.2) is necessary, too, since the only other semantic structure that might determine subtypes is that which determines the performative status of a proposition, and this semantic structure is not available for subcategorization of performative types because additions to the first major branch would undercut the account of performativeness. Such additions would either restrict performativeness to certain special cases of performative subtypes or, worse, eliminate the potential of performative sentences to satisfy their own unconverted condition.

We shall now set up some parts of the classification of performative types based on the principles (6.1) and (6.2). We make no pretense to completeness either at the level of types or subtypes. I am not here concerned with the question of how many distinct kinds of act we can use our language to perform. Rather, the emphasis is on making the general claims expressed in (6.1) and (6.2) plausible and on preparing the background for the philosophical implications to be sketched in the next section. Moreover, a closure principle restricting the kinds of acts we can perform in the use of sentences involves complex questions about the relation between cognition, grammar, and linguistic change that we cannot try to answer here.

In Austin's classification of speech acts, warning and advising are lumped together with requesting and ordering in the category called *Exercitives*.[15] Vendler follows Austin's lead by classifying verbs like "warn", "advise", "counsel", and so on (and the sentences they give rise to) with verbs like "request", "order", "urge", "beg", and so on (and the sentences they give rise to) in his category of exercitives.[16] Austin's basis for such a classification is merely that each of these speech acts involve the exercising of powers. Vendler's is:

> The infinitive construction in the nominal once more conceals an auxiliary (in this case the "subjunctive equivalent" *should*), and the subject of the nominalized sentence again appears as the direct object of the performative. This, at least in the performative occurrence, is always *you.*[17]

There is no point in commenting on these criteria. It is clear that they conflate quite different performative types. Searle put his finger on the real difference in observing that

15. Austin, *How To Do Things with Words*, p. 150.
16. Vendler, *Res Cogitans*, pp. 20–21.
17. Ibid., p. 20. Austin's basis is stated on p. 150.

Contrary to what one might suppose advice is not a species of requesting. . . . Advising you is not trying to get you to do something in the sense that requesting is. Advising is more like telling you what is best for you.[18]

Thus we distinguish *Requestives*, under which are included besides "request" such verbs as "order", "command", "urge", "beg", "entreat", and so on, from *Advisives*, under which are included such verbs as "warn", "advise", "recommend", "suggest", "counsel", and so on. We shall now apply our principle (6.1) to represent the difference between the requestive type and the advisive type. We then apply its corollary (6.2) to distinguish various subtypes under the requestive type.

Searle does not quite get the characterization of advisives right. Advising, recommending, and so on, is *like* telling you what is best for you (especially if the contrast is with requesting) but it is not telling you what is best for you. If it were, sentences like (6.3) would be semantically anomalous or contradictory.

(6.3) It is best for you to sell the car but I advise you not to because it would be unfair to George.

They are not, which shows that the grounds for advice, recommendations, and so on, is not always prudence. We want to represent the purpose of the act in advisives as something broader, such as making the recipient realize that the (future) course of action in question is the best of the available choices, leaving open whether the evaluation is prudential, moral, or something else.[19] We also want to represent the fact that, in advising, recommending, and so on, the agent expresses his or her belief that the recipient should perform the act in question, since sentences like (6.4) are not semantically anomalous.

(6.4) It is best that you explain your conduct but I'm not saying that you should do it (advising that you do it).

Together, these two semantic features provide plausible accounts of the meaning of typical examples like (6.5) and (6.6).

(6.5) I advise you to take off your hat here.
(6.6) I recommend that you not sell the car.

18. Searle, *Speech Acts*, p. 67. He seems to reverse himself in "A Taxonomy of Illocutionary Acts," p. 369, but this is a mistake.
19. Particular evaluations are specified by "if clauses" such as in "I advise you to dress better if you wish to get the job", "I advise you to keep less for yourself if you wish to distribute them fairly".

Therefore, we provide (6.7) as a hypothesis about the second major branch in the lexical reading for *Advisive* verbs.[20]

(6.7)

$$
\begin{array}{c}
((\text{Act})_{[\text{NP, S}]}) \\
(\text{X}) \\
\langle(\text{Sentient})\rangle \\
| \\
(\text{Purpose}) \\
| \\
(\text{Achievement})
\end{array}
$$

$$
\begin{array}{cc}
(\text{Effort}) & (\text{Success}) \\
| & | \\
(\text{Act}) & ((\text{Believes})_{[\text{NP, S, VP, S}]}) \\
& (\text{X}) \\
& \langle(\text{Sentient})\rangle
\end{array}
$$

$$
\begin{array}{cc}
((\text{Best Choice})_{[\text{VP, S, VP, S}]}) & ((\text{State})_{[\text{NP, S}]}) \\
\text{X} & (\text{X}) \\
\langle\ \rangle & \langle(\text{Sentient})\rangle \\
& | \\
& (\text{Nature}) \\
& | \\
& (\text{Psychological}) \\
& | \\
& ((\text{Believes})_{(\text{Should Do})[\text{NP, S, VP, S}] \ [\text{VP, S, VP, S}]}) \\
& (\text{X}) \quad , \quad \text{X} \\
& \langle(\text{Sentient})\rangle \quad \langle\ \rangle
\end{array}
$$

Advisive verbs like "warn" and "caution" in sentences like (6.8) and (6.9) have the same semantic structure except that they involve the notion that the agent is attempting to get the recipient to recognize some sort of danger in other choices.

(6.8)   I warn you not to stick your nose into other people's business.
(6.9)   I caution you against associating with total slobs.

20. As indicated earlier, repetition of a semantic marker like (Act) represents reference back to the same act. Note also that we make no mention of the agent's motive. This is because it may be almost anything; for example, one can advise, recommend, and so on, for the benefit of the recipient, for his or her detriment, for one's own benefit, for no reason at all, and so on.

The difference in meaning between warning (cautioning, and so on) people not to do something and advising them not to is that the former but not the latter specifies that the indicated choice is preferable to other choices because it poses least danger to the recipient. We may formally represent this aspect of the meaning of sentences like (6.8) and (6.9) by writing the lexical readings of verbs like "warn" or "caution" in the same form as (6.7) but with the semantic marker (6.10) or something similar attached directly under the semantic marker (Best Choice) in (6.7).

(6.10)   (Reason)
             |
((Dangerous to) [VP, S, VP, S] [NP, VP, S])
          A /   X   ,   (X)
               〈 〉   〈 〉

The "A/. . ." is the antonymy operator, so that the term that results from the substitution of a reading for the first categorized variable and the antonymy operation on this reading represents the notion that any choice is better than the one specified.

This sets up a subtype of *Advisives*, which we may refer to as *Negative Advisives*. It might also be possible to set up a complementary subtype of *Positive Advisives*. It is not unreasonable to suppose that a sentence like (6.6) specifies that the reason for indicating not selling the car as the best choice is that it offers more benefit to the addressee. But it is difficult to decide which semantic properties and relations of the examples provide the critical test of whether this supposition is true. That is, it is unclear whether (6.11) is contradictory.

(6.11) I recommend your not selling the car but, of course, you can expect no benefit from this course of action.

Thus, I will leave this question open.

These principles do not allow differences in the meaning of performative verbs concerning aspects of their semantic structure that would be represented in the first major branch of their lexical reading, or differences in the meaning of performative sentences concerning aspects of the semantic structure that would be represented in the readings of terms (that is, those that provide information about the agent, addressee, and so on), to be the basis of distinctions between subtypes under the various types in the class of performatives. This, I think, accords with our intuition. Generally, subtypes are distinguished by the same kind of considerations employed to distinguish the types themselves. Since performative types are distinguished from one another by differences in the purpose of communication, it is reasonable that their subtypes be distinguished by finer differences within each kind of purpose. But we do not suppose that subtypes proliferate each time there is an appropriate difference in meaning between two performative verbs of the same type. We do not think that the semantic differences among, say, "advise", "counsel", and "recommend", or between "warn" and "caution", whatever they are, ought to compel us to recognize new subtypes under *Advisives*. Nor is it necessary that the semantic differences that do not give rise to new subtypes all appear within the system of semantic roles. A further principle will be required to determine which kinds of information about purpose create new subtypes and which kinds merely create new performative verbs. But until we have carried our analyses of performative types and subtypes considerably further, we shall not see on what lines such a principle should be based.

We may define "advisive proposition" as in (6.12).

(6.12) A proposition P is *advisive* just in case P is performative and the propositional content of P has the form (6.7) except that the categorized variables are replaced by the appropriate values.[21]

Requestive propositions are built out of the meaning of performative verbs like "request", "beseech", "ask", "beg", "command", "bid", "order", "invite", "implore", "entreat", "instruct", "call on", "demand", "dare", and "challenge", and also out of the meaning of sentential structures like the imperative and interrogative forms. Clearly, there are nowhere nearly as many subtypes under *Requestive* as there are semantically distinct verbs and sentential structures associated with requestiveness.[22] We shall concern ourselves with two subtypes, *Erotetics* and *Provocatives*.

21. To say that the propositional content of P is of the form (6.7) allows for the occurrence of semantic markers like (6.10) as described above in connection with the meaning of "warn".

22. We might briefly consider nonsubtype differences between requestive performative verbs. These performative verbs are good examples of how features of the semantic roles determined by verbs can account for their semantic differences without introducing new subtypes. Accordingly, it is sometimes suggested that verbs like "order" and "command" contrast with verbs like "beg", "entreat", "implore", and so on, in that the former express the fact that the agent occupies a position of authority over the recipient, whereas the latter expresses the opposite relationship. Actually, the situation is somewhat more complicated, but not in ways that suggest the creation of further subtypes. The main deficiency of this overly simple view is that, whereas verbs like "order" and "command" contain the concept of an agent in a position of authority over the recipient, verbs like "beg" or "entreat" do not involve the concept of the agent's being under the authority of the recipient. Sen-

The verb "ask" exhibits an ambiguity that reflects the *Erotetic* subtype of requestive propositions. A sentence like (6.13) can mean either that she requested some action to be done, as in (6.14), or that she posed some question, as in (6.15).

(6.13) She asked.
(6.14) She asked, but he flatly refused to do it.
(6.15) She asked, and he answered her question.

In the former, "ask" is synonymous with "request something", whereas in the latter "ask" is synonymous with "ask a question". Since asking a question is requesting the answer to the question, that is, requesting that the recipient provide the information constituting an answer to the question, the sense of "ask" in (6.15) is of the requestive type, like the sense of "ask" in (6.14), but because the purpose in standard uses of the former sense (including uses of the interrogative sentential form) is considerably more specific than the purpose of requests generally, our corollary (6.2) dictates the introduction of an appropriate subtype of *Requestive*. This will be the *Erotetic Requestive*.

We can construct a reading for the erotetic sense of "ask" and the interrogative sentential form by elaborating the second major branch in (5.14). According to previous discussions of questions,[23] this elaboration will contain further semantic markers under the semantic markers (Achievement)–(Success) that represent the concept of the requestee's producing a true token of a sentence S that stands in the possible answer relation to the question Q asked (as determined by the semantic representation of the sentence that asks Q).[24] Therefore, the reading we wish to construct ought to have (6.16) as its second major branch.

---

tences like "I beg your forgiveness for doing it" or "He implored her not to wave farewell" make requests and state truths when the agent has authority over the recipient or when neither has authority over the other. The recipient's acknowledged right to withhold compliance seems to be confused with authority in such cases. This together with an element of urgent appeal for compliance might be all there is (beyond the concept of request) to the meaning of verbs like "beg". (We note that "plead" is probably not a performative because its sense contains the concept of the agent offering considerations to show that the request ought to be granted.) Thus, the differences between these verbs provide no basis for subtypes: the notions of authority (the power to compel compliance) and of urgency have to do with the bringing about of compliance, not with features of the purpose fulfilled in compliance.

23. See J. J. Katz, *Semantic Theory* (New York: Harper & Row, 1972), chap. 5. The relation "S is a possible answer to the question Q" is formalized there.

24. Although we use the notion of a sentence here, the proper notion is that of the reading that PRAG assigns as the utterance meaning of the token.

(6.16)

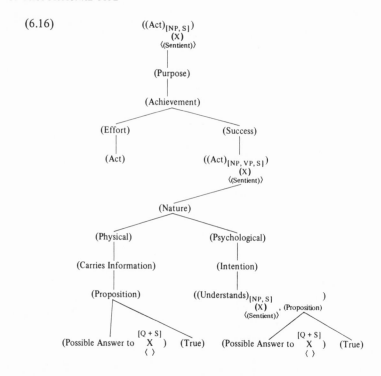

The categorizing grammatical functions in (6.16) are written as if (6.16) were the lexical reading for "ask" because we do not wish to take any stand on the issue of how to syntactically represent the interrogative form. The expression Q + S is thus an abbreviation of the grammatical function that picks out the interrogative constituent, for example, the italicized constituent in the sentence (6.17).

(6.17) I ask you *who told the police about our plot.*

Before turning to *Provocatives*, it will be worthwhile considering the connection between this account of erotetic propositions in the framework of our theory of performativeness and our previous treatment of the logical structure of questions.[25] On the structural definition of the notion "P is the presupposition

25. Katz, *Semantic Theory*, pp. 201–232.

of the question Q" in *Semantic Theory*,[26] the presuppositions of (6.18), (6.19), and (6.20) are, respectively, the truth of the statements (6.21), (6.22), and (6.23).

    (6.18)   Who killed Cock Robin?

    (6.19)   What hit the fan?

    (6.20)   When did you stop beating your wife?

    (6.21)   Someone killed Cock Robin.

    (6.22)   Something hit the fan.

    (6.23)   You beat your wife at some (earlier) time.

The question arises, what interpretation to place on such conditions. What logical property of the question depends directly on its presupposition *in this sense*? One answer is that it is *the property of succeeding in making a request for information*, and another is that it is *the property of making a request for information that can be complied with*. In the case of the first alternative, the structural definition of such presuppositions would be included in the illocutionary success conditions for interrogative sentences, whereas in the second, we would add an interpretive definition to the effect that such presuppositions are conditions under which the compliance condition for a request can, in principle, be satisfied. Choosing the first makes the truth of (6.21)-(6.23), respectively, the condition under which (6.18)-(6.20) can be used to make a request for information. Choosing the second makes the truth of (6.21)-(6.23), respectively, the condition for there to be an answer, that is, a true possible answer, to (6.18)-(6.20).

Our previous treatment of the logic of questions opted for the first of these alternatives,[27] but the theory of performativeness in this book repudiates this earlier choice and commits us to the second. This is because our characterization of the notion of illocutionary success conditions makes the truth of propositions like (6.21)-(6.23) irrelevant to whether interrogatives like (6.18)-(6.20) can perform the illocutionary act of asking a question. All that is required for a sentence expressing an erotetic proposition to satisfy (5.33) is that its referring terms designate appropriately and that its unconverted condition be satisfied by these designata. Now, the reading of an erotetic proposition has the form of a marker whose first major branch is the same as that in (5.14) and whose second major branch is that in (6.16). Hence, the first clause of (5.33) requires that there be an agent (a questioner) and an addressee, and the second clause requires that the use of the sentence be an act of communication whose

26. Ibid., pp. 210–211.

27. Ibid., p. 210.

purpose is to bring about another communication in which the addressee produces a token of a sentence that is a true possible answer to the original question. Therefore, nothing in our condition for illocutionary success requires the satisfaction of presuppositions like (6.21)–(6.23). The truth of (6.21), or even that Cock Robin is dead, has nothing to do with whether someone succeeds in requesting information in uttering a token of the interrogative (6.18).

That our theory of performativeness is correct in preferring the second alternative can be seen from the following. Consider the classic case in which such presupposition fails, namely, (6.20). You are on trial and the prosecution lawyer directs a token of (6.20) to you on the witness stand. You, of course, reply by denying the truth of the presupposition (6.23). But in so doing you do not establish that the lawyer failed to ask a question. Rather, you acknowledge that the lawyer asked a question but imply that he or she asked a *loaded* one. Fleshed out, your reply is that you have been put into a double bind: the question is a request for an answer, namely, a *true* possible answer, but because you never beat your wife, every possible answer to the question is false, and you cannot, in principle, comply with the request to provide a *true* sentence that is a possible answer.

The definition (5.39) of "compliance condition" already implies that a necessary condition for compliance is the truth of the presupposition in this sense. As requestive propositions requesting a true possible answer, cases like (6.18)–(6.20) can be complied with only if the requestee produces a true possible answer. But if the requestee does produce one, then every necessary condition for doing so must be satisfied, and in particular, the presupposition in this sense must be, since the existence of a true possible answer entails the truth of such presuppositions.

Actually, the situation is in no way unique to *Erotetics*. What we have just said applies equally well to the use of nonerotetic requestives like (6.24).

(6.24)   I request that you stop beating your wife.

Given their reading and (5.39), one of the conditions necessary for compliance will be (6.23). If this condition is not met, it will be impossible to satisfy the compliance condition for the request made in the use of (6.24). Therefore, presuppositions in the sense of (6.21)–(6.23) are better thought of as clauses of the compliance condition associated with a proposition, rather than as presuppositions in the sense of (2.60)–(2.61).

These considerations eliminate an argument formerly used to justify a presuppositional account of propositional structure.[28] Geach claimed that Russell's

28. As indicated at the beginning of our discussion of presupposition, the loss of this argument is not significant. For the earlier use of it, see Ibid., pp. 33–34.

account of propositional structure commits the fallacy of "many questions".[29]
According to Geach, the prior question of whether the addressee had been
beating his wife is involved in (6.20), so that the act of asking (6.20) presupposes
an affirmative answer to this prior question, in the sense that the question (6.20)
"does not arise" if the answer to the prior question is negative. But, as we have
seen above, the question does arise, at least in what seems to be the sense Geach
intended, namely, that the act of asking a question by the use of (6.20) succeeds.
Geach also says that when a question does not arise, an affirmative answer or
negative answer "though grammatically and logically possible, is *out of place"*.
But such a property of a possible answer is independent of whether an affirmative answer to the prior question is presupposed in asking the question. A judge,
for example, may rule the lawyer's question "out of place", that is, a question
that the defendant does not have to answer, without at all denying that there
was a question asked. Indeed, there has to be a question for there to be something that is out of place. Now, the counterpart of successfully using an interrogative sentence to ask a question is successfully using a declarative to make
a statement, and therefore, if the failure of such presuppositions is not a condition under which the interrogative fails to ask a question, in declaratives the failure of such a presupposition ought not to be a condition under which the
declarative fails to make a statement.

Nonetheless, it seems reasonable to say that Geach was making an important
observation in distinguishing the prior question of whether the addressee had
been beating his wife. The claim I wish to make is that this observation is not
about presupposition in the sense of this notion that develops out of a rational
reconstruction of Frege's original ideas. Thus, it might be best to distinguish a
new semantic relation, that of a question having a prior question. We can say
that when the prior question cannot be answered affirmatively, the question to
which it is prior is "out of place". Hence, we can say that (6.20) does not
presuppose that John beat his wife, but asserts it in the way that asking whether
something melted asserts it was solid or in the way· that asking did John run
fast asserts that John ran. There is no need to take the affirmative answer of
the prior question as a presupposition. Predications stack up and we can explicate the notion of a prior question in terms of the ordering relation in a series
of stacked predications. Such an explication accounts for the real intuition
speakers have that questions like (6.20) do involve prior questions.

The subtype *Provocatives* are propositions that express requests for someone
to try something in order to show that they can do it. The meaning of "dare" in
(6.25) comes very close to such an expression.

29. P. Geach, "Russell's Theory of Descriptions," *Philosophy and Analysis*, ed. M. Mac-
Donald (New York: Philosophical Library, 1954), pp. 32–36.

(6.25)   I dare you to eat everything there is on your plate.

Its lexical sense can be represented by a reading such as (6.26).[30]

(6.26)

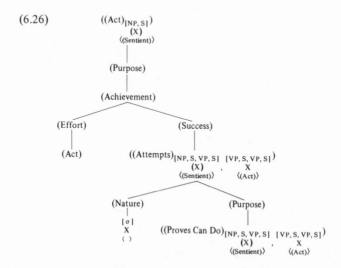

Thus, we can define the subtypes *Erotetic* and *Provocative* as in (6.27) and (6.28):

(6.27)   A proposition P is *erotetic* just in case P is requestive and the propositional content of P has the form (6.16) except that the categorized variables are replaced by their appropriate values.

(6.28)   A proposition P is *provocative* just in case P is requestive and the propositional content of P has the form of (6.26) except that the categorized variables are replaced by their appropriate values.

The verb "dare", as suggested by the meaning of the nominalized form "daring", may be more specific semantically than indicated in (6.26) because it

30. The occurrence of the categorized variable in (6.26) with the categorization indicated by σ is intended to create the position at which a reading representing the nature of the attempt appears. The function σ, which has been left unspecified, will express the principle that the nature of an attempt to perform an act is the same as the nature of the act attempted (for example, if what is attempted is physical, like jumping over a chair, then the nature of the attempt is also physical). A specification of σ would, accordingly, pick out the semantic markers that represent the nature of the act in the reading of the complement sentence [of cases like (6.25) and (6.30)].

involves the notion of a demonstration of courage on the part of the recipient of the dare. We could handle this lexical fact by a further branch of the form (6.29) added to a semantic marker of the form (6.26) under the semantic marker describing the success (as a third branch).

(6.29)

$$\diagdown$$

(Goal)

$$|$$

$$((\text{Establishes Courage})_{[\text{NP, S, VP, S}]})$$
$$(\text{X})$$
$$\langle(\text{Sentient})\rangle$$

The semantic marker (Goal) describes what goal is attained when an act achieves its purpose. Thus, in a sentence like (6.30), the purpose, bringing about an attempt to stay in the ring, has the goal of demonstrating the courage of the recipient.

(6.30) I dare you to stay in the boxing ring with someone your size.

The goal is, as it were, the recipient's purpose in making the attempt.

Let us make one final point about *Provocatives* before turning to the third performative type that we shall consider. In our account of *Provocatives*, their purpose is to get the requestee to attempt to do something. It seems reasonable, for a sentence like (6.25), to say that the compliance condition is satisfied if the recipient tries to eat everything on the plate. If the recipient fails to finish the food, it seems wrong to say that he or she did not take the dare. This treatment is further supported by the fact that utterances like "I dare you to try it" and "I dare you to do it" do not differ in meaning (in the way that "I tried it" and "I did it" do). Note that this will require us to have a stronger selection restriction than $\langle(\text{Act})\rangle$ on the categorized variable $\overset{[\text{VP, S, VP, S}]}{\underset{\langle(\text{Act})\rangle}{\text{X}}}$ in (6.26) and other lexical readings for *Provocative verbs*, since we do not want readings for acts of trying to appear as their value. What we want, in fact, is the part of the reading of the constituent [VP, S, VP, S] that specifies the goal of the act, in the sense discussed in connection with (5.23). The trouble is, as pointed out then, that the definition of this notion is uncompleted. Thus, the further specification of this selection restriction will have to wait until this definition can be completed.

Expressives are conveyed by explicit performative sentences like (6.31).

(6.31)   (i)   I thank you for giving me such a nice present.
         (ii)   I congratulate you on your win in the chess match.
         (iii) I apologize to you for missing our appointment.

These performative propositions are defined in terms of the purpose of making the recipient aware (causing the recipient to realize) that the agent feels a certain way about something the recipient has done (or played a role in the doing of or is affected by) and attaining the goal of adequately compensating the recipient for the debt consequently incurred. The aspect of this notion of expressive propositions that requires explanation is its construal of the event about which the agent communicates his or her feelings as something that makes the agent subject to a debt of some sort. The case of apologies is clearest. I miss an appointment with Sally. Contrite at having done her this harm, I try to make amends by apology, uttering (6.31)(iii). In performing this illocutionary act of apologizing, I am paying the debt incurred by standing her up. In saying, "It's O.K." or some such thing, she is indicating that this act is sufficient compensation for the harm done. (Note that this judgment is not a matter of her estimation, since she might wrongly accept my apology or wrongly refuse to accept.) Compensation also seems to be the basis for thanking. I go to the store for you, which is some trouble for me and saves you valuable time. You say "thanks" and then I say "You are welcome". Again, it seems clear that I am indicating to you that sufficient compensation has been made by your performing this speech act of thanking me: I consider your debt to me, incurred by my taking the time and trouble to go to the store for you, to be paid. Note that "Don't mention it" can be a way of indicating that the debt is too small to bother about.

Congratulations, although somewhat more subtle, are also compensation or cancellation of a debt. You do something fantastic, say you win the Nobel Prize or you break a sports record. This, I submit, creates a debt on the part of some people to provide you deserved praise. If I am one of these people (your parent, friend, colleague, and so on) and congratulate you for your achievement, I am paying my portion of the generalized debt owed you. When you say "thanks" or some such thing in response to my congratulations, you thereby indicate to me that my act of congratulating you compensates adequately for this debt. Note that the ritualistic use of the expression "It was nothing" is often like saying "It was not enough of an achievement to warrant such compensation". Also, note that the mechanism of "damning with faint praise" depends on the debt/payment relation, since it is the use of "underpayment" to indicate that the actual value of the achievement is well below what the debt has been taken to be.

This type differs from the previous two types in that no single lexical item conveys the pure form of expressive propositions in the way that "request" conveys the pure form of *Requestives* and "advise" the pure form of *Advisives*. There seems to be a gap in the language in connection with *Expressives*: there is no syntactic device in English for performing an illocutionary act of compensating someone by making him or her aware that one has a certain feeling. There might be such a verb, just as there might be (but, in fact, there isn't) a verbal counterpart of "to starve" meaning "to die of thirst". Hence, the formal structure that defines the type *Expressive*, (6.32), is not the lexical reading of any performative verb in current English.

(6.32)

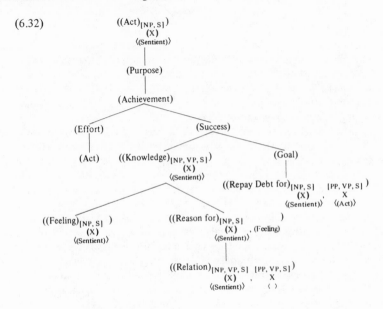

This, of course, does not prevent us from introducing the definition (6.33).

(6.33) A proposition *P* is *expressive* just in case *P* is performative and the propositional content of *P* has the form (6.32) except that the categorized variables are replaced by their values.

The lexical readings for the performative verbs "thank", "congratulate", or "apologize" (in this case the categorization of the variable associated with

(Knowledge) in (6.32) has to be [NP, PP, VP, S]), can be written as expansions of (6.32): (6.34)(i) is attached under the semantic marker representing the fact that the agent's having a feeling is one aspect of the knowledge the act imparts; (6.34)(ii) is attached under the semantic marker representing the relation that further specifies the reason for the agent's feeling.

$$(6.34) \quad \text{(i)} \quad \text{(Appreciation)}$$

$$\text{(ii)} \quad ((\text{Benefits})_{[\text{PP}, \text{VP}, \text{S}]} \quad [\text{NP}, \text{S}])$$
$$X \quad , \quad (X)$$
$$\langle \ \rangle \quad \langle(\text{Sentient})\rangle$$

Two things should be noted here. (6.34)(i) must be attached under each occurrence of (Feeling) in (6.32), and the two occurrences of the variable categorized with the function [PP, VP, S] in the lexical reading for "thank" must take the same value; hence, by the coincidence convention (5.15), these readings refer to the same act. For example, in the case of (6.31)(i), it is the past act of the recipient giving the agent a nice present.

The lexical readings for "congratulate" and "apologize" overlap with that of "thank" with respect to the structure marking them as *Expressives*, namely, (6.32), but differ from that of "thank" and from one another with respect to the semantic markers that represent the kind of feeling the agent seeks to communicate and the reason for that feeling. In the case of "congratuate", the feeling would appear to be some form of admiration or approval and the reason some accomplishment of the recipient's. Some standard reference dictionaries suggest that the feeling might be pleasure or happiness and the reason might be the recipient's good fortune, but this is doubtful. There seems to be something odd about *congratulating* someone for winning a million in a chance lottery but no such oddity about congratulating a Nobel Prize winner. Some of these dictionaries suggest also that congratulating is wishing happiness, but this seems wrong, too, since (6.35) is clearly nondeviant.

(6.35) I wish you a lot of happiness with your lottery winnings but there is nothing to congratulate you for.

The feeling in the case of "apologize" is regret and the reason is the agent's role in some event that has proven (or will prove) to be harmful to the recipient (either directly or indirectly). Note, further, that the act referred to in specifying the reason in both "thank" and "apologize" will be represented as past relative to the speech point of the sentence, for example, (6.31)(i) and (6.31)(iii), whereas in "congratulate" this may not be so. The question at issue is whether one can congratulate someone for something, say, winning an election, that has not occurred yet (but is virtually certain to occur), or whether such "congratulations" take effect only when the event does occur. Another question that we leave open is whether there is a division under the category *Expressives* similar to the positive/negative division under *Advisives*. One might claim that "thank" and "congratulate" involve positive emotions, whereas "apologize" and, say, "offer condolences" (the feeling is sympathy and the reason is the grief the recipient is suffering over some event) involve negative emotions. A slightly different distinction might be made between whether the expression of feeling is about something that is good for the recipient or something bad. We leave all these questions for further study.

We have now elaborated three types in our taxonomy of performatives, *Requestives*, *Advisives*, and *Expressives*. In the remainder of this section, we shall consider four more, *Permissives*, *Obligatives*, *Expositives*, and *Stipulatives*. In the category of *Permissives*, we find senses of explicit performative sentences with main verbs like "permit", "authorize", "allow", "grant", and so on. The definition of this performative type will be in terms of the illocutionary act's having the purpose of freeing the recipient from blame and/or penalty possibly associated with an act by virtue of the agent's assuming responsibility for that act's taking place. The notion of "blame and/or penalty associated with an act" is intended to carry the following interpretation. If I use (6.36) to give you permission to use my car, I am not thereby absolving you from blame or penalty for driving recklessly, or under the influence of alcohol, or running down school children, only for whatever blame or penalty might otherwise be associated with your using it that day, for example, the moral censure for depriving me of its use, the legal penalty for theft, and so on.

(6.36) I give you permission to use my car today.

I do not know how to explicate this notion of associated blame and/or penalty, but it seems clear that there is an intuitively clear notion to work with.

The analysis of purpose in this case cannot assume the form it took earlier where the agent's communicative act plays a causal role in achieving the purpose of the act. With *Permissives* (and *Obligatives*, too), there is nothing causal in the fulfillment of the purpose. Rather, its fulfillment is brought about in the performance of the communicative act when the conditions under which the performance occurs are appropriate (that is, when the agent has the proper authority to grant such permission). Moreover, the license granted to the recipient imposes no pressure on him or her to exercise it. Unlike being requested to use the car or advised to do so, the recipient is under no constraint or influence to exercise the new option. We may thus represent the lexical reading for "permit" as in (6.37), and we may define the permissive type as (6.38).[31]

(6.37)

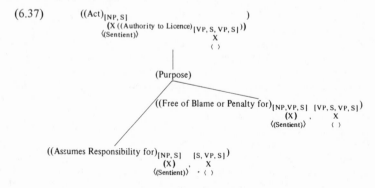

(6.38) A proposition *P* is *permissive* just in case *P* is performative and the propositional content of *P* has the form (6.37) except that the categorized variables are replaced by their values.

In the category *Obligatives* are the senses of explicit performative sentences with main verbs like "promise", "vow", "swear", "pledge", "resolve", "guarantee", and so on. The lexical reading for "promise" and the definition of this type can be given, following Searle's treatment of promising,[32] in terms of a purpose of the agent undertaking the obligation to perform the future act, that is, (6.39) and (6.40).

(6.39) $((Act)_{[NP, S]}$)
                    (X)
                ⟨(Sentient)⟩

                    |

                (Purpose)

                    |

        $((Assumes\ Responsibility\ for)_{[NP, S]}$ $[S, VP, S]}$)
                        (X)   ,   X
                    ⟨(Sentient)⟩   ( )

---

31. It is probably worth mentioning here that "prohibit" and "forbid" are not *Permissives* but (negative) *Requestives*. "Forbid" means, roughly, "order not to". "Prohibit" seems to differ only in that it involves a notion of institutional authority with jurisdiction over the class of acts in question (thus it might be closer to "command not to"). Clearly, neither means "withhold permission from". It should also be observed that the agent may be acting as a proxy in assuming responsibility for the recipient's act.

32. Searle, *Speech Acts*, pp. 57–61.

(6.40) A proposition P is *Obligative* just in case P is performative and the propositional content of P has the form (6.39) except that the categorized variables are replaced by their values.

This treatment relates verbs like "permit", "allow", and so on, and verbs like "promise", "vow", and so on, plausibly without implying a stronger connection than exists, that is, the illocutionary act of promising, unlike that of permitting, does not free the recipient from an obligation to do the act but only obligates someone else. For example, my promise to pay the rent for you does not free you from the obligation to pay it, whereas permission to skip the rent does.

We treat the senses of explicit performative sentences with main verbs like "bet", "wager", and "offer" as a subtype, *Proposive*, of *Obligatives* rather than as requiring an independent performative type. They may be so treated because their purpose is the assumption of responsibility for some future act(s) contingent on the recipient's agreeing to assume responsibility for some related future act(s) (or simply agreeing that the agent should assume such responsibility). Thus, if I say (6.41), your response of "You're on" or something of the kind is sufficient for me to undertake the obligation to pay you five dollars in the event that he does call.

(6.41) I bet you five dollars that he doesn't call.

After you have said something constituting an expression of your acceptance of the proposal, the options are exactly those of a conditional promise, such as would be made in a normal use of (6.42).

(6.42) I promise to come over if you call to remind me.

The relation between *Proposives* and conditional *Obligatives* generally can be seen from the virtual synonymy of sentences like (6.41) and (6.43).

(6.43) I promise to pay you five dollars if he calls providing you agree to pay me five dollars if he does not.

Another indication of this relation is that the verb "welch" is the specialized term for reneging on a promise where the promise is to fulfill the obligations of a bet.

On this treatment of performative verbs like "bet", "offer", "wager", and so on, acts of betting, offering, or wagering are not, strictly speaking, illocutionary acts, but the joint product of the illocutionary act of one person's making a conditional promise and the illocutionary act of another person's making the complementary promise.

Under *Expositives* are the propositions expressed by explicit performative sentences with main verbs like "declare", "claim", "insist", "state", "affirm", and "concede". The definition of this type is formulated in terms of the purpose of putting the agent on record as endorsing that something is the case. In connection with sentences having "declare", "claim", and so on, as their main verb, the agent goes on record as holding that the state of affairs described in the complement sentence is the case, whereas in connection with sentences having "deny", the agent goes on record as holding that some incompatible state of affairs is the case. Thus, we might represent the lexical reading of a verb like "declare" as (6.44) and define the expositive type as (6.45).

(6.44)

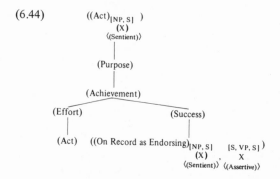

(6.45) A proposition *P* is *Expositive* just in case *P* is performative and the propositional content of *P* has the form (6.44) except that the categorized variables are replaced by their values.

The negative verb "deny" can be represented with a reading of the form (6.44) where the categorized variable $\underset{\langle\ \rangle}{\overset{[S, VP, S]}{X}}$ is in the scope of an occurrence of the antonymy operator.

It is interesting to compare this treatment of verbs like "declare", "claim", and so on, with the treatment we would give for "lie". What emerges is a new and better explanation than Vendler's of why "lie" is nonperformative.[33]

---

33. I thank George Smith for this suggestion.

Vendler says:

> I cannot say "I lie. . ." and be lying. For, to repeat, by saying "I lie. . ." I would cancel the claim for belief, which, again, is essential to lying.[34]

Vendler's explanation may be a good explanation of why sentences like "I allege that Jones did it" fail to make an allegation, but it cannot explain why the use of "lie" fails to perform an illocutionary act of lying. For his explanation presupposes that the speaker utters an appropriate sentence, something of the form "I lie. . ." but commits "illocutionary suicide" in so doing. But, in fact, there is no such meaningful sentence. That is, there is no way to fill in the blank in Vendler's formula "I lie. . .". Sentences like "I lie that Jones did it" are semantically anomalous. Hence, some new explanation is required. Ours will have the double advantage of explaining why "lie" is not a performative on the grounds that sentences that result from filling the blank in "I lie. . ." are semantically anomalous.

Given the generally accepted meaning of "lie" and the framework for representing the sense of action verbs, the lexical reading for "lie" would be something like (6.46).

(6.46)

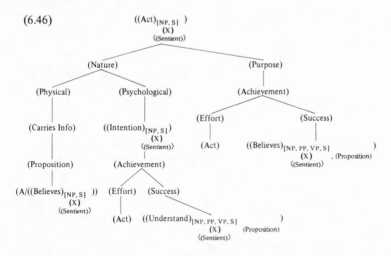

If this is a reasonably accurate account of the meaning of "lie", it follows that "lie" is not a performative because (6.46) fails the condition (5.41)(i) in just the

34. Vendler, *Res Cogitans*, p. 208.

way that (5.110) does, *viz.*, by containing a semantic marker in its first branch that is not in the first branch of (5.14).

The last performative type I shall consider are the *Stipulatives*. These propositions are the senses of explicit performative sentences with main verbs like "name", "baptize", "dub", "christen", and "call". The definition we give for this type is in terms of the purpose of affixing a name to the recipient to make the recipient the bearer of that name. The question arises whether this type is too narrowly defined. Searle, as we have seen, proposed the class of *Declarations*, which includes naming, baptizing, dubbing, and presumably the other illocutionary acts described in what we are calling stipulative propositions, but also firing, resigning, nominating, marrying a couple, declaring war, finding someone guilty, and so forth.[35] We have chosen to risk narrowness rather than follow Searle because his characterization of *Declarations* is so broad it is hard to see how it can exclude anything. Searle's characterization is:

> Declarations bring about some alteration in the status or condition of the referred to object or objects solely in virtue of the fact that the declaration has been successfully performed.[36]

Thus, firing someone is a declaration because the status of his or her employment is altered by virtue of the illocutionary act. But, then, aren't promising, permitting, apologizing, daring, claiming, and so forth, also *Declarations*, insofar as in promising my condition is altered because I am under an obligation, in permitting the condition of both the agent and the recipient is altered by the fact that the former has gained a responsibility and the latter a license, in apologizing the condition of the agent is altered because he or she no longer owes this expression of regret, in daring the condition of the recipient is altered because he or she is now faced with a challenge, and in claiming the condition of the agent is altered because he or she is on record as endorsing the proposition? It may be that something can be done about this slippery slope, but, unable to see how to do it while preserving the cases Searle includes as *Declarations*, I have chosen to follow the safer course.

We shall treat stipulatives as cases in which the illocutionary act brings it about that the recipient bears the name. We distinguish between someone thinking up a name for someone, or first calling someone by a particular name, on the one hand, and someone *naming* them, on the other. Even in cases where one of the former acts is responsible for initiating a practice culminating in the person bearing the name, we make this distinction. The ability to confer a name

35. Searle, "A Taxonomy of Illocutionary Acts", pp. 358–360.
36. Ibid., p. 358.

in a particular act seems to lie in the position of the agent, that is, whether or not the agent has the proper position of authority in the circumstances. In this respect, *Stipulatives* are like *Permissives*. We suggest (6.47) as the lexical reading of "name" and in terms of it we propose the definition (6.48) for the *Stipulative* type, where the subscripts with the symbol NP are simply a way of covering our ignorance about the nature of the grammatical relations of the noun phrases NP_1 and NP_2 in sentences of the form "I name you (= NP_1) John (= NP_2)".

(6.47) $((Act)_{[NP, S]}$ $)$
                $(X$ $((Authority\ to\ Name)_{[NP_2, VP, S]}))$
                $\langle(Sentient)\rangle$ X
                                                                      $(\ )$

                                          |

                                 $(Purpose)$

                                          |

                    $((Confers\ on)_{[NP_1, VP, S]}\ [NP_2, VP, S]})$
                              (X) X
                              $(\ )$ $(\ )$

(6.48)   A proposition P is *stipulative* in case P is performative and the propositional content of P has the form (6.47) except that the categorized variables are replaced by their appropriate values.

No particular selection restriction is indicated for the categorized variables marking the positions for readings of the name and the thing named. It is not clear either what things are nameable or what things can count as names.[37]

We said we would not offer a complete classification of performative types, and we have been true to our word. But suppose that we had. We would then have a principled basis for enumerating every performative type and every sub-type under each type. We could classify each performative proposition, each performative sense of each sentence of the language, under some type and possibly under some subtype. What, then, about the project that Austin, Searle, and others undertook? How would we stand with respect to the project of classifying illocutionary *acts*? I wish to claim that we would have accomplished it, too.

Each distinct illocutionary act corresponds to a distinct utterance meaning of the use of a performative sentence in the null context. The performative type and subtype of an illocutionary act is that of the utterance meaning to which it corresponds. This is so because the act, which is a sequence of muscular contractions producing an acoustic disturbance in the air, obtains its semantic properties

37. For a discussion of some of the issues concerning a theory of names from the perspective of semantic theory, see J. J. Katz, "A Proper Theory of Names," *Philosophical Studies* (in press).

from the utterance meaning to which it is assigned when it communicates the speaker's message to the listeners. A complete classification of performative propositions would be a complete classification of the illocutionary acts that can be performed in the null context. Now, consider an illocutionary act in a non-null context. The act is performed by the use of some sentence S, but the proposition P expressed by S does not determine the character of the illocution. Its type, subtype, and other features of its linguistic interpretation are determined on the basis of another proposition, P', which is assigned as the utterance meaning of this use of S. P' is the proposition that speakers of the language assign as the proper semantic interpretation of the utterance by virtue of their knowledge of pragmatic principles.[38] Since the structure of P' determines the illocutionary character of this use of S and since P' is *ex hypothesi* fully treated in our classification of performative propositions, a complete classification of performative propositions is also a complete classification of illocutionary acts.

Therefore, the orientation of our study of illocutionary force does not abandon the old goals of linguistic philosophy. It rather pursues them by new and more purely linguistic means.

PHILOSOPHICAL
IMPLICATIONS

In the first chapter of this book, we conjectured that speech act theory as handed down by Austin and more explicitly formulated by Searle does not constitute an autonomous theory. We claimed that it has the status of a hybrid, a grafting of semantics onto pragmatics. We argued that such a heterogeneous composition ought to be "reduced away" in favor of a grammatical theory of the compositional meaning of sentence types, on the one hand, and a pragmatic theory of the contextual meaning of their tokens, on the other. By way of establishing initial plausibility for such a reduction, we pointed out that Searle's rules for the use of illocutionary force-indicating devices divide, exhaustively, into rules about the grammatical meaning of syntactic structures and rules about use. We conjectured that the former are simply semantic rules of the kind already available in semantic theory or rules that can be formulated on the basis of natural extensions of existing apparatus in semantic theory, and that the latter are essentially Gricean principles,[39] principles that explicate the general reasoning

38. See the discussion of pragmatic theory in Chapter 1.

39. H. P. Grice, "Logic and Conversation," in *Syntax and Semantics*, vol. 3, ed. P. Cole and J. L. Morgan (New York: Academic Press, 1975), pp. 41–58. It is worth making the point here that Gricean principles, as set out by Grice, do not take the form of a performance theory but that I imagine them extended and given a different formulation. (Grice's formu-

that speakers and hearers go through to utilize extragrammatical information to mean something different by the utterance of a sentence than it (literally) means in the language. Finally, we conjectured also that the main obstacle to the semantic representation of illocutionary force is the failure of speech act theorists to draw a sharp competence/performance distinction to separate questions of semantics from pragmatics.

Therefore, we set the goals for our study in terms of such a distinction. We fixed the boundary between semantics and pragmatics in the same way that the boundary between grammar and use is fixed at the phonological and syntactic levels, namely, by taking grammatical rules (here semantic rules) to comprise the idealized speaker-hearer's perfect knowledge of the language and taking performance principles to comprise part of their ability to exercise this knowledge of grammatical rules and performance principles in real speech situations. Within this framework, we could pursue the study of the illocutionary force of sentences independently of considerations of the practical reasoning that exploits features of the speech context to accord the utterance of a sentence a different meaning in the context from what it has in the language.

In the chapters that followed, we developed a theory of the illocutionary potential of sentences strictly within the framework of the study of formal grammatical structure. The principal question we dealt with was whether a natural extension of already existing grammatical apparatus, particularly, semantic apparatus, can provide the necessary formal machinery for a revealing account of illocutionary potential. I think these chapters show that semantic theory can be naturally extended so as to provide a homogeneous grammatical theory that does account for the illocutionary potential of sentences.

Here, then, we may turn to the question of what some of the advantages are in dispensing with speech act theory in favor of such a grammatical theory. One, which follows directly from the conjectures with which we began, is that we thereby obtain a uniform view of the relation between the structure of language and the use of language. The same view of the role of phonological and syntactic competence in models of speech production and recognition can be taken about the role of semantic competence: the grammar supplies the information about the structure of sentences while the performance theory provides a real-time model showing how sentence structure and contextual factors enable speakers to assign sentence tokens to grammatical types. Speech act theory insists on a radi-

---

lations too much reflect his controversy with philosophers of logic like Strawson, that is, his attempt to meet their objections to the use of formal devices from logic as accounts of the logical properties of their counterparts in natural languages. Grice formulates a theory of the different kinds of implication to show that these objections are based on the wrong kind.)

cal disparity between the role of phonological and syntactic competence, on the one hand, and semantic competence, on the other.[40]

Another advantage is that we are no longer forced to treat linguistic facts of the same kind as different. For example, linguistic facts like those mentioned in connection with (1.36)–(1.46) are, in Searle's speech act theory, treated one way in connection with constative sentences and another way in connection with performatives: the condition of undertaking an obligation is admitted to derive from the meaning of "promise" in sentences describing or reporting someone's act of promising but is denied this status in explicit performative sentences expressing an obligative proposition.

On the other hand, we are no longer forced to treat essentially different linguistic facts as facts of the same kind. If we compare the kind of information in semantic representations on our account with the kind that Searle expresses in his speech act rules for the use of the illocutionary force indication devices associated with requesting, promising, stating, questioning, and so on,[41] we find that, except for minor disagreements about details, the following strong generalizations hold: Searle's propositional content and essential rules expressed the kind of information that falls properly within the grammar's representation of the lexical meaning of performative verbs and other syntactic devices for indicating illocutionary force, whereas his preparatory and sincerity rules express essentially different information, that is, facts and guidelines that speakers use in working out utterance meanings on the basis of assumptions about each other's beliefs and intentions. To put the point another way, on speech act theory, the basis on which sentences (6.49)–(6.51) perform, respectively, the acts of requesting the removal of the log, promising to be there, and requesting the window to be closed, is the same as that on which (6.52)–(6.54) perform these acts.

(6.49) Can you take this heavy log off my foot?
(6.50) I will be there on time.
(6.51) The window is wide open and flies are getting in.
(6.52) I request that you remove this heavy log from my foot.
(6.53) I promise that I will be there on time.
(6.54) I request that you close the window.

---

40. J. Searle, "Chomsky's Revolution in Linguistics," in *On Noam Chomsky*, ed. C. Harman (New York: Anchor Books, 1974), pp. 28–29. Note, however, that Searle has recently taken the further step of claiming that syntax, too, is not a formal system, but contains rules of use. See J. Searle, "The Rules of the Language Game," *Times Literary Supplement*, 10 September 1976, p. 1119.

41. Searle, *Speech Acts*, pp. 67–68.

There would, of course, be differences in degree of complexity. The construal of (6.51) as a request might be explained by assuming the speaker uses a two-stage reasoning process in which the utterance of (6.51) is first analyzed as a statement about the window and then reanalyzed as a request because the statement cannot be made to square with features of the context, but, in general, speech act theory has to account for the meaning of the utterance at each stage strictly within the same framework of rules for the use of illocutionary force-indicating devices.[42] Outside the framework of speech act theory, the explanation of a use of (6.54) to make a request to close a window is different *in kind* from the explanation of a use of (6.51) to make this request: the former appeals only to the sound-meaning correlation in the language, whereas the latter appeals also to pragmatic principles and to information about the particular situation where the use occurs. Such an approach offers a far neater distinction between the two explanatory paradigms, and one that coincides with Grice's distinction between what is directly implicated by the conventional meanings of words and what is implicated by the conversational maxims and the situational facts in conjunction with conventional meaning.[43] Searle's position is, as it were, the other extreme of that taken by Gordon and Lakoff.[44] As Bever and I argued,[45] Gordon and Lakoff hold a *grammatical monism* on which every linguistic fact is a grammatical fact, so that the explanation of performance facts, like the occasional use of (6.51) to perform the same speech act (6.54) standardly performs, is given on the basis of "conversational postulates" *in the grammar*, just as the explanation that (6.52) and (6.54) both make requests might be given on the basis of "meaning postulates" in the grammar. Searle, at the other extreme, holds a kind of *contextual monism* on which every semantic fact about illocutionary force is a contextual fact, so that the explanation of competence facts, for example, that (6.52) and (6.54) both standardly make requests, is given on the basis of extragrammatical rules of use, just as the explanation of the fact

42. Recently, Searle has proposed such a multiple-stage account of these cases in J. Searle, "Indirect Speech Acts," *Syntax and Semantics: Speech Acts*, pp. 59–82. This proposal follows the proposal Bever and I made, also in reply to Gordon and Lakoff ("Conversational Postulates", *Papers from the Seventh Regional Meeting of the Chicago Linguistics Society*, University of Chicago, 1971, pp. 63–84), in "The Fall and Rise of Empiricism," Indiana University Linguistic Club, February 1974, published in *An Integrated Theory of Linguistic Ability* (New York: Thomas Y. Crowell, 1976), pp. 53–57. It should be pointed out that, although Searle uses expressions like "literal meaning" and "sentence meaning", he makes it quite clear (pp. 60–61) that these are to be unpacked strictly within his earlier account of speech acts.

43. Grice, "Logic and Conversation," pp. 44–45.

44. In "Conversational Postulates."

45. Katz and Bever, "The Fall and Rise of Empiricism."

that (6.51) can sometimes be used to perform the same speech act as (6.54) does standardly might be given on the basis of extragrammatical rules of use.

Still another advantage is that, outside the framework of speech act theory, we have a formal representation of any proposition. If speech act theory were correct about the relation between grammar and pragmatics, it would not be possible to claim that every proposition, performative propositions included, is the sense of some sentence in natural language and consequently that each proposition is formally represented by a reading of the sentence in an optimal grammar of the language.

The fact that we can have not only a formal representation of performative as well as assertive propositions but one of the same kind for both reconciles highly desirable features of the artificial language tradition and of the ordinary language tradition. The former tradition, exemplified by Carnap, is concerned with erecting formal systems whose formulas can be related by rules of the system in such a way as to mirror a wide range of the valid inferences people make. This tradition sees natural languages as imperfect devices for inference and theory construction because they contain ambiguities, vagueness, truth value gaps, logically misleading grammatical forms, and perhaps even inconsistencies. Their program is, roughly speaking, to replace reliance on natural languages with reconstructions of inference patterns and steps of theory construction framed in a perfect artificial language. The ordinary language tradition, exemplified by Austin, is concerned with describing the use of natural language. This tradition sees natural languages as the home of meaning, and denies that the meaningfulness of sentences in natural language depends on their translation into some appropriate artificial language. They argue that, conversely, the meaningfulness of the formal objects in artificial languages depends on explanations relating them to meaningful parts of a natural language. Ambiguities, vagueness, and truth value gaps are features of natural languages that are essential to their functions as living languages. The majority of such functions, it is claimed, cannot be reconstructed in lifeless formal systems. These at best reconstruct the more pedestrian, scientific uses of language.

The desirable feature of the artificial language tradition is its demand for a formal theory of logical structure. The desirable feature of the ordinary language tradition is its insistence that meaning is an inherent feature of natural language and that the test of an account of meaning is how well it does justice to standard uses of words. The conflict between these traditions has made it seem necessary to sacrifice one or the other of these features; so philosophers have chosen one side or the other depending on which feature they find more desirable. But I think it can be shown that the conflict, and hence the rationale for taking sides, stems from a fundamental mistake on each side and further that, once these mistakes are corrected, we no longer have to sacrifice either desirable feature.

The artificial language tradition makes the mistake of thinking that natural languages are highly imperfect devices that can and should be replaced by perfect ones. They seem to believe that this case is analogous to the replacement of piggy-back by cars, buses, and trains. But their formal systems are no more replacements for natural languages than the theories of natural scientists are replacements for phenomena in nature.

The mistake of the ordinary language tradition is twofold: first, to swallow the conception of formal theories as paradigmatically the statement-logics developed by Carnap and others, and second, to assume that an adequate approach to natural language requires us to account directly for use.[46]

The philosophical viewpoint of the present book conceives of natural languages as the proper objects to theorize about in studying meaning and of theories of natural languages as properly formal objects. By abandoning the chimera of a perfect language, the restriction to formal systems designed exclusively for inferences with statements, and the commitment to understanding meaning directly in terms of use, we wed these conceptions in a view of semantics as the formal study of meaning in natural language. It is thus possible to obtain formal theories that do not achieve their formal status at the expense of saying nothing about performative uses of language. The goals of such theories can be framed so that a theory that achieves them says what can be said about the illocutionary potential of sentences. In this way, we give content to the claim that each type of proposition is expressed by some class of sentences in a natural language and each propositional type can be formally described in terms of semantic representations of sentences in the class.

The next implication I wish to discuss is a consequence of framing our goals in this way and of having developed the particular theory of propositional structure in the preceding pages. In abandoning a constative/performative distinction, speech act theorists missed the opportunity to develop one of the more promising ideas to hit philosophy in a long time. The promise latent in this idea is that of a more comprehensive theory of logic than the present, orthodox theory, which restricts the domain of logic to deductive relations among statements, taking logic to be about truth-preserving inferences between sentences that express them. Such a more comprehensive theory of logic is

---

46. This direct approach is illustrated by the fact that, although Austin recognized the concept of a performative as an abstraction, he did not treat it as an idealization in the way physicists treat abstractions like an ideal gas or a perfect vacuum, but as an "extreme marginal case". See Austin, *How To Do Things with Words*, pp. 185–188; and Searle, "A Taxonomy of Illocutionary Acts," p. 359.

precluded by the treatment of performative information as exclusively a matter of contextual determination, for then questions about the logical structure of performative arguments cannot be dealt with in the same manner as questions about the logical structure of arguments involving only assertive propositions. There arises, then, the bizarre notion that there are two logics, one of the kind pictured in the orthodox theory and the other a "natural logic".[47] I want to show now how the broad outlines of such a more comprehensive logic, which is both formal and natural, emerges from the constative/performative distinction developed in terms of the classification of performative types in the previous section.

Let me begin with a connection to earlier work, where I tried to argue that the orthodox theory neglects the logical relations between questions, requests, and in general, nonassertive propositions of each type.[48] I argued that merely because such propositions are truth valueless ought not make us conclude that they do not enter into logical relations nor form a legitimate part of the domain of logic, insofar as the same semantic relations that underlie the inheritance of truth in connection with assertive propositions also underlie implication relations between nonassertive propositions. For instance, the semantic relation by virtue of which (6.56) must be true if (6.55) is true underlies the implication of (6.58) by (6.57).

(6.55)   John is having a nightmare.
(6.56)   John is having a dream.
(6.57)   Is John having a nightmare?
(6.58)   Is John having a dream?

The difference in the case of arguments like (6.57)-(6.58) is that affirmative answerhood is inherited rather than truth. That is, just as the truth of (6.55) makes it necessary that (6.56) is true, so an affirmative answer to (6.57) makes it necessary that the answer to (6.58) is affirmative. In general, an aspect of answerhood is what is inherited under deductive relations between erotetic propositions. Thus, the implicational relations between erotetic propositions, and as we shall see below, between other nonassertive propositions, are a function of aspects of the structure of these propositions, in essence, the same aspects on which the implicational relations between assertive propositions depend. Moreover, the notion of validity based on inheritance of truth is nothing more than the particular extensional interpretation appropriate for implicational relations between

47. This is the notion to which Grice is referring in "Logic and Conversation," p. 43.
48. J. J. Katz, "The Logic of Questions," in *Logic, Methodology, and Philosophy of Science*, ed. B. Van Rootselaar and J. F. Staal, vol. 3 (Amsterdam: North-Holland, 1968), pp. 463–494; revised in Katz, *Semantic Theory*, chap. 5.

assertive propositions (that is, those that bear truth values). Other notions of validity, based on the inheritance of something corresponding to truth, will have to be introduced as the appropriate extensional interpretation for implicational relations between nonassertive propositions.

We may carry this line of thinking a step further. If these reflections are correct, then the subject matter of logic is simply the semantic structure of sentences. Accordingly, the picture presented by a variety of studies, called "statement logic", "the logic of imperatives", "deontic logic", "erotetic logic", and so on, is misleading in suggesting a number of distinct subject matters. A better picture is that of a single study whose aim is to represent formally the logical form of sentences in natural language and investigate the laws according to which these forms are deductively related and to which the appropriate property in the case of each propositional type would be inherited in a valid argument involving propositions of that type.

Here, then, is where our theory about propositional type, performative type, and, in particular, the classification of performative types, has its most important application to philosophical logic. It provides a basis for defining the full range of what we may call *inheritance properties*, that is, the full range of those properties on which the special notions of validity depend. Each type of proposition, *Assertive*, *Requestive*, *Advisive*, *Permissive*, and so on, determines one type of *pure argument*. An argument is pure just in case the premises and the conclusion are of the same propositional type; otherwise, it is a *mixed argument*.[49] For the class of pure arguments, each type of argument is determined by the type of proposition making up its premises and conclusion. Each type of argument in this class has its unique inheritance property and hence its own distinct notion of validity (that is, inheritance of this property). Thus, just as truth is the inheritance property in statement arguments, so the counterparts of truth, answerhood, and so on, will be the inheritance properties in each of the types of performative argument. Accordingly, to say that a pure performative argument is valid is to say that the appropriate counterpart property of truth is preserved in the transition from its premises to its conclusion. These new notions of validity provide extensional interpretations for intensionally determined deductive connections.

The desire for generality plus the existence of mixed arguments will lead us to collapse truth, answerhood, and all of the other inheritance properties into one abstract inheritance property and to define a single overall notion of validity. We shall turn to this shortly.

In requestive propositions, the counterpart of truth is obviously compliance. Consider the argument from (6.59) to (6.60).

49. A mixed argument is one in which at least two of the propositions are of different propositional type.

(6.59) I request that you eat breakfast.
(6.60) I request that you eat a meal.

Here validity has to be understood as preservation of compliance; that is, any act that satisfies the compliance condition for the requestive proposition expressed by the premise (6.59) must satisfy the compliance condition for the requestive proposition expressed by the conclusion. Since, as we have seen above, erotetic propositions are a subtype of *Requestives*, namely, that subtype in which the request has the purpose of eliciting information constituting a true possible answer to the question, preservation of compliance ought to provide the proper notion of validity for erotetic arguments like (6.57)-(6.58). But, in fact, it does not. The inheritance property for *yes-no* questions is a true possible *affirmative* answer. A true possible negative answer is no more preserved in valid arguments like (6.57)-(6.58) than falsehood is preserved in valid arguments like (6.55)-(6.56). On the other hand, a true possible negative answer can satisfy the compliance condition for the request issued in (6.57). Thus, it is not always the case that the inheritance property is satisfaction of the converted condition itself. Nonetheless, the inheritance property for a propositional type T, as we shall argue below, is, in general, satisfaction of the converted condition of T. This exception is, I think, a reflection of the fact that erotetics are subtypes, and in the case of subtypes we can have satisfaction of a component of the converted condition as the inheritance property. Earlier we raised the question of what principles might distinguish a subtype under a performative type. I would now like to propose the hypothesis that one such principle is that in the case of a genuine subtype (for example, "ask" as opposed to "order" or "command") the inheritance property may be less than satisfaction of the converted condition of the type to which it belongs. If the inheritance property is less, then we are dealing with a genuine subtype, but the converse may not hold. There may be other sufficient conditions for subtypes.

Now, modulo this feature of subtypes, we can provide a theoretical deduction of the principles we established in earlier studies,[50] especially for the logic of questions. There we claimed that answerhood is the inheritance property in erotetic propositions and that the validity of erotetic arguments consist in the fact that anything counting as an answer to the premise question must count as an answer to the conclusion question. These claims follow directly from (6.27) and (5.39), on which the compliance condition for an erotetic proposition is essentially that the requestee produce a true possible answer to the question.

The case of *Assertives* and *Requestives* suggest the general principle that the inheritance property for a particular propositional type is determined by

50. Katz, "The Logic of Questions," and idem, *Semantic Theory*, chap. 5.

the converted conditions for that type. This principle immediately implies the principle tacitly employed in the preceding paragraphs, namely, that the inheritance property for any subtype of a propositional type T is either the same as the inheritance property for T or a simple modification of it.[51]

Let us see now what the application of this general principle says about the extensional interpretation of each of the propositional types that we characterized in the previous section. The converted condition for *Advisives* will be a *heeding condition* (intuitively, the condition that determines whether the advice is heeded). We may define it as (6.61).

(6.61) The *heeding condition* for an advisive proposition P is that (a) there is an advisee (that is, a designatum for the advisee reading in the reading of P),[52] (b) the advisee realizes the significance of the advice for his or her purposes, and (c) on the basis of this realization, the advisee acts in accord with the course of action presented as the best choice.

This definition is general enough to allow a wide range of behavior to count as heeding a warning such as that issued in a use of (6.62)(i), for example, anything from getting rid of one's cash to trying to borrow more cash (since it is thought that muggers become more hostile if they find their efforts are poorly rewarded), but specific enough to disallow going downtown from counting as heeding a warning such as that issued in a use of (6.62)(ii).[53]

51. Thus, since according to (6.28), *Provocatives* are a subtype of *Requestives*, their *acceptance condition* is a species of compliance condition (just as the answerhood condition of erotetics is a species of compliance condition). The acceptance condition, on this account, is, therefore, the recipient's attempt to do the act in question to prove that he or she can do it and to make the attempt in part for the reason that the agent issued the challenge. The notion of validity for provocative propositions is that if something is a case of taking up the challenge expressed in the premise, it is also a case of taking up the challenge expressed in the conclusion. For example, if one child uses the sentence "I dare you to shout while the teacher is in the room" to dare Charlie and another child uses the sentence "I dare you to make a noise while the teacher is in the room" to dare him, Charlie can comply with both requests at once by shouting while the teacher is in the room.

52. "Advisee reading" can be defined in analogy to the definition of "requestee reading".

53. We intend "on the basis of" to imply a correspondence between the standard underlying the agent's notion of what the advisee should do and the standard underlying the advisee's own choice in the situation. If these standards conflict, we ought not allow that the advisee acts on the basis of the realization. A masochist does not heed my warning to watch out for the hot stove when he or she responds to the warning by gleefully putting both hands on the stove.

(6.62) (i) I warn you that muggers are lurking downtown.
(ii) I warn you not to go downtown.

On the basis of this converted condition, the inheritance property for *Advisives* will be heeding. That is to say, the notion of validity that applies to an argument like (6.63)–(6.64) is that an act that counts as heeding the premise must count as heeding the conclusion.

(6.63) I advise you to buy a table and some chairs.
(6.64) I advise you to buy some furniture.

The converted condition for *Expressives* is what we shall call a *compensation condition*. We may define it as (6.65).

(6.65) The *compensation condition* for an expressive proposition P is that (a) there is a designatum for the recipient reading, (b) this person has received the knowledge that the agent has the specified feeling about them and that the agent has this feeling for the specified reason, and (c) as a consequence the act attains its goal of adequately compensating the recipient.

Thus, the inheritance property will be compensation. Accordingly, if one expressive proposition entails another, such as with (6.66) and (6.67), then if the utterance of the former compensates for a debt to the recipient, the utterance of the latter compensates for the same debt.[54]

(6.66) I apologize for having stepped on your foot.
(6.67) I apologize for having stepped on a part of your body.

The converted condition for *Permissives* will be a *license condition*. We may define it as (6.68).[55]

54. Sentence (6.66) also entails "I apologize for stepping on a physical object". We claim that this, too, inherits compensation, even though its use might rub the recipient the wrong way. The insult inherent in the compensation does not lessen the compensation any more than my repaying with coins you are allergic to reduces the payment value of the money.

55. Someone might argue as follows. If A gives B permission to do Z, then B has permission but it does not follow that B has license, that is, is actually free to do it. For instance, in an elaborate bureaucracy with many agencies having overlapping and not too well-defined jurisdictional spheres, it might happen that one agency gives B permission to do Z without B's thereby having license because license depends on permission from another agency. We would reply that the first agency had only given *their* permission, not permission, because in such situations permission is joint permission of each of the agencies having jurisdiction. Therefore, the agent in this example was not in a position to permit B to do Z. (Authority to License) in (6.37) stands for the concept of full authority.

(6.68) The *license condition* for a permissive proposition P is that (a) there is a designatum for the recipient reading, (b) the agent's communicative act frees the recipient of any blame or penalty of the kind normally associated with the specified act, and (c) the agent's communicative act gives the agent responsibility for the recipient's doing the specified act.

License is the inheritance property and thus if one permissive proposition like (6.69) entails another like (6.70), then the license given in the use of the former is also license to do the act described in the latter (that is, includes the license given in a use of the latter).

(6.69) I permit you to use any tool of mine.
(6.70) I permit you to use any hammer of mine.

The converted condition for *Obligatives* will be a *fulfillment condition*. We may define it as (6.71).

(6.71) The *fulfillment condition* for an obligative proposition P is that the agent of the communicative act perform some (future) act that dispenses the obligation undertaken in the communicative act.

There is no required recipient here, since one can make a promise without promising anyone (for example, vows, resolutions). An addressee is, of course, required, but this can be oneself. Fulfillment is the inheritance property, and thus if an obligative proposition like (6.72) entails one like (6.73), then any act that dispenses the responsibility undertaken in making the promise (6.72) dispenses the responsibility that would be undertaken in making the promise (6.73).

(6.72) I promise to hire a south-paw.
(6.73) I promise to hire a left-hander.

The converted condition for *Expositives* will be an *acknowledgment condition*. We may define it as (6.74).

(6.74) The *acknowledgment condition* for an expositive proposition P is that (a) there is a designatum for the recipient reading, (b) the recipient(s) indicate that they take notice of the fact that the agent takes it that the proposition in question is the case (or is not) and (c) this indication is a consequence of the agent's communicative act.

The acknowledgment condition for (6.75) would be satisfied if the relevant people acknowledge that, in the act using (6.75) to declare, the speaker has put it forth that the side to which he or she belongs will win.

(6.75) I declare that we shall be victorious.

When no recipient is specified in the sentence, as in the case of (6.75) but not (6.76), the relevant people are the addressees and other interested parties.

(6.76) I declare to our people that we shall be victorious.

The addressees can be disjoint from the recipient as when (6.76) is used by a patriot facing death, surrounded by the enemy. Since acknowledgment is the inheritance property, the validity of an argument like that from (6.77) to (6.78) consists of the fact that any acknowledgment of the declaration expressed in (6.77) is also an acknowledgment of that expressed in (6.78).

(6.77) I declare that France has no monarch.
(6.78) I declare that there is no king of France.

Finally, the converted condition for *Stipulatives* will be a *nomenative condition.* We may define it as (6.79).

(6.79) The *nomenative condition* for a stipulative proposition P is that (a) there is a designatum of the recipient reading, (b) people identify the recipient by the name in P (assuming that a sense of a sentence like (6.80) and (6.81) contains information specifying the name mentioned in the sentence), and (c) people do so in part as a consequence of the communicative act in which the recipient becomes the bearer of the name.

As we might expect, however, stipulative propositions do not enter into nearly as wide a range of logical structures as other performatives. This is because they involve proper names and proper names do not have a meaning in the language.[56] But there are some trivial implications, like (6.80)–(6.81).

(6.80) I christen you "James Smith".
(6.81) I name you "James Smith".

Thus, we can speak about an inheritance property "being identified by the specified name": the name someone would be called as the result of a successful

56. Katz, *Semantic Theory*, pp. 381–382, and idem, "A Proper Theory of Names."

use of (6.81) would be the same as that he would be called as a result of the successful use of (6.80).

We observe that (6.79) provides the causal or historical theory of the reference of proper names with a rationale for connecting "baptisms" (successful illocutionary acts of name-stipulation) and uses of a name with the appropriate reference (actions that satisfy the nomenative condition for such illocutionary acts). Kripke rightly insists on the intention of the user of a name "to use it with the same reference as the man from whom he heard it"—going back to the person who originally conferred the name.[57] This condition on the intention of the user of a name is, I claim, a consequence of the more general condition that compliance conditions, fulfillment conditions, nomenative conditions, and other converted conditions all require that the action be done in part because of the illocutionary act (See pp. 152–156.)

On our theory, the concept of validity has a constant and a variable component. Regardless of the type of argument, that is, the type of proposition appearing as premises and conclusion, validity is always a matter of semantic relations between the premise and conclusion on which the latter inherits an extensional property from the former. The variable component, which is a function of the type of argument, is the particular inheritance property, for example truth in statement arguments, compliance in requestive arguments, fulfillment in obligative arguments, and license in permissive arguments. The general notion of validity is that of the preservation of the appropriate extensional property.

It is here that the abstraction we made in constructing the notion of converted conditions becomes more than a useful general term to cover truth conditions, compliance conditions, and so on. It provides us with a specification of this extensional property, namely, *satisfaction of the converted condition*. Truth is satisfaction of the converted conditions in the case where they are truth conditions. Compliance is satisfaction of the converted conditions where they are compliance conditions. And so on. Therefore, we can say *a pure argument is valid just in case it preserves satisfaction of the converted conditions.*[58]

This notion of validity offers a completely general treatment of logical structure. The reasons are clear in the case of the semantic entailments we have been considering, that is, arguments like (6.55)–(6.56), (6.57)–(6.58), (6.59)–(6.60), and so on. In these cases, the logical form of the conclusion is part of the logical form of the premise. In propositional logic, too, we can

57. S. Kripke, "Naming and Necessity," in *Semantics of Natural Language*, eds. D. Davidson and G. Harman (Dordrecht-Holland: D. Reidel Publishing Co., 1972), p. 302 and p. 349, footnotes 42 and 43.

58. Or, for both pure and mixed arguments, *an argument is valid just in case satisfaction of the converted conditions of its premise(s) makes the satisfaction of the converted conditions of its conclusion necessary.*

have such a completely general treatment. We use the propositional variables "p", "q", "r", . . . to stand for propositions of any type, not merely assertions or statements, as in standard versions of propositional logic. We introduce the connectives with what we shall call *satisfaction tables* instead of truth tables, with "1" for the value of satisfied converted condition and "0" for the value of nonsatisfied converted conditions. The table for conjunction may be the standard (6.82), where the symbols are interpreted as indicated.

(6.82)   p   q   p & q

1	1	1
1	0	0
0	1	0
0	0	0

Table (6.82) says that the *satisfaction value* of a conjunction is "satisfied converted condition" just in case both of its components have a satisfied converted condition. It is clear that this table will be adequate in case p and q are assertions, and it is also clear that it will be adequate in case p and q are propositions of any other type. Thus, for instance, the conjunctive question (6.83) has a satisfied converted condition (compliance condition) on the basis of a response that is an answer to both the component questions, and only on this basis.[59]

(6.83)   Where are the demonstrators and where are the police?

The power of the theory lies in the full generality of the inheritance property. The propositional variables are really variables for any proposition, and so the satisfaction tables represent the meaning of connectives like "and" even in arguments that involve propositions of different types, "mixed arguments". Consider an example like the "mixed proposition" (6.84). Table (6.82) says, quite correctly, that its satisfaction value is "satisfied converted condition" just in case the promise is fulfilled and the assertion is true.

(6.84)   I promise that I will go and I will go.

---

59. On the difficult question of determining components, see Harnish's "Logical Form and Implicature."

The satisfaction table for disjunction is the familiar (6.85).

(6.85)   p   q   p $\lor$ q

p	q	p $\lor$ q
1	1	1
1	0	1
0	1	1
0	0	0

Although the treatment is straightforward in the case of "pure arguments" like (6.86), the case of mixed arguments calls for some comment.

(6.86)   Fix the table or fix the chairs!

A sentence like (6.87) is normally taken as "or else" and so construed as a threat; a sentence like (6.88) seems odd in the way that (6.89) does not; and so forth.

(6.87)   Fix the table or I will eat at the restaurant.
(6.88)   I promise to drive you to the station or I congratulate you on the good job you did.
(6.89)   I promise to drive you to the station or I permit you to use the car to drive yourself there.

I would suppose that these are matters for a pragmatic theory's account of how Grice's maxim "Be relevant", which he rightly observes is as difficult as it is terse,[60] is applied in determining utterance meaning. I think that the grammatical meaning of (6.88) and (6.87) is computed, just as the grammatical meaning of (6.86) and (6.89) is, using the table (6.85), but that in (6.87) and (6.88) the resulting grammatical meaning is rejected as the utterance meaning because it fails to be relevant. One of the difficult problems a pragmatic theory has to solve, then, is why the utterance meaning of (6.87) but not (6.88) can be obtained reasonably easily. But, however such problems turn out to be handled, the sentences must be treated as cases where the context supplies information that determines a way in which the audience preserves the assumption that the speaker is being relevant. Any such treatment thus presupposes that the sentences must be construed, since taking their grammatical

60. Grice, "Logic and Conversation," pp. 46–47.

meaning to be the message would make their use irrelevant. Hence, some such interpretation as the account of the meaning of "or" in (6.87) is necessary as an explanation of the irrelevance that has to be overcome contextually.

The case of negation is where our theory has surprising consequences. In a way, this is to be expected. In natural language, negation is not a mechanism for forming compound propositions. Logicians treat negation as a propositional connective even though it does not connect propositions, but in constructing artificial languages one is free to do what one wants, and furthermore, in the kind of artificial languages acceptable within the orthodox conception of logic there is no choice. These systems have to treat negation as applying to propositions as wholes because their restriction of the vocabulary for expressing logical form to the logical particles precludes the kind of internal term and predicate structure that makes it possible to treat negation as a means of changing around concepts inside the meaning of terms and predicates.

In describing the structure of natural languages, one has to be faithful to the facts, and the facts, as linguists have found,[61] are that negative elements do not behave like the connectives "and" and "or" but like adverbs and adjectives. Negative elements enter into construction with words, thereby creating a sense that contributes to the structure of simple propositions. For this reason, in the past[62] I framed my semantic treatment of negation as a uniform operation from the morpheme to the clause level of converting concepts into incompatible ones. On this treatment, "not" and other negative elements are assigned a lexical reading consisting of the antonymy operator and a specification of its scope. As discussed in connection with (3.1), this operator is designed to represent how negation interacts with the component concepts in the meaning of constituents in its scope. The operator transforms a reading of such constituents into an alternation of disjunctions of the other semantic markers in the antonymous n-tuples to which the semantic markers in the reading belong.

On this treatment, we would predict that when the performative component of the meaning of a sentence is in the scope of a negative element, the proposition expressed by the sentence comes out assertive.[63] This is indeed what

61. E. Klima, "Negation in English," in *The Structure of Language: Readings in the Philosophy of Language*, eds. J. A. Fodor and J. J. Katz, (Englewood Cliffs, New Jersey: Prentice Hall, 1964), pp. 246–323; and more recently, but along the same lines, A. Akmajian and F. Heny, *An Introduction to the Principles of Transformational Syntax*, (Cambridge, Mass.: M.I.T. Press, 1975).

62. Katz, *Semantic Theory*, pp. 157–168.

63. The antonymy operator will convert the semantic markers in performative structures into alternations of the semantic markers in their antonymous n-tuples, thereby making the reading of such a sentence fail (5.41). See pp. 177–178.

happens. For example, the requestive proposition expressed by (6.90) in construction with a negative element, as in the proposition expressed by (6.91) or (6.92), comes out assertive.

  (6.90) I request that you deliver it.
  (6.91) I do not request that you deliver it.
  (6.92) It is not the case that I request that you deliver it.

Sentences (6.91) and (6.92) assert that the speaker forbears making the request. The same is true with other performative types, for example, (6.93) and (6.94).

  (6.93) I promise to bring it.
  (6.94) I do not promise to bring it.

A surprising consequence is that there is no satisfaction table for negation corresponding to the truth table for negation. The table (6.95) cannot receive the interpretation that "1" stands for satisfaction of the converted conditions of a proposition and "0" stands for their nonsatisfaction.

  (6.95)   p   ~p

1	0
0	1

For instance, the compliance condition for (6.90) can fail to be satisfied while at the same time the truth condition for (6.91) can fail to be satisfied. A case of this kind is where the recipient has been requested to deliver the object but fails to comply with the request.[64]

On the other hand, it is clear that the converted conditions of such propositions cannot be jointly satisfied. The converted conditions of (6.96) are necessarily unsatisfied.

  (6.96) I request and do not request that you deliver it.

The antonymy operator treatment of negation together with our theory of the constative/performative distinction implies that propositions like (6.90) and

---

64. Note that the time span covered in (6.91) and similar cases is broader than the speech point. If I requested you to deliver it ten minutes ago, and now (perhaps forgetting) utter (6.91), I say something false.

(6.91) are contraries in the sense that they cannot both have satisfied converted conditions.

The question arises whether double negation holds. Do (6.97) and (6.98), respectively, express the propositions expressed by (6.90) and (6.93)?

>   (6.97) I do not not request that you deliver it.
>   (6.98) I do not not promise to bring it.

I have not been able to satisfy myself one way or the other on this question. English speakers seem to divide into those for whom such double negations are semantically equivalent to the original sentences (6.90) and (6.93) and those for whom such double negations express the speaker's refusal to assert (6.91) and (6.94). Moreover, such double negations are hard examples for people to work with, and it is also possible that they are ambiguous.

Thus, I shall not try to choose between the possible positions here. One position is that the effect of negating (6.91), in the way that we negated (6.90) to obtain (6.91), is to bring us back to the proposition expressed by (6.90). Supporters of this position would argue that (6.97) can issue requests just as (6.90) can. They can argue that someone who uses (6.97) in some context performs an act that includes the condition that the truth conditions of (6.91) are not satisfied in that context. The truth conditions of (6.91) being that no request to deliver it is made in the context, if they are not satisfied, it must be that such a request is made in the context, and that it is the use of (6.92) that made it. They can also argue that the strangeness in using a double negative like (6.97) to perform such an act is real enough but amounts to nothing more than a clash with pragmatic constraints against the use of complex, difficult constructions when simple, standard ways of performing the illocutionary act are available.[65]

The other position would claim that the negation of (6.91) denies that the speaker asserts a refusal to request the delivery. Supporters of this position would reply that someone who uses (6.97) is contradicting the claim of (6.91), but that this in no way brings about the act of requesting.

To obtain a denial of a proposition like (6.90), we have to negate the complement sentence rather than the sentence itself. Thus, (6.99) expresses the denial of (6.90): the converted conditions of one are satisfied just in case those of the other are not.

>   (6.99) I request that you do not deliver it.

65. See Grice, "Logic and Conversation," pp. 47–56.

We should mention that this redefinition of the metalogical concept of denial is paradigmatic: in each case, we obtain the new metalogical concept by replacing the notion of truth with that of satisfied converted conditions. Thus, the concept of tautology becomes that of a compound proposition whose converted condition is satisfied no matter what the pattern of satisfaction and nonsatisfaction for the converted conditions of its component propositions. For example, (6.100) is a tautology as much as (6.101).[66]

(6.100) I request that you deliver it or that you do not deliver it.

(6.101) Jones delivered it or Jones did not deliver it.

It should be noted that a mixed inference like (6.102) to (6.103) is valid on our theory.

(6.102) I request that you, Jones, deliver the goods at midnight.

(6.103) Jones will deliver the goods at midnight.

This might be thought counter-intuitive. Since the conclusion (6.103) can be false even though the premise (6.102) makes a request, it might be objected that we count an invalid inference as valid. But this objection does not hold: it confuses the success of making the request of (6.102) with the truth of (6.102) (it confuses an illocutionary success condition with a truth condition). The inference in question, on our notion of validity, is valid: satisfaction of the converted condition of the conclusion (6.103), namely, Jones's delivering the goods at midnight, cannot fail to obtain if satisfaction of the converted condition of the premise (6.102), namely, Jones's delivering the goods at midnight in compliance with the speaker's request, obtains.

I think it is clear even without going further than the sketch above that the standard notion of validity is just a special case of the general notion of preservation of satisfaction of converted conditions. The conclusion I draw from this is that accounts of logic that represent logic as the subject concerned with the most general class of truths, or with implications in which the truth of the implying proposition(s) makes it necessary that the implied proposition is true, give a false picture of the essential features of this subject.[67] Since the most general characterization of the subject abstracts away from truth and

66. I provide no satisfaction table corresponding to the truth table for the material conditional because of the difficulties considered in Chapter 3, pp. 107–108, and similar problems.

67. W. V. Quine, *Mathematical Logic*, rev. ed. (Cambridge, Mass.: Harvard University Press, 1951), pp. 1–8.

pictures logic as the study of the semantic structures underlying relations be-tween sentences in which satisfaction of the converted conditions of one sen-tence makes it necessary that the converted conditions of the other is satisfied, the only thing standing in the way of accepting the most general characterization of logic is the philosophical view I have been calling the orthodox conception of logic. This view says that logical form is determined by nothing beyond properties of the so-called logical vocabulary, the logical particles. It thus says that the rest of the vocabulary and grammar of sentences, the nouns, adjectives, verbs, sentence types, and so on, do not contribute to logical form, and that logical forms are constative forms. It therefore restricts implication relations between sentences to those in which truth is preserved. If, therefore, we wish to adopt the most general characterization of logic, it will be necessary to reject the orthodox conception. This, of course, does not mean that we have to reject any highly sophisticated formal theories of implication between statements, but only that they cannot be comprehensive accounts of logical implication.

INDEX